All Grown Up and
No Place to Go

Other Books by David Elkind

The Hurried Child: Growing Up Too Fast Too Soon
Parenting Your Teenager
The Ties That Stress: The New Family Imbalance
Child Development and Education: A Piagetian Perspective
Children and Adolescents
Grandparenting: Understanding Today's Children
*Images of the Young Child: Collected Essays on
Development and Education*
Miseducation: Preschoolers at Risk
The Child and Society
The Child's Reality: Three Developmental Themes
Understanding Your Child from Birth to Sixteen

David Elkind

All Grown Up and No Place to Go

Teenagers in Crisis

Revised Edition

PERSEUS BOOKS

Cambridge, Massachusetts

Many of the designations used by manufacturers and sellers to distinguish their products are claimed as trademarks. Where those designations appear in this book and Perseus Books was aware of a trademark claim, the designations have been printed in initial capital letters.

Permissions acknowledgments appear on pages 276-277.

Library of Congress Cataloging-in-Publication Data
Elkind, David, 1931-
    All grown up and no place to go: teenagers in crisis / David Elkind.—Rev. ed.
      p.   cm.
    Includes bibliographical references and index.
    ISBN 0-201-48358-8
    1. Teenagers—United States. 2. Adolescent psychology—United States. 3. Stress in adolescence—United States. I. Title.
HQ796.E535   1997
305.253—dc21   97-40872
                                             CIP

Perseus Books is a member of the Perseus Books Group.

Cover design by Suzanne Heiser
Text design by Faith Hague
Set in 10.5-point Palatino by Faith Hague

      4   5   6   7   8   9   10–03 02 01 00 99

Perseus Books are available for special discounts for bulk purchases in the U.S. by corporations, institutions, and other organizations. For more information, please contact the Special Markets Department at HarperCollins Publishers, 10 East 53rd Street, New York, NY 10022, or call 1-212-207-7528.

Find us on the World Wide Web at
http://www.perseusbooksgroup.com

To Lara, and to all the other
adolescents who have successfully
battled their past and won a
brighter future.

Contents

Acknowledgments

A book is always written alone, in the privacy of one's work room. But the writer also carries in his or her head all of the many collaborators who contributed facts, thoughts, ideas, challenges, support, and criticism. The writing time is like the slender part of the hourglass, where all the collected thoughts have to go through one narrow channel, a single mind, before they return to the larger population from which they came. It is not possible to thank all my collaborators by name. First and foremost are the teenagers I have known and worked with over these many years. Then there are the parents, sometimes busting their buttons, sometimes angry, and sometimes just outright scared. And there are the many teachers and administrators who have taught me so much about young people's lives in their homes away from home—the schools. And finally I have to acknowledge the health professionals, nurses, social workers, physicians, psychologists, and psychiatrists who give so much of themselves to the children and youth they serve. To all of you, my thanks and appreciation.

I also want to thank my former departmental assistant, Louise Clancy, for typing an early draft of the book and Dorothy O'Toole who typed later versions. Susan Oleksiw and Kendra Crossen provided valuable editorial help on the manuscript.

I want to thank the editors at Perseus Books: Doe

Coover who worked with me on the first draft, and Anne Eldridge, who took over from there and saw the first edition through its final stages. Both were unfailing in their support and encouragement. John Bell encouraged me to update the book and gave a thoughtful and helpful reading of the revised manuscript.

I also want to thank my wife and sons who always tolerate, with grace and understanding, my mental absences while I am working on a new project. My sons Paul, Robert, and Rick were adolescents when I first wrote this book; they taught me how easy it is to give advice and how hard it is to follow it.

Finally, it is important to acknowledge all of the adolescents, their parents, and their teachers whom I have had the good luck to meet and work with since the last writing. They have been a constant source of both inspiration and raised spirits. Although I have sounded many notes of warning and concern in this book, these parents and teachers have never surrendered their adult role. My prayer is that as a society, hopefully sooner than later, we can follow their example and once again provide a secure and supportive place for adolescents to be young.

Preface

Over the past thirty-five years I have worked with young people in many different settings. I have worked with teenage patients at psychiatric hospitals and with delinquent teenagers who were being brought to court. I have also seen teenagers who came with their families to child guidance clinics or to my private practice. And, with colleagues, I have conducted research with students who were attending junior and senior high school. That research often involved interviewing large numbers of young people. I have reported my observations and concerns about teenagers in articles, book chapters, and books for professionals and for parents. I know, and care, about young people.

Since the publication of *The Hurried Child*, I have had a very different kind of interaction with teenagers, with their parents and teachers, and with professionals in many different fields who provide for their health needs. I had many requests to speak, from all parts of the United States and Canada. I have now traveled to every state in the Union and to all the Canadian provinces. Everywhere I go, I make it my practice not only to speak but also to listen.

What I have heard, and what I am still hearing, gave me the impetus for writing this book. Not only are children still being hurried, but the phenomenon is becoming more common and accepted. Mothers-to-be are deluged with literature assuring them that if they use the right materials they will be able to raise their babies' IQs and have them reading, swimming, and doing gymnastics before they are three months old. There is, of course, no evidence to support the value of such early pushing. There is, however, considerable evidence that children are showing more and more serious stress symptoms than ever before.

Even more discouraging has been the realization that many of these hurried children are now teenagers. Now, more than two decades after the hurrying began, we are getting a truer measure of the cost of acceleration as we look at the threefold increase in stress symptoms among young people. What I have seen and heard is frightening enough. Many parents and many schools and much of the media have been hurrying children to grow up fast, but they have also been abandoning teenagers. There is simply no protected place for teenagers in today's hurried and hurrying society.

The result is a staggering number of teenagers who have not had the adult guidance, direction, and support they need to make a healthy transition to adulthood. We always lost a certain number of teenagers in the past, for all kinds of reasons. But we are losing too many teenagers today. We are producing too many young people who may never be productive and responsible citizens, much less lead happy and rewarding lives. When 50% of our youth are at one time or another abusing alcohol or drugs, then something is seriously wrong with our society.

That is why I wrote this book. The one encouraging experience I had, wherever I traveled, was meeting many parents, teachers, and health professionals who are deeply committed to young people and who really care. But they need help and support to continue and to resist the social pressure to foist a premature adulthood on teenagers.

It has been thirteen years since the first edition of *All*

Grown Up and No Place to Go was published. I have been pleased and encouraged by the continued receptive audience the book has found among parents, teachers, and health professionals. Because the book has apparently been useful to a wide audience I welcomed the invitation, of Addison-Wesley editor John Bell, to revise and update it. I have rewritten the entire text and have updated the references and the discussions wherever this seemed dictated by the most recent statistics, research, and conceptual innovations. For example, the work of Carol Gilligan and her colleagues has fundamentally altered the ways in which we look at gender differences and the ways in which we interpret research on issues such as moral development. I have incorporated her work into my treatment of these topics.

In addition to updating references and statistics and to revising discussions, I have also introduced a new conceptual framework for looking at and understanding the pressures on contemporary children and youth. In the interim since the first edition, I have had the opportunity to rethink the issues that I addressed in this and my other books on stress in young people, namely, *The Hurried Child* (1981/1988) and *Miseducation* (1987), and to present these pressures in a broader social and cultural context in *Ties That Stress* (1994). Accordingly, in this book, I have also introduced the idea that the stressors confronting young people today are part of a larger social phenomena, namely, the shift from a modern to a postmodern society. Put rather simply, during the late modern period, which ended roughly around mid-century, the needs of children and youth were weighted more heavily than those of parents and adults. As we have become postmodern this need imbalance has shifted in the other direction. Today the needs of children and youth are often weighted less heavily than are the needs of parents and the rest of adult society.

PART I

Needed:
A Time to Grow

CHAPTER 1

Teenagers in Crisis

There is little or no place for adolescents in American society today—not in our homes, not in our schools, and not in society at large. We have, in effect, all but eliminated this age period as a distinct stage in the life cycle. In our homes we increasingly treat teenagers as equals, rather than as young people who, despite their physical maturity, are still psychologically immature. Contemporary high schools provide little in the way of teacher-organized activities (with the exception of sports) that speak to the need of young people for adult guidance and direction. The larger society offers few places for young people to "hang out" and to socialize with their peers. In contemporary society, therefore, we effectively ignore the unique needs of the age group who are no longer children, yet who have not yet attained full adulthood.

Changing Perceptions of Adolescence

This was not always the case. For a brief period, beginning in the latter part of the last century and extending through the first half of this century, there was what might well be called the "golden age" of adolescence. In part, this era was the result of universal, free public education that, for the first time, gave adolescents a distinct role: that of student. In part, it grew out of nineteenth-century humanitarianism and the revulsion against the exploitation and degradation of child labor. In part, it could also be traced to the social science depiction of adolescence as a period of immaturity, of storm and stress, and of religious conversion. Last, but certainly not least, the golden era of adolescence coincided with the prevalence of urban life and the ascendance of the nuclear family as the dominant family form. The nuclear family was regarded as a safe haven for the immature young before they ventured into the cruel, harsh, and competitive outside world.

This view of adolescence was mirrored in the larger society. Clubs for adolescents were to be found in most cities. Boy Scouts of America was founded in 1910 and Girl Scouts of America in 1912. 4H clubs, and church, or synagogue-related youth groups were very popular. High school teachers ran debating, gardening, stamp, chess, and other clubs after school hours. The legal system protected young people by passing and enforcing child labor and compulsory school attendance laws. The media made its own contribution to this view of adolescent immaturity. In films such as the Andy Hardy series, a young adolescent got into youthful scrapes from which he was rescued by his father, the judge.

Likewise, the literature of this period in some ways glorified adolescence in stories for boys such as Alger's *Tattered Tom* (1871) and its successors, *Tom Sawyer* (Twain 1876), *Huckleberry Finn* (Twain 1885), the Stratemeyer syndicate's Rover Boys (Winfield 1899) and Hardy Boys (Dixon 1927) series, and toward the end of the period, *A Catcher in the Rye* (Salinger 1951). For young women there were books like *Little Women* (Alcott 1869), *Anne of Green Gables* (Montgomery 1908), and the Nancy Drew series (Keene 1930).

These stories tended to portray young people as good-hearted, hard working and well-meaning, but within the context of a larger, protective adult world.

As a consequence of this enlightened view of adolescence, young people came to be regarded as "the next generation," the future leaders of America. Adolescents' intellectual, social, and moral development was considered important, and therefore was protected and nurtured. Young people's occasional foibles—scrapes with the law and emotional excesses—were looked upon as a healthy expression of youthful spirit, as a necessary Mardi Gras before they assumed adult responsibility and decorum. Adolescents were thus given the time needed to adapt to the remarkable transformation their bodies, their minds, and their emotions were undergoing. Society as a whole recognized that the transition to adulthood was a difficult one and that adolescents needed time and adult support and supervision in this endeavor.

All this began to change after mid-century. The 1960s was the era of the civil rights and women's liberation movements. Both movements were long overdue demands for equality for minorities and for women. The egalitarian ethos ushered in by these two movements was extended to children and youth as well. The depictions of adolescents as immature was judged to be as demeaning as the portrayal of minorities as inferior and of women as dependent. Portrayals of adolescence as a period of immaturity and storm and stress (which characterized the golden era) were now seen as infantilization, an underestimation of the knowledge and abilities of young people. Hereafter, adolescence would be recognized as a period of social sophistication and technological savvy.

Other changes contributed to the passing of the golden age of adolescence. The second sexual revolution of the sixties (the first took place in the nineteenth century when young people began to choose their own marital partners) resulted in the social acceptance of premarital sex. This change in sexual mores had extraordinary social consequences. Prior to the second sexual revolution, virginity was a commodity; it had exchange value. It could be bartered for marital commitment. Thanks to the social acceptance of premarital sex, virginity lost its exchange value. This lessened commitment to marriage has played its part in the rapid rise in the divorce rate. At the same time, because adolescents pattern their behavior after adults, it encouraged a new social phenomenon—large numbers of sexually active teens. Whereas prior to the 1950s the majority of adolescents were virgins when they left the teen years, the reverse is true today. The postmodern acceptance of adolescent sexual activity has contributed to our new perception of this age group as sophisticated.

These changes in our way of looking at adolescents were mirrored by other institutions in society. At the same time that they introduced sex and drug education courses, high schools also did away with many adult-organized activities. Some high schools have begun to dispense condoms. The media too now portrays adolescents in a different way than they did before. After the sixties, teenage vamps began appearing in the "soaps," and "soft porn" films were produced for, and marketed to, teenagers. Today young people have access to X-rated films on videotape and late-night cable television and to a variety of magazines featuring female and male nudity, not to mention rock music and rock videos that might, conservatively, be called uninhibited. With so many sexually active adolescents, with so many young people experimenting with alcohol and other drugs, the perception of teenage immaturity had to be abandoned.

In today's society, therefore, the perception of adolescent sophistication has divested this age group of its lost erstwhile status. Instead, adolescents often have a premature adulthood thrust upon them. Young people are now required to confront life and its challenges with the maturity once only expected of the fully grown, but without any time for preparation and with little adult guidance. Given the changed economic landscape, today's parents must spend longer hours working and retraining than was true in the past. This is required in order for them to maintain a reasonable quality of life for themselves and their children. Parenting time must be sacrificed. It has been estimated that over the last twenty years young people have lost about twelve hours of parental interaction each week (Fuchs 1988). Most parents want to spend more time with their children but cannot do so without denying their adolescent offspring some of the educational and vocational opportunities they believe are essential for young people to succeed in today's extremely competitive marketplace.

The media and merchandisers have rushed to fill this parental vacuum. In part because parents are reluctant to ask teenagers to contribute to household expenses, a large percentage of working teenagers' income is disposable. Adolescents are now seen as a "niche market" whose emerging sexuality, need for peer-group approval, and search for idols can all be manipulated to motivate them to buy a variety of goods from clothing to CDs. High schools that once afforded many different adult-organized activities have become, in many communities, centers for theft, violence, sex, and substance abuse. In a variety of ways, therefore, the world of adolescents today is continuous with, rather than separate from, the world of adults.

I have, of course, somewhat overstated the case to make a point. It has to be emphasized that there are many parents and many communities in our society that remain committed to offering adolescents the time, protection, and guidance they require to traverse this difficult developmental period. But even well-meaning adults and communities often meet seemingly insurmountable barriers to effective parenting and many feel powerless to provide the kind of guidance they believe their teenagers need. For example, the mother of a teenage boy asked me what to do with her fourteen-year-old son who was staying up late to watch X-rated movies on cable television. I suggested that if she did not want him to watch the movies she should not permit him to do so and give him the reasons for the prohibition. Her next question surprised me. She asked what she should do if he watches the films after she goes to bed. This mother clearly felt helpless to monitor her son's television viewing. She felt, mistakenly, that because she could not do everything, she could do nothing. The truth is, however, that even though we can't do everything we can do something.

Growing Up Today

It will be argued, of course, that growing up in the world today is a far different affair from growing up even a half century ago. And this is certainly true. Thanks in large part to television, films, magazines, and music lyrics, even young children are witness to brutality, violence, and sexuality on a scale that would have been unimaginable four or five decades ago. By the time they are adolescents, therefore, most contemporary teenagers have already been exposed to more violent and seamier sides of life than their parents and grandparents had seen or heard of in a lifetime.

In addition, from an early age, children are being made aware of the dangers in our society. Even preschoolers are now taught what behaviors constitute child abuse. School-age children learn about the risks of cigarette smoking, of getting high on inhalants, and of drugs. They know about sexually transmitted diseases (STDs) and AIDS. Children and adolescents hear daily what is happening to the world they will inherit: the destruction of the ozone layer and the rain forests, the extinction of species, the rapid depletion of irreplaceable natural resources. Young people are also learning about the global economy and the fact that America has moved from a position of preeminence to one of equality with other economic giants.

In these respects, it is certainly true that by the time they are adolescents, today's young people are more sophisticated than were their peers of a half century ago. And it would indeed be a mistake to treat contemporary adolescents as if they were growing up in the world of the 1950s. Yet adolescents today are still adolescents in many respects. They are still undergoing enormous changes in their bodies, their intelligence, and their emotions. They still need a period of relaxed, unpressured time to deal with these changes and to put them together in some meaningful way.

Social Change and the Perception of Adolescent Sophistication

The perceptions of adolescence, and the family of which teenagers are a part, are a reflection of society. When society changes, so too must that family and the perceptions of adolescence. Over the past half century we have moved from a society founded on the beliefs of modernity to one grounded in the tenets of postmodernity. Just as the beliefs of modernity were the fundamental assumptions for all facets of modern society from the arts to the sciences, so the tenets of postmodernity are now the generative themes in all facets of our postmodern world. And just as the beliefs of modernity were the foundation stones of the *nuclear* family, those of postmodernity are now the underpinnings of the *permeable* family. The movement from the golden era of childhood and adolescence to the present was, therefore, mediated by this social transformation from the modern to the postmodern.

The Modern Era

The modern era began with the Renaissance and the Enlightenment and was founded on the beliefs in *progress, universality,* and *regularity.* These beliefs grew out of the new science, which took its guidance from nature rather than from the authority of church or state. Science progressed by gathering increasingly more accurate and useful information about the natural world. Scientific knowledge was also believed to be universal, to encompass principles of nature that transcended time and place. Finally, scientific laws were believed to be regular, or uniform, admitting no exceptions. The laws of gravity, for example, cannot be defied. Society progressed as well, and it was believed that this progress would bring health and happiness to all its members.

The principles of progress, universality, and regularity were built into the modern conception of the nuclear family. The nuclear family (a married couple with two or more children and the mother staying home to care for them) was regarded as the end result of a progressive evolutionary process. It was extolled as the ideal family form most suited to the rearing of children who would become responsible, productive citizens. The nuclear family was also seen as the family arrangement that would eventually be universal, found in every country and culture. In addition, the nuclear family also took on moral dimensions; it was seen as the most regular and best parenting arrangement. Any family form that deviated from this ideal was not only irregular but also less morally justified.

The sentiments of the nuclear family (Shorter 1975) echoed the idealistic aura that surrounded this family structure. According to the sentiment of *romantic love*, marriages were made in heaven. Once the fated couple met, they fell in love and lived happily ever after. Mothers were endowed with the sentiment of *maternal love*, an instinct that insured their willingness to subordinate their own needs for self-fulfillment to those of their children and spouse. The home was seen as a refuge of *domesticity*; Christopher Lasch (1977) termed it a *Haven in a Heartless World* where family members could receive unconditional love and acceptance whenever they came in out of the cold, cruel, outside world. Finally, the value of *togetherness* insured that the family as a unit was more important than the needs or aspirations of any individual family member.

Harmonizing with these sentiments and values were the perceptions of parents, children, and adolescents. Parents were regarded as *intuitively* knowledgeable about child growth and development. They were, as pediatrician and psychiatrist D. W. Winnicott (1987) wrote, "Good Enough Parents" even if they had not attended college or university. Those who wrote for parents during this era, like Arnold Gesell and his colleagues (1956), gave parents exacting descriptions of children at successive age levels but few if any childrearing directives. It was assumed that if parents were given the *how do's* of child development, the *how to's* would follow naturally. And many parents *were* intuitively knowledgeable thanks to having grown up in large, extended families surrounded by many children of different age levels.

The sentiments of romantic love, maternal love, and domesticity were consistent with a perception of childhood *innocence*. Childhood, beginning in the latter part of the last century, came to be seen as a very special, almost magical, period that had to be protected and cherished. This perception of childhood was reflected in the literature of the time in stories such as *Peter Pan* (Barrie 1902), *The Secret Garden* (Burnett 1911), and *Winnie the Pooh* (Milne 1926). Adolescence, as we saw it, was looked upon as a period of *immaturity* in preparation for adulthood. Young people were permitted a certain license, given their need to experiment and to learn about the world outside of the nuclear haven.

The Postmodern Era

Mid-century is a convenient, if not very precise, time at which to mark the beginning of the postmodern era. Two World Wars, the Holocaust, the atomic bomb, the population explosion, the deterioration of natural resources, and the deterioration of the environment challenged the modern belief that science would provide uninterrupted human progress and betterment (e.g., better living through chemistry). The advancement of science and the growth of knowledge, we now recognize, can be used for self-seeking as well as for benevolent purposes. As a consequence the assumptions associated with science, progress, universality, and regularity have all been critiqued and modified.

While progress does indeed occur, it happens in specific domains rather than in all facets of life. Thus a new concern with *difference* has replaced the overarching belief in an unbroken course of social progress. In America we now recognize that progress does not involve the "melting" of all nationalities into some common American identity. Rather we now appreciate that people do not melt and that cultural, ethnic, and racial differences are to be valued rather than fused into a common amalgam. Likewise, while there is still a place for universal laws and principles, there is also room for *particular*, domain-specific theories and explanations. Finally, we now acknowledge that *irregular* phenomena, such as the weather, are inherently chaotic and do not conceal an underlying uniformity.

These new fundamental ideas of the postmodern world helped transform the nuclear family into the *permeable* family (Elkind 1994). Unlike the nuclear family that was walled off from the rest of society, the permeable family is open to any and all social influences. The permeable family includes a variety of kinship structures such as two-working-parent families, single-parent families, adoptive families, remarried families, and so on. We increasingly appreciate the fact that it is the emotional climate of the family, rather than its kinship structure, that is critical for effective childrearing and that no one family form can claim to be superior to the others. A nuclear family with fulfilled, loving parents is perhaps the least stressful family arrangement. But if these qualities are absent, the fact that the family is nuclear is no guarantee of successful parenting.

The second sexual revolution that made premarital sex socially acceptable also undermined the sentiment of romantic love. Romantic love was predicated on the belief in saving oneself sexually for one's destined partner. The exchange premium of virginity has lost its value for contemporary marriages. What has replaced romantic love is what might be called *consensual love*, a relationship between equals entered into with the understanding that either partner might at some time decide to end it. In a similar fashion the sentiment of maternal love has been transformed into the sentiment of *shared parenting*. The sentiment of shared parenting recognizes the reality of women in the workplace and the fact that childrearing is not the sole responsibility of the mother, but of the father and of nonparental caregivers as well. As these sentiments began to dominate family life, and as the outside world entered the home—in a way unprecedented by radio—first through television and increasingly through other electronic means, the sentiment of the family changed from one of domesticity to one of *urbanity*.

These changed sentiments entailed new perceptions of parents and of their offspring. Most fathers and mothers entering permeable family relationships did not grow up in extended families and had little intuitive knowledge about childrearing. Such parents began to look to experts for advice not about *how do* children grow and develop, but rather about *how to* parent, discipline, toilet train, and so on. Those writing for parents were happy to oblige and we have had an outpouring of books providing a variety of techniques of childrearing. Unfortunately, many of these books about children and adolescents say little about child development and suggest that the same techniques and verbal formulae are appropriate for preschoolers, children, and adolescents.

It is because of the changed sentiments and parental perceptions that the perceptions of children and adolescents have altered as discussed earlier. When 50% of marriages have a probability of ending in divorce, when parenting is shared with non-parental caregivers, and when children can no longer be protected or shielded from the violence, brutality, and sexuality of the world as conveyed by the media, children, in order to deal with these experiences, are perceived as competent. Adolescent immaturity, in turn, is no longer a fitting sequel to childhood competence. Moreover, the many postmodern realities described earlier contribute to the present-day perception of *adolescent sophistication*.

Other social changes have also transformed the context in which young people are growing up. Starting in the sixties a new youth culture emerged, spearheaded by a new musical form: rock and roll. Until the advent of that musical style young people had modeled their musical choices, their language, their clothing, and their behaviors (smoking, drinking) after that of adults. With the creation of a new youth culture and the elevation of that culture's heroes, adults were no longer the models emulated by adolescents. Indeed, it might be contended that the new youth culture was created precisely because adult society no longer provided a place for adolescent social experimentation. From this standpoint, the emergence of a unique youth culture expresses young people's need to have a place of their own, even if it is primarily an electronic one.

Social Change and Teenage Identity

The shift in orientation from a modern to a postmodern family is mirrored in the altered social science depictions of adolescence. As suggested earlier, modern writers described adolescence as a period of storm and stress, of emotional turmoil and conflict. The late Erik Erikson, the last of the preeminent advocates of modern adolescence, described the period as one during which the adolescent's task was to construct a sense of personal identity (1950). In Erikson's view, the adolescent must bring together all of the various, and sometimes conflicting, facets of self into a working whole that at once provides continuity with the past and a focus and direction for the future. This sense of personal identity includes various roles (son, daughter, student, athlete, musician, artist, and so on), various traits and abilities (quiet, outgoing, timid, generous, high-strung), as well as the teenager's personal playbill of likes and dislikes, political and social attitudes, religious orientation, and much more.

In Erikson's view, the task of constructing an identity

is a difficult and complex one. It is not undertaken until the teen years in part because the young person has not yet acquired all the necessary experiential ingredients and in part because, prior to adolescence, young people lack the requisite mental abilities. Only in adolescence do young people attain the new mental operations that Inhelder and Piaget (1958) termed "formal operations" that enable young people to construct theories. It is not unreasonable to characterize the sense of personal identity as a theory of the self. Constructing an identity, inventing oneself if you will, is a creative endeavor and takes much time and concentrated effort. That is why Erikson has suggested that teenagers either make or find a "moratorium," a period of relatively unencumbered time for themselves during which they can engage in the process of identity formation.

Erikson was writing during the modern period and his conception of adolescence was colored by the prevailing societal perception of this age group. Now that we have moved into the postmodern era and see adolescence as sophisticated, rather than as immature, the social science depictions of adolescence have changed as well. The following is the stereotypic depiction of modern adolescence:

> The adolescent presumably is engaged in a struggle to emancipate himself from his parents. He therefore resists and rebels against any restrictions and controls they impose upon his behavior. To facilitate the process of emancipation, he transfers his dependency to the peer group, whose values are typically in conflict with those of his parents. Since his behavior is now largely under the control of peer group members he begins to adopt idiosyncratic clothing, mannerisms, lingo and other forms of peer group fad behavior. Because of the conflicting values and pressures to

which the adolescent is exposed, he is ambivalent, frightened and unpredictable. (Bandura 1964)

This portrayal of young people has been challenged by many postmodern psychiatrists. Daniel Offer and his colleagues have collected data to demonstrate that the adolescent years are no more conflictual than are other age periods (1975). Likewise, Robert J. Lifton argues that in today's world young people have to postpone various facets of identity formation, particularly the occupational, until young adulthood (1976). Finally, psychoanalyst Heinz Kohut contends that adolescence is a transition period like other transition periods in life and is no more or no less important for personality development than any other life period (1972).

And it is certainly true that in today's world young people cannot postpone identity formation until adolescence. As we have noted earlier, from an early age children are confronted with the most sordid facets of life's continuum. From the first few years of life they must begin to build some protective, immunizing structures. At the same time, as Lifton suggests, important identity construction must continue throughout life given that large numbers of people will change vocational and family identities in the course of a lifetime.

In addition, some of the emotional conflict between adolescents and parents is also likely to be less today than was true in the past. In the nuclear family, emotional bonds were very close and adolescent rebellion was required, in part at least, to loosen those attachments. Family emotional ties are less intense today, thanks to the facts that many children have been cared for by non-parental adults from an early age and that, given today's economic pressures, parents are spending less time with their offspring.

In many respects, therefore, the postmodern social science portrayal of adolescents as sophisticated is more accurate than was the modern portrait of adolescent immaturity. It is also more particular and individualized, in contrast to the overgeneralized stereotype of the modern adolescent. We are more ready today, than in the past, to recognize the diversity among young people and the many paths they take to maturity. This said, it is also true that adolescence is a unique life passage. No other transition is witness to the extraordinary physical, physiological, and psychological transformations of this period. And even if identity formation begins earlier, and continues far longer than it once did, the teen years are still a period of great vulnerability and fragility. It remains an epoch when young people are still very much in need of adult authority and commitment.

Two Ways of Growing

When we speak of a "mature" person, we usually mean, to some extent, an individual with a healthy sense of identity and self acquired during adolescence. Likewise, when we speak of an immature person, we have in mind someone who lacks a strong base of personhood. The sense of personal identity is constructed by one of two means. One of these is the process of *differentiation* (the process of discriminating or separating out concepts, feelings, and emotions) and *integration* (putting the separated parts together into a higher-ordered whole). The other path to identity formation is the process of *substitution* (merely replacing one set of concepts, feelings, or emotions for another). In general, a healthy sense of identity is achieved when growth by differentiation and integration takes precedence over growth by substitution.

Clearly, the young person's abilities and talents, the kind of parenting he or she receives, and the social climate in which the teenager grows up are critical in determining which of these two paths of development will predominate. Growth by integration is conflictual, time-consuming, and laborious. An illustration from the cognitive domain will illustrate the process. A child who is acquiring the concept of *squareness*, for example, must first differentiate among a variety of different shapes before he or she can separate squareness from roundness and pointedness. Once this is accomplished, the child must begin to integrate all the different types of squareness, large and small squares, red and black squares, windows, boxes, and so on into a general concept of squareness that includes squares of many different kinds and excludes other shapes.

The principles of differentiation and integration operate with respect to the attainment of a self-concept. To acquire a consistent sense of self, children must experience many different social interactions that allow them to differentiate their own feelings, desires, thoughts, and beliefs from those of other people. At the same time, however, young people also need to discover how much they are like other people. Children need to discover that other people don't like insults any more than they do and that other people do appreciate compliments as much as children themselves do. As a result of this slow process of differentiating the self from others, learning how one is both like and different from others, children are prepared, in adolescence, to construct a stable and unique perception of themselves.

Once growth by integration, including the construction of a sense of identity, has been accomplished, it is difficult, if not impossible, to break down. In the physical realm, once children have acquired the concept of squareness in the manner described earlier, they will not lose it. The concept is now a part of their view of reality. In the social realm, the same holds true. People who have acquired a sense of identity largely through a process of differentiation and higher-order integration do not lose their sense of self even under the most trying circumstances. Some survivors of concentration camps and of brainwashing have had such well-grounded self-concepts that even isolation, starvation, and torture did not break them.

Mental structures, whether physical or social, that are achieved through differentiation and integration also conserve energy and reduce stress. Once we know what a square is, we can identify it immediately; we don't have to worry about what it is and what to do with it. In the same way, once we have attained an integrated sense of self, we know how to behave in a variety of different social situations. We know how to show respect to those in authority, how to be courteous at social gatherings, and how to resist those who are trying to get us to do something that is not in our own best interest. A well-developed sense of personal identity thus provides us with many strategies for dealing with psychological stress, the bane of postmodern society.

Growth, however, can also follow the path of substitution. An example is the transition from the dial to the push-button telephone. Learning to dial a number by turning a wheel is not a preparation for getting that number by pushing buttons. Both actions have the same result, but the first skill is neither required to learn the second, nor is it incorporated within it. Both skills exist side by side. Either skill can be drawn upon as needed. This type of learning is clearly of value, particularly in a society with rapidly changing technology. In adapting to a new technology, say an upgraded version of a word processor or spreadsheet, it is an advantage to be able to replace old habits with new ones.

The same path can be followed in social growth. Indeed, substitution is the kind of process suggested by the well-known adage, "When in Rome do as the Romans do." In some social situations where we do not know the rules, it is generally considered wise to follow the example of others who are familiar with the situation. But this type of learning is not adaptive when it comes to constructing a sense of personal identity. A sense of self constructed by the simple compilation of feelings, thoughts, and beliefs appropriated from others amounts to a *patchwork* self. A young person who has constructed a sense of self in this way has no inner sense of self to fall back on for guidance and direction. Such individuals are easily influenced by others, both because they have no inner gyroscope and because they have developed the habit of following others rather than making their own decisions. Each new situation is a fresh challenge, and they are always looking for external direction—which may not be forthcoming. Adolescents with a patchwork self are vulnerable to stress because they must always look to others for coping strategies. These young people lack the history of differentiation and higher-order integration that would prepare them to deal with new situations on the basis of past experiences and reality constructions.

Obviously development is not an "either/or," and young people fall all along the continuum from growth by integration to growth by substitution. Nevertheless, those young people who have progressed largely by integration have a strong sense of personal identity and are able to postpone immediate gratification for the attainment of long-term goals. They are future-oriented and inner-directed. In contrast, those whose development was predominantly by substitution often acquire a patchwork self. Young people with this history are less able to postpone immediate gratification. They tend to be present-oriented and other-directed, easily influenced by peers and by fads and trends. Unfortunately, the sentiments and perceptions of the postmodern family, as these are reflected and mirrored by institutions within the larger society, are more conducive to growth by substitution than they are to growth by integration. Although the majority of young people are still growing up with an integrated sense of self, many more than in the past have elements of the patchwork self.

The foregoing discussion provides the basic argument of this book, namely, that there is little or no place for adolescents in today's postmodern society. This has contributed to many more young people than in the past acquiring elements of the patchwork self that make them more vulnerable to stress. At the very same time we are also exposing young people to new and more demanding forms of stress at ages when they are the most vulnerable.

The New Morbidity

The evidence for both the ascendance of the patchwork self and the increased stress upon the young is what has been called the *new morbidity*: the dramatic postmodern rise in stress-related dysfunctions in this age group (Haggarty, Roughman, and Bless 1975). During the modern era, most young people who contracted diseases such as polio or tuberculosis died. Fortunately, thanks to modern medicine, we can now largely prevent these diseases. Nonetheless, today we lose as many or more adolescents through stress-related behaviors. Stress-related death, disease, and injury among teenagers constitutes the new morbidity.

Perhaps the clearest evidence of the rise of both the patchwork self and stress among young people is their abuse of drugs. Young people use drugs for the same reason adults do, to reduce stress. In this postmodern era, when young people have lost their special place and many opportunities to grow by integration, substance abuse has become epidemic. Alcohol is the most abused substance and plays a leading role in the new morbidity. Substance abuse-related automobile accidents are by far the largest contributor to the new morbidity. Many different studies concur in finding, through postmortem examination, that at least half of those teenagers killed in car accidents had been drinking alcohol before the accident. But that is only the tip of the iceberg. The National Safety Council estimates that there were 630,000 nonfatal motor vehicle accidents in the 15- to 24-year-old age group in 1991. About half of these accidents were alcohol related and many of the injuries were permanent or disabling. Recent surveys suggest that 33% of high school seniors, 24% of tenth graders, and 13% of eighth graders admit to getting drunk—drinking five or more drinks every two weeks (O'Malley, Johnston, and Bachman 1993). "Teenage social drinking is a myth. Teenagers drink to get drunk," as one reporter put it (Cobb 1982).

Another contributor to the new morbidity is teenage suicide. Between the years 1960 and 1988, the suicide rate for 15- to 19-year-olds more than tripled. More than 5,000 adolescents take their own lives each year, and for every adolescent who succeeds, some 100 make an unsuccessful attempt. One in ten teenagers has, at one or another time, contemplated suicide. Gender differences in mode of suicide are changing. Young women, who in the past resorted to pills and slashing their wrists, are now using the more violent means employed by young men: hanging and shooting (Tishler 1992). In 1994, two teenage girls took their own lives by placing their bodies across railroad tracks. Many apparently "accidental" teenage deaths may also be, at least in part, suicidal.

Perhaps the most frightening contributor to the new morbidity is teenage gun violence. Firearms were the second highest cause of death (after car accidents) for all children from 10 to 14 years of age as well as for teenagers and young adults. Among teenagers and young adults, one in every four deaths was from a gunshot. Just between the years 1985 and 1990 deaths due to guns has tripled for young black males and almost doubled for white youth. Murders by juveniles have also increased at a frightening rate. Between 1986 and 1991 murders by 14- to 17-year-olds more than doubled (Jenkins and Bell 1992). Murders are only part of the story of gun violence; the number of young people injured or maimed by guns is far greater, ranging from 30 to 67 incidents per day nationwide (Jenkins and Bell 1992).

The new morbidity is but one measure of the stress experienced by contemporary young people. There are many other, nonfatal behaviors that offer evidence of the crisis of contemporary youth. Our teenage pregnancy rates are the highest of any Western country, almost seven times that of the Netherlands (U.S. Department of Health and Human Services 1990). The Center for Disease Control reports a continued high rate of STDs among adolescents associated with earlier and more widespread sexual activity. Although AIDS is not a major problem among adolescents, it is now recognized that many young people contract the virus during the teen years.

The new morbidity and the other problem behaviors of young people are frightful evidence of the stresses they are experiencing. In the succeeding chapters we will first look at some of the enduring developmental aspects of adolescence and then at some of the postmodern social and institutional changes that increasingly ignore the perennial and all-important characteristics of this unique stage of life.

CHAPTER 2

Thinking in a New Key

Getting comfortable with new ways of thinking is one of the most difficult tasks confronting young adolescents. This is not an obvious fact. Indeed, we adults tend to assume that coping with the physical and hormonal changes they are experiencing is what gives teenagers the most trouble. Rapid changes in their height, uneven changes in their facial features (the nose grows more rapidly than the chin, making many young people look nose-heavy), and frequent changes in their moods are far more obvious than the changes in their mental abilities. Accordingly, when young people are irritable, sullen, and uncommunicative, we are likely to consider these reactions by-products of rapid physical growth.

We may, however, be putting the blame on the wrong culprit. The changes in mental ability that accompany adolescence are as emotionally troubling, or even more so, than the physical and physiological transformations. Starting at about the age of eleven or twelve, adolescents develop the ability to think at a higher, more abstract level than they did as children—to think in a new key. These new mental abilities bring about a Copernican revolution in the way young people think and feel about themselves, others, and the world in general. Indeed, the ways in which young people react to their reconfigured bodies and emotions are very much affected by the fresh ways in which they see themselves and the world. For example, the self-consciousnes so common in the early teen years is a result of changes in their thinking, not just of physical changes (or lack of them) in their bodies. In a letter asking for help, a boy named George reflects how his late physical maturity interacts with his new concern for peer group approval:

> Help, I don't have any pubic hair that shows. The boys call me "Baldy" and the girls want to know why, and it's so embarrassing. I'm fourteen, shouldn't I have it by now? (Winship 1983)

George's new mental powers, which in his case are in advance of his physical maturity, underlie the manner in which he reacts to his comparatively slow growth rate. He has constructed an ideal standard of physical development and is troubled that he does not measure up to it. He is also very distressed over what he assumes his peers think about him. Both of these concerns derive from his new ability to think in a new key.

It is important to remember that young people are as unfamiliar with their expanded thinking abilities as they are with their reconfigured bodies. Moreover, to become proficient in, and at ease with, thinking on a higher level takes a lot of practice. Adolescents need to regularly exercise their expanded powers of thinking just as they need to exercise their bodies to be comfortable with their increased height and muscle power. And just as adolescents are sometimes awkward and clumsy in maneuvering with their newly elongated arms and legs, they are sometimes equally awkward in their use of their newly expanded intellectual powers. As adults we have to be careful not to mistake young people's gaucheness—which may sometimes pop out in the form of ill-thought-out or insensitive remarks—as anything more sinister than inexperience.

Formal Operational Thinking

Since ancient times, the age of six or seven has been known as the age of reason, for it is at this age that children are first observed to employ logical thinking. Particularly observed was the ability of children to employ the syllogistic logic of Aristotle. Syllogistic reasoning is the basis for the classifications that made up the bulk of Aristotelian science. For example, the classic syllogism

All men are mortal	(Major Premise)
Socrates is a man	(Minor Premise)
. . . Socrates is mortal	(Conclusion)

enables us to classify Socrates as mortal once we have first categorized him as a man. Up until relatively recent times, syllogistic reasoning was regarded as the only form of reasoning. In the nineteenth century, however, new forms of logic were invented. These new forms of logic, Boolean algebra and symbolic logic, dealt with many variables rather than the two to which the syllogism is limited. They also introduced the idea of logical truth that is independent of actual events. Within symbolic logic, for example, the statement "It is raining" can be true regardless of the weather.

It was Jean Piaget who discovered that a second age of reason appears in adolescence resembling the operations of symbolic logic (Inhelder and Piaget 1958). This new level of thinking enables adolescents to understand the logic of propositions and of truth tables. Whereas children can reason about two properties or relations at the same time, adolescents can reason about many variables simultaneously.

In addition, this new mode of thinking permits them to consider possibilities, to imagine what *might be* rather than what *is*. If, for example, you say to a child, "Let us suppose we live in a world in which coal is white, what color do you think snow would be?" the child, unable to deal with conditions contrary to fact, will object, "But coal is black." An adolescent, in contrast, can accept the contrary-to-fact statement as a purely logical proposition that can be reasoned about regardless of its factual truth.

Piaget attributed young people's ability to engage in propositional thinking to their attainment of a new system of mental abilities that he termed *formal operations.* These new mental operations empower young people to expand their thinking in many different and more abstract ways than was possible when they were children. To illustrate, these new operations permit young people to go beyond the here and now, to truly understand the concepts (e.g., centuries) of historical time and those (e.g., light-years) of celestial space. They also enable young people to deal with second-symbol systems—with symbols for symbols. Armed with formal operations, adolescents can learn subjects like algebra and calculus, interpret literature, understand allegory, and enjoy satire and parody. In each of these achievements young people's newly attained power to understand that a symbol (say the algebraic symbol A) can represent another symbol (say the number 10) reflects their capacity to think in a new key.

A personal anecdote may help to illustrate this adolescent mode of thinking. Some years ago, when my sons were young, we were sitting at the dinner table and my oldest son, who was thirteen at the time, was talking about a book he was reading, Tolkien's *The Hobbit.* His brother, who was eight, misheard Paul and asked "What is a Hobble?" In a rare moment of comic inspiration I made what I thought was a pretty funny joke. I said, " A Hobble is a Hobbit with a sore foot." My older son grimaced at this terrible pun, but his brother remained mystified until his brother explained what a Hobbit was. The understanding of puns, the lowest form of humor, nonetheless requires the highest level of intellectual development. Puns, like simile, metaphor, irony, and satire, demand that young people grasp that words can have both literal and suggestive meanings, can be symbols for symbols. This awareness requires the attainment of formal operations.

Many of the lyrics of contemporary music targeted at adolescents are rife with sexual, sadistic, and satanic metaphors that, fortunately, are missed by younger children. The rock group AC/DC, for instance, has recorded a song titled "Let Me Put My Love Into You." Indeed, salacious wordplay is so common in heavy-metal music that it has been parodied in such comedic portrayals of adolescent "headbangers" as *Wayne's World* ("Ex-squeeze me?") and *Beavis and Butt-head* ("Heh heh, he said 'hole.'"). Through these broad satires a teenage audience can both enjoy spotting a word's double meaning and laugh at the characters for enjoying it a little too much.

One reason teenagers enjoy wordplay so much, aside from the sexual innuendo in much of it, is that it allows them to practice their mental abilities at the same time that it enables them to differentiate themselves from the adult world. This is particularly true of words that young people themselves create. Each generation has its own words for certain experiences (e.g., what one generation described as "the cat's meow" a later generation described as "awesome," and what one generation called a "brain" a later one called a "nerd"). With these words young people begin to define their own generation's unique take on values, tastes, and preferences, as well as on their antipathies.

Interestingly, as young people come to be treated more as equals in postmodern society, they seem to go to greater and greater lengths to distinguish themselves from adults in their language, dress, and behavior. From ear and nose rings to slam dancing and jeans with holes in the knees, young people give clear evidence of their new understanding of the importance and power of symbolism. That is why it is important not to take all of this symbolism at face value. Even the most garishly attired adolescent may be a pussycat who feels that he or she is only parodying adults' erroneous stereotypic impressions of teenagers.

Adolescents also appreciate the symbolism created by others. It is the symbolism of the lyrics of rock or rap groups that appeals to adolescents when adults find their literal meanings outrageous. For many young people, the lyrics express what they themselves are feeling and thus can have a therapeutic effect. As one young man put it:

> Groups like Suicidal Tendencies and Black Flag and Dead Milkmen. They're sort of a parody group, but you listen to it and you know what they are trying to say. It's sort of a parody on life, I mean there's something wrong with the world and they know it. But they're trying to find a bit of solution and you hear it and you are pretty sure of yourself after you listen for a while. (Louv 1990)

The appearance of formal operational thinking enables young people to express gender differences more fully than was possible when they were children. For example, in their self-descriptions, as in their literary and musical preferences, adolescent males and females begin to move quite far apart from one another. We don't really know to what extent these differences are culturally and socially transmitted, or to what extent they may represent more basic gender differences. Whatever their origin, the differences are real enough. Consider the following two interviews conducted by Carol Gilligan and her colleagues. A fourteen-year-old boy and a fourteen-year-old girl were both asked, "How would you describe yourself to yourself?"

> JACK: What am I? [pause] That's a hard one . . . Well, I ski—think I am a pretty good skier. And basketball, I think I'm a pretty good basketball player. I'm a good runner . . . and I think I'm pretty smart. My grades are good . . . I get along with lots of people and teachers . . . And, I'm not too fussy, I don't think—easy to satisfy usually, depending upon what it is.

Compare this with Beth's response to the same question:

> BETH: I like to do a lot of things. I like to do activities and stuff. I like people. I like little kids and babies. And I like older people too, like grandparents and everything: they're special and stuff. I don't know, I'd guess I say I like myself. I have a lot going on. I have a lot of friends in the neighborhood and I laugh a lot. (Gilligan, Ward, and Taylor 1988)

Boys are likely to be competitive and achievement oriented, and to measure themselves against an absolute standard. In contrast, girls are more socially focused and tend to evaluate themselves from the perspective of their empathy for others and their interpersonal skills. Obviously there is a lot of overlap between young men and women in this regard and the differences are heavily conditioned socially, but the differences are real.

In addition to providing young people with symbolic means of expression and comprehension, formal operations also allow young people to use language in more colorful and creative ways than was true during childhood. Adolescents can use puns, metaphors, sarcasm, and satire without fully realizing they are using an allegorical mode of speech. They also can create poetry of great power and beauty, of great sadness and of great joy:

A Dream in the Clouds

You may laugh at my dream
Yet I am more than what I seem
I may look like a weak lamb
But I am sure of what I am
I am hidden among the trees
And my heart is not at ease
But I will rise above the rest
And fly free of the sheltered nest
All will see my grace and beauty
As I go about my duty
Clip not my wings that I may not fly
For now I am soaring up in the sky.
(Rich 1995)

As these examples make clear, teenagers' new mental abilities transform and color the way in which they deal with their changing bodies and their social relationships. In the following pages we will look at other ways in which young people's new intellectual abilities affect the way they think about themselves and about other people and the world in general. We should not be surprised if teenagers are sometimes naive in using their new mental powers. Young people need to practice these expanded thinking abilities before they feel entirely at ease with them.

Idealism and Criticalness

Formal operations enable young people to go beyond the real and the immediate to the possible and to the future. Now adolescents can envisage a world where families are intact and happy, where communities are safe and welcoming, and where countries are concerned with preserving natural resources and protecting the environment. Young people contrast this ideal world with the ugly realities of the experienced world in which they live. Not surprisingly, adolescents blame adults for these failings and they become critical of adults in general and of parents in particular.

With respect to adult society, young people center their attention upon the hypocrisy and deceitfulness of some adults, particularly those in public life. They attack these failings with merciless satire and parody. *Mad* magazine voices the kind of attacks adolescents make against well-known figures in society. In an article entitled "Why Do We Believe?" we read the following:

> Why Do We Believe . . . A National Rifle Association that says it promotes gun safety and personal security . . . when the main freebie that comes with membership is a $20,000 insurance policy for accidental death or dismemberment? . . .
>
> Television programmers who refuse to run ads for condoms or public service announcements for safe sex because their audiences wouldn't stand for it . . . when the other 23 hours and 59 minutes of their schedule is filled with drooling lustbags doing every smutty thing possible (except watching condom ads)? (Devlin 1995)

Young adolescents also turn their critical spotlight upon their parents. Even when young people have a good relationship with their parents and when they are given a voice in decision making, the need to be critical and to belittle parents is irresistible:

> TANYA: Why don't we visit Grandma and then go someplace exotic like the Everglades?
>
> WILLIE: Do you know how hot it is in Florida in August? I vote to skip the family visit this year and go to Acapulco. That's a real vacation.
>
> DAD: I could sure use some time on the beach.
> WILLIE: Right, Dad, but you don't want to share it with a crocodile, do you? (Cobb 1995)

This new faultfinding derives in part, as in the above example, from the adolescent's need to feel more competent than parents in dealing with life's practicalities. In this way adolescents reassure themselves that they are indeed able to assume adult roles and responsibilities. Adolescents also criticize their parents out of their concern about the impression their parents will make on their friends. The respectful, loving, ten-year-old for whom parents can do no wrong becomes the disrespectful, critical twelve-year-old for whom parents can do no right. Suddenly a boy who never washed, changed his shirt, or used a fork without a battle becomes a connoisseur of manners, dress, and behavior. Out of the blue, as it were, parents are told that they do not know how to talk, walk, or dress.

A personal example can illustrate this motive for faultfinding. My own parents were Russian immigrants. This never bothered me until I became a teenager and discovered, as if I had never heard them speak before, that they spoke with heavy accents. They also looked different from my friends' parents. My mother grew her hair long, down to the floor, as she had in Russia, and wore it in two large braids that she then made into a bun at the back of her head. I still remember now, with lingering shame and regret, how embarrassed I was to introduce my parents to my friends.

Faultfinding has other roots in young people's new thinking abilities. With formal operations, adolescents can now reconstruct their childhood and see it quite differently from how they did when they were younger. Children tend to deny or ignore parental transgressions, but once they become adolescents they reconstruct their childhood and pay us back for all the sins, real or imagined, that we committed against them:

> Buba is now the ripe age of 11. Yesterday my husband and I received a note from her (a common form of communication around here when one is particularly upset) that was so mature and such a plea for understanding that we both wept at the passing of our little girl.
>
> In it she thanked us for all of the wonderful things we have done for her (good opening, lull parents into feeling good) and then hit us right between the eyes, the old one-two about never listening and never understanding and blaming her for everything and yelling too much and feeling left out of the family and not being sure we loved her too much (if at all) (take a breath for effect) what are we going to do about it? (*Parent* 1983)

There is still another dimension of adolescents' criticalness of their parents that has to do more with their feelings than with their thoughts. Given the hormonal surges of this age period young people often form romantic

"crushes" on members of the opposite sex. Formal operations aid and abet such attachments by enabling young
people to idealize the person to whom they are attracted.
Yet such attractions cause problems in a teenager's relationship with parents. Many adolescents believe that love
comes in a fixed amount that will neither increase nor de-
crease. Accordingly, if they have only a pound of love and
give half of it to the mother and half to the father (forget the
siblings), there is none to give to the new idol. Where is the
love going to come from? Clearly, it has to be taken from
the love allotted to the parents. When adolescents develop
a crush, they also feel that they are taking something that
they owe to their parents and giving it to someone else.

Not surprisingly, when this happens, young people
feel guilty. After all, their parents have taken good care of
them all of these years and are entitled to their half-pound
of love apiece. Or are they? One way to resolve the issue
without feeling guilty is to find fault with the parents. If
they are unloving, insensitive, demanding, and so on, they
do not deserve their half-pound of love apiece. By measuring parents against an ideal, the teenager is justified in
withdrawing some love from the parents and giving it instead to a friend of the opposite sex.

The benefits of this process of measuring society
against ideal standards and finding fault with parents are
only reaped later in young adulthood. Adolescents who
have looked at their society and its institutions with a critical eye will be more responsible citizens than if they had
never challenged authority. In the same way, young people
who have recognized that their parents are both wonderful
and flawed are better prepared than they would otherwise
have been to enter into positive and rewarding relationships. Tolerance for the flaws of parents extends to others
and eventually to oneself.

Although teenagers' criticisms of their parents have positive long-term outcomes and should not be taken too seriously, they should also not go unanswered. When young people attack our appearance or behavior, various responses are appropriate:

"I am very happy with the way I am, so I guess you will have to accept it. That is what growing up is all about."

"Okay, I am perfectly willing to hear your complaints against me. But I demand equal time to voice my complaints against you."

Such replies can help young people to differentiate their point of view from ours. Speaking up can help them to see that we may be as unhappy with them as they are with us.

Argumentativeness

At each stage of intellectual development, young people are motivated to practice and use the abilities they have newly acquired. Parents who could not wait for their one-year-old to speak cannot wait for their three-year-old to be silent. Likewise, the five-year-old who is learning to count will ask repeatedly, "Do you want to hear me count to a thousand?" And he or she will do so at the slightest invitation. Children find, or create, the opportunity to practice their new mental abilities. The same is true for adolescents.

Thanks to formal operations, young people now have the ability to marshal facts and logic in support of the argument they are forwarding. In addition, in contrast to children who tend to see things as black or white, good or bad, and right or wrong, adolescents come to appreciate shades of gray, and degrees of goodness and badness, as well as gradations of rightness and wrongness. As a result, teenagers will no longer be content with the parental mandate, "Do it because I tell you to." Rather, they want to know the reason for why they should or should not do something, and they want more than one.

> "Mom, can I go over to Noah's house?"
>
> "No, you haven't finished your homework, it's a school night, and you need to get up early."
>
> "But I have done most of my homework, and I can do the rest in study hall, and I can't fall asleep anyway."
>
> "No dice, not going out on school nights is the rule, and you really have to have a good reason to break it."
>
> "It is important, he has a new video game."
>
> "Sorry, you'll have to do better than that."
>
> (Winship 1983)

Such arguments, while painful for parents, have to be understood, at least in part, as an effort by the adolescent to use his or her new powers of argumentation.

Indeed, parents of teenagers often say to me, "But he (or she) is arguing for the sake of arguing." I tell them that they are entirely correct—that is just what the teenager is doing! It is not just the wish (to go out on a weeknight) that prompts teenagers to challenge their parents, but the need to argue for the sake of practicing these confrontational skills. Once we appreciate the motivation behind much of the argumentativeness of young teenagers, we can handle the issue in ways that help facilitate constructive growth by integration. We can help teenagers to distinguish between argumentation as an exercise in logic and argumentation that is an attempt at persuasion.

Young people need to argue, but we should make clear to them that we are more than willing to argue about matters of principle, but not about emotional positions. Homework should be done as a matter of principle—it is a responsibility to which a young person commits himself or herself to by virtue of being a student. A teenager may want to argue about these principles, and that is fine. What we as parents must do is avoid arguing about matters of taste, preference, or interest. It is really not productive to argue about a young person's taste in music. On the other hand, it is legitimate to argue about whether or not song lyrics that seem to celebrate suicide are conducive to such actions on the part of listeners. By arguing about principles, rather than emotionally linked matters of taste or preference, we provide a model for young people for distinguishing productive from nonproductive argument.

Self-Consciousness

Another characteristic of young adolescents that is a direct outgrowth of their ability to think in a new key is self-consciousness. Formal operations make it possible for teenagers to think about thinking. Children think, but they do not think about thinking. For example, in a study I conducted regarding children's conceptions of their religious denomination, I asked, "Can a dog or a cat be a Protestant (or Catholic, or Jew depending upon the child's own religious affiliation)?" Regardless of religious affiliation, children responded that a dog or a cat could not be a Protestant, Catholic, or Jew because the minister, priest, or rabbi would not allow the animal in the church or the synagogue. "They would make noise and run around," one child explained.

Teenagers, on the other hand, uniformly offered a different answer: "They are not intelligent; they would not understand religion." Others said, "They don't believe in God." Words like "intelligence" or "understanding" or "belief" are terms for mental states that children rarely use but that adolescents employ with increasing frequency. Teenagers can think about thinking; about what goes on in their minds and what goes on in the minds of others.

Because adolescents are caught up with the transformations that they are undergoing—in their bodies, in their facial structure, in their feelings, and in their emotions, as well as in their thinking powers—they become self-centered. They assume that everyone around them is preoccupied with the same subject that engrosses them: namely, themselves. I call this assumption, that everyone is watching you and is concerned with your behavior and appearance as you are yourself, the *imaginary audience*. It is the imaginary audience that accounts for the teenager's extreme self-consciousness. Teenagers feel that they are always on stage and that everyone around them is as aware of, and as concerned about, their appearance and behavior as they are themselves.

All of us retain some remnants of the imaginary audience fantasies even after we are fully grown. I recall sitting alone in a restaurant in a strange city. I accidentally dropped my knife, and it hit the marble floor with what sounded to me like an ear-rending clang. For a moment I was sure that everyone was looking at me and thinking, "What a klutz!" Some adults even become dependent upon the imaginary audience. The fading motion picture star may become depressed because he or she is sure the audience will see every new wrinkle, gray hair, and blue vein. Other men and women, puffed up with their success, are sure that everyone recognizes and admires them. At a restaurant, they loudly call the headwaiter by his first name, make a show of being seated at the best table, and so on. In many ways, such actions create the audience that the individual already believes is watching.

Of course, at times we all succumb to the imaginary

audience fantasy, whether in a positive or a negative sense. Most of us recognize, however, that in fact we are in other people's consciousness for only a brief moment or two, if at all. Most people spend the majority of their time preoccupied with their own lives, their own problems, their own hopes, and their own frustrations. Of course, people admire a good actor, an outstanding athlete, or a superb musician. But this admiration is fleeting and does not occupy most of our waking moments. That insight, however, usually comes later in life, and young adolescents stubbornly believe that they are the focus of everyone's abiding attention and concern.

The imaginary audience helps explain a lot of early adolescent behaviors and preoccupations. A girl may believe that everyone noticed that she stayed in the school rest room too long. She may believe that the audience noticed the spot on her skirt and that everyone noticed that one of her bra straps was loose. Boys, in turn, often wear their shirts out to cover up unwelcome, involuntary erections. In the following fictional passage from Paula Danziger's *The Cat Ate My Gymsuit*, a sensitive, overweight girl handles the problem of avoiding gym in a manner that speaks poignantly of the teenager's sometimes overwhelming self-consciousness:

> I just sat there. Trying to change into a gymsuit while hiding my mini bra and fat body would have been a gymnastic feat in itself.
>
> Once the class started, I walked up to the gym teacher, Schmidt.
>
> "All right, Lewis, what is it this time?"
>
> "The cat ate my gymsuit."
>
> She shook her head, frowned and wrote another zero in her marking book.

I sat down to watch my eighty millionth volley-
ball game. (1973)

For this teenage girl, as for many others, the imaginary audience looms so large, she has to get off the stage.

The imaginary audience helps us to understand several otherwise puzzling changes in teenagers' behavior. For
example, how are we to explain the boy for whom every request to take a bath or to put on fresh clothing once pro-
voked a battle and who now, overnight it seems, begins
spending hours in the bathroom, bathing and combing his
hair? When adolescents stand in front of a mirror, they
imagine the audience's reaction to their appearance. They
are also much more sensitive about public exposure. That
is why it is so important for adults who deal with young
teenagers to avoid public correction or criticism. If we have
to speak to a teenager about behavior, the considerate thing
to do is to wait until we can speak in private.

As teenagers grow older, their concern with the imaginary audience begins to diminish. Through broader experience and expanded social relationships they come to
focus less upon themselves. This change has been demonstrated in a number of studies using the Imaginary Audience Scale (IAS). The scale consists of items such as, "You
have been looking forward to going to a party for over a
month. Once you arrive, after an hour-long drive, you discover a grease spot on your slacks or skirt. Do you stay, or
return home?" The results from the different studies are
fairly consistent. Most preteens are generally unconcerned,
and responded that they would go to the party anyway.
Similarly, older teenagers (sixteen to seventeen years) generally answered, "They are my friends, no one would care."
But many young teenagers (thirteen to fourteen years) said
they would go home or stand in a dark corner or pour

something on themselves to explain the spot.

Clearly, the imaginary audience mirrors teenagers' inability to differentiate between their own preoccupations and those of others. We can best help teenagers make these distinctions if we take a middle ground between fully accepting the young person's point of view or completely rejecting it. Suppose a teenage girl has a blemish on her cheek and states that she is ugly, that the whole world knows she is ugly, and that she won't leave the house. We won't get very far if we try to reassure here that she is pretty. Nor will she appreciate it if we agree with her assessment of herself as ugly. If we take a middle position and say something like, "Well, you certainly don't look ugly to me, but that is my opinion. What do other people do? Do they make faces, say things to you, snicker or what?" In this way we encourage the young woman to test the audience fantasy against reality. This testing of the imaginary audience against the real audience helps young people to discover the difference between fantasy and reality. In this way adolescents learn a strategy for dealing with impressions, gain objectivity, and free themselves from some of the more negative effects of the imaginary audience.

Speciality and Invulnerability

Because young adolescents are so convinced that other people are intent upon observing and thinking about them, they get an inflated opinion of their own uniqueness and invulnerability. They begin to think that they are special, different from other people. "Other people will grow old and die, not me. Other people will never realize their burning ambitions, not me. Other people will get hooked on drugs, not me." The teenage boy who is sure that the pretty girl at the party is admiring him, reflects this kind

of thinking. Another teenager may believe that her admired teacher really likes her better than the other students
in the class but is unwilling to show her preference. Many
young people (and many adults) smoke under the belief
that they are invulnerable to any harm from this habit. I
call this feeling of speciality and invulnerability the *personal fable*.

Like the imaginary audience, the personal fable, in a
somewhat more realistic form, stays with us for the rest of
our lives. It is our legacy from adolescent thought. Given
all the dangers of contemporary life, we would hardly ven-
ture outside our homes if we did not clothe ourselves in a
personal fable, a shield of our own speciality and invulnerability. It is the fable that convinces the soldier going into
battle that though other men will be killed or wounded, he
will survive. Likewise, many of us would probably never
get on an airplane if we did not believe we were shielded
by some special providence. Quite simply, the fable gives
us the courage to participate in many necessary but frightening activities.

Also, like the imaginary audience, the personal fable is
much more powerful in early adolescence than at any other
stage of life. We recently surveyed large numbers of children and adolescents with a Personal Fable Scale (PFS). It
had items that measured a sense of speciality and invulnerability and a willingness to take risks. We measured the
positive and negative sides of these beliefs. A positive speciality item was "Sometimes I think my teacher looks at me
in a special way." A negative speciality item was "When I
mess up, I think no one in the whole world could be as stupid as me." We found that the belief in speciality and invulnerability (both positive and negative) and the
willingness to take risks was particularly high among the
thirteen-, fourteen-, and fifteen-year-old students.

The personal fable can have both positive and negative effects upon young people. For example, a young woman may keep a detailed diary with the expectation that it will one day be published as successfully as *The Diary of Anne Frank*. Or a girl may tell her mother, "Mom, you just don't know how it feels to be in love." In both examples, the young teen has the impression that her experience is unique and special. Revising the fable and bringing it into line with reality is part of maturing, of slowly finding out how much we are like everyone else rather than different from them. Only in finding out how much we are like other people, paradoxically, can we really discover our true speciality and uniqueness. When I was a young man, my mother suffered a heart attack, and I had to come to grips with my fable that my parents would never die. Serious illness happened to other kids' parents, not to mine. It wasn't right somehow; I was supposed to be protected. It was only when I confronted my own sense of speciality, recognized how much I was like everyone else, that I could master my own anger and help my mother cope with her illness. Thank God, she did recover.

Sometimes young people tend to reinforce their sense of speciality and of being observed by an audience through their clothing and appearance. The purple hair, odd clothing, and body decoration affected by some young people serve both to assert their uniqueness and to invite audience reaction. Richard Louv had the following conversation with a young man dressed in an original way:

> I told him I liked his clothes. He was wearing quite an outfit. I asked him how he would describe his style.
>
> "Everything is pretty dirty." He laughed.
>
> What kind of boots were those? Combat boots right?

"Yeah."

And the pants?

"These are, I guess paratrooper pants, they have little tabs all over them that you can tie to your parachute and they don't rip off."

He was also wearing bright suspenders and a loud purple shirt, and a little white cap with a short brim turned upright.

"I'm glad you asked about the hat, a dead person's hat. I get a lot of my clothes from dead people."

I asked him to explain.

"Well, my granddad died, and I liked him a lot, and this was his hat. If I like somebody then I adopt their clothing. Like my stepfather, I liked him so I took his field jacket. And I like looking dopey because a lot of girls think it is sexy."

He described his haircut as "white sidewalls." "I went to Jim the Barber on fifteenth, he's the Republican barber on Capitol Hill." He grinned. "I like the haircut because George Orwell had one and Dashiell Hammett and T. S. Eliot and girls like it. It's nice to look dumb. Spencer Tracy looked like a sack of potatoes, but everybody liked him. I kind of have to utilize my dumbness and strange traits to be more— likable. You know?" (1990)

This young man, like most teenagers, feels that he is different from his peers (his dumbness and strange traits) yet wants very much to be accepted and liked by them. Young people's belief in their speciality also contributes to a feeling of being apart, lonely, even when in the midst of peers. At the same time the personal fable also makes us feel powerful, that our presence changes things.

In the deep facet way in which feeling becomes stronger than thought, I had always felt that Devon School came into existence the day that I entered it, was vibrantly real while I was a student there and then blinked out like a candle on the day I left. (Knowles 1960)

The fable, then, can suggest that we are special in both a positive and a negative way. Our problems are special because no one else has it so bad. But our joys are special too; no one else has it so good.

The personal fable, in a weaker form than during adolescence, stays with us throughout our lives. It is constantly being modified and adjusted in keeping with new life experiences. The process by which we reconstruct the fable during our lives is the same one used to build our sense of personal identity: differentiation and higher-order integration. Understandably, adolescents regard their fable as an unalterable truth, and we should not challenge it head-on even when it is clearly self-destructive. Such an approach will only entrench them in their position. Arguing with someone else's reality simply does not work.

Rather than argue with young people about how they are not special in either a positive or a negative way (a denial of their fable), we can verbalize our own fable experiences. "When I was an adolescent, I was convinced that I would be the one to write the great American novel, and if I only had the time I might still do it." Or to voice the other side: "You know, sometimes when I make a mistake, I feel like the dumbest person in the whole world, that no one else could have done anything that stupid." Hearing our adult fable experiences helps young people to appreciate that they are not as different as they had believed. While in a way this is a letdown, it is also a considerable relief.

Pseudo-Stupidity

Adolescents, particularly young ones, have trouble making decisions. It is excruciating trying to decide what to wear, what to eat, sometimes even what to say. Teenagers' ability to think in a new key is the cause of this indecisiveness. Now that they can keep many choices in mind simultaneously, they have trouble choosing among them. In this respect, teenagers are like the child in the candy store who can see so many different kinds of candy, all of which look and smell delectable, that it is almost impossible to make a choice. Adolescents, in effect, now carry the potential for multiple options around in their heads, so that the decision-making problem is ever present. To adults, young people's difficulties in making decisions often resemble feeblemindedness. But this is really a pseudo-stupidity because it is a product of young people's enhanced mental capacity, not the lack of it.

As a result of having so many options, and because they lack a choice strategy (or strategies), adolescents often make choices that appear bizarre. Clothing choices provide a good example. A girl who doesn't know what to wear to school will ask her mother for advice and will then choose the opposite of her mother's suggestion. A boy will insist upon wearing a jacket when it is hot and on taking it off when it is cold because he is "boiling." Food choices provide another example. Many teenagers are addicted to fast-food restaurants because they require very few choices. Once a teenager decides on a preferred menu—hamburger, large Coke, small fries, and a cherry pie—the problem is solved for now and for eternity. A regular restaurant menu, in comparison, provides so many choices that teenagers will usually revert to their preferences and order something as close to the fast-food menu as possible.

The difference between the teenager and the adult in making decisions is largely a matter of experience. As we mature, we develop a number of strategies for dealing with routine decision making. In regard to clothing, for example, some people dress according to their mood, some use a rotation method (a different color combination every day), and some dress according to the calendar—Brown Monday, Blue Tuesday, and so on. When adults have had little experience in a particular decision-making arena, however, they may act like adolescents. Computer technology is changing so rapidly that making intelligent, experienced choices is often very difficult for adults. Those computer companies that offer the most comprehensive packages, eliminating the need to exercise many options, are often the most successful.

It is not just experience, strategies, and rules that help us to make decisions; we also use emotional cues. In choosing what to wear, what to eat, and where to go for entertainment, we listen to our feelings. If we are feeling depressed, we may want to wear something with a bit of dash to counteract the mood. If we feel like celebrating, we may choose to go to a really nice restaurant and order an expensive bottle of wine. If we are feeling lonely, we may want to watch a romantic comedy to revive our spirits. Teenagers, however, don't know their feelings all that well and may not be able to identify and label them. Moreover, their moods change with such rapidity that choices made on the basis of the feeling of one moment may not be suited to the feelings of the next. As a result, there is often a poor fit between the teenagers' decisions and feelings, which can often be disconcerting to adults. "But you just said you wanted to see a movie and now you want to stay home!"

With experience, adolescents become better able to recognize their different moods and feelings. With time and increasing maturity, the rapid emotional swings will subside. We can help teenagers discriminate between some of their emotions by suggesting to them how they might be feeling. It is important *not* to play psychologist and go into deep interpretation. Rather, labeling the feeling and offering young people a way of dealing with it is more acceptable and less intrusive. A concerned parent might say, "You are looking a little down. Would you like to go shopping with me or join us for a movie?" Helping young people to recognize and cope with their moods is every bit as important as helping them do the same with their thoughts.

Apparent Hypocrisy

Young people become very idealistic once they have attained the level of formal operational thought. Although they are usually quite vocal in expressing their ideals, they often fail to carry out the actions that would seem to follow logically from those professed ideals. To use an expression popular in my generation, they "don't put their money where their mouth is." To adults this discrepancy between young people's voiced ideals on the one hand, and the lack of any action to realize them on the other, seems hypocritical.

It is, however, only an apparent hypocrisy. Again let me use a personal example to illustrate both the appearance of hypocrisy and the developmental honesty that underlies it. This happened a few years ago when there was a great deal of concern about the use of endangered species for fur coats and about the way in which baby seals were killed. On Boston's Newbury Street there is a well-known furrier. After a long harsh winter, spring finally arrived. On one of the first warm sunny days, a number of adolescents appeared in front of the furrier bearing placards to the effect that we should save the animals and not buy furs. What struck me as I watched the earnest young people parading in front of the store was that they had waited until the weather had turned nice to express their outrage!

It would be easy, but incorrect, to call these young people hypocritical. Rather, they did not see the difference between marching on a warm, sunny day and parading on a cold, wintry day. For adolescents, the expression of the ideal is important, not the personal sacrifice that working toward the ideal entails. Because young people do not fully appreciate the difference between the expression of an ideal and the effort and self-denial of working toward its realization, their behavior appears hypocritical. We can help young people become more realistic by encouraging them to engage in community service. Some schools make such service a requirement for graduation. When young people volunteer to work with the young, or with the elderly, or in environmental clean-up efforts, they learn the difference between merely expressing an ideal and the effort that helps to make it a reality.

Personal Religion

Attitudes toward parents are not the only things that suffer as a result of adolescents' ability to construct ideals; attitudes toward religion suffer as well. The child who went to church or synagogue without question now understands that religion is more than an activity, that it involves belief. Adolescents distinguish between institutional religion, which is social and public, and personal religion, which is individual and private. They become aware of the difference between the accoutrements of religion—the clergy, prayers, and rituals—and a personal God who is nondenominational and omnipresent. The personal God is the one we all refer to in times of crises; it is the same for the soldier in the fox-hole, the frightened patient awaiting surgery, and the miner's wife awaiting news from the cave-in.

Like the imaginary audience and the personal fable, the belief in a personal God is much more powerful in adolescence than it is in adulthood. Teenagers, who for the first time realize that they can think in their heads without anyone knowing their thoughts, relish this newfound privacy and guard it zealously. Parents are often put off by adolescent offspring who seem unwilling to share even the most commonplace details of the day's or evening's events.

Parent: Where did you go?

Teenager: Out.

Parent: What did you do?

Teenager: Nothing.

Nonetheless, despite the pleasure young people take in keeping their thoughts to themselves, they also have a need to share those thoughts, to put them into words. For adolescents, a personal God is the ideal listener. No matter what you tell God, however silly, however childish, however frightening, God will listen and will not tell. At this age, God is the ultimate confidant.

When young adolescents turn away from institutional religion, this is often interpreted by adults as an antireligious act. It is not. Adolescents do not want to be treated as children and made to go to Sunday School or to religious classes. They still want and need adult guidance and direction but not directly in religious matters. Religious programs for youth should be more social or intellectual than Bible studies. Although young people seem averse to institutional religion, a great many are deeply religious in a very personal sense. They simply need a moratorium from institutional religion.

In general, most young people return to the faith of their parents once they become young adults and particularly when they become parents. But other teenagers, particularly in our increasingly secular society, have had little or no religious training as children and, in the absence of effective parenting, turn to gangs for leadership, guidance, and a sense of community. As parents and as caring adults, we can help young people during these transition years by encouraging a religious orientation when they are children and by granting them a moratorium from institutional religion when they are teenagers. During this period, parents and youth ministry should move away from religious instruction and use the time instead for discussing social and moral issues. Such discussions, which often can and should be heated, help young people to better define themselves. Although it is counterintuitive, a sabbatical from formal institutional religion may be the best guarantee that young people will later integrate their personal religion with that of the church or synagogue.

CHAPTER 3

Perils of Puberty

Children fret, teenagers worry. Children fret about what they can and cannot have, where they can and cannot go. Adolescents worry about their appearance, their social acceptability, their future, and much more. Worry is a new emotion made possible by their ability to think in a new key. Young people begin to worry when their newly attained formal operations enable them to conjure up many hypothetical outcomes for the physical transformations they are undergoing. Puberty presents young people with a full slate of possible eventualities. Moreover, as soon as one physical hurdle is past, another looms into view. If boys are not worried about height, they are worried about penis size; if girls are not worried about menstruation, they are concerned about their weight, and so on. Each of these changes, and their potential outcomes, constitutes a peril of puberty.

Worry about the perils of puberty is magnified by young adolescents' exaggerated need for peer group approval. As they attempt to demonstrate that they are no longer children and have their own lives, teenagers feel a closer affinity with peers than with the family. Peer approval becomes as important, or more so, than family acceptance. When a girl worries about whether she will ever get her period, she is concerned about being less "cool" than her friends who have already "got it." In the same way, when a boy worries that he is too short, he is worrying about being left out of activities with his taller and stronger friends.

The changes associated with puberty effectively encourage growth by differentiation and hierarchical integration. Pubertal alterations force young people to ask, "How am I different, how am I the same?" During the early part of puberty, teenagers tend to focus upon differences; this is often painful because they usually compare themselves unfavorably with peers, even when this is unjustified. Toward the end of the pubertal period, teenagers begin to appreciate the ways in which they are the same as their peers and thus complete the process of hierarchical integration. Though painful, the process of differentiation and integration allows for the construction of a solid sense of personal identity. On the other hand, those isolated teenagers who avoid peer interaction may have a continuing struggle with self-definition throughout adolescence and beyond.

Perils for Girls

For girls, the perils of puberty include the unknown outcomes of the pubertal changes upon their bodies— height, weight, menstruation, breast development, hair growth, body shape and configuration, facial features, skin conditions, and much more. Each facet of development is a focus of worry and concern. Perhaps the most frequent strategy girls employ to handle these myriad anxieties is to focus upon a single feature. They often lament, "If only my breasts were smaller (or larger, or firmer), all my problems would be solved and I would be happy for ever and ever."

I call this strategy finding an *emotional lightning rod*. When girls take this approach, the feature in question becomes supercharged, capturing the emotions that might otherwise be divided amongst several different physical attributes. If she has focused on breast size, any remark remotely associated with breasts may send her into unspeakable ecstasy or sink her into an inferno of depression. Breast size becomes the icon for all of the perils of puberty, and as a result her reactions to allusions to breasts become, in Freudian terms, overdetermined, because her reactions reflect a concentration of different emotions, not just one.

Height and Weight

The perils of puberty begin for girls around the age of nine or ten, when physical growth begins to accelerate. Until this age there is little difference between boys and girls in height, weight, or strength. Both boys and girls have reached about four-fifths of their adult height and somewhat more than half of their adult weight. But as they move into puberty, the relative uniformity of growth during childhood explodes into a fireworks of different growth rates in adolescence. Some young people shoot straight up, some have delayed fuses, and some hardly get off the ground at all. Although 95% of all girls show at least one sign of puberty between the ages of 9 and 13½, it is still normal for some girls to confront their first peril after the age of 13.

On average, the growth in height for girls begins at age 10½ and ends at age 14. By age 14, most girls have attained their adult height. Some girls, of course, continue to grow beyond that age but seldom beyond age fifteen. Self-consciousness about height may be one of the first teenage concerns if a girl feels she is above or below average:

> I would give my eyeteeth to be two inches shorter. I
> hate being 5'9" with very long legs. Most of my
> problems with friends and boyfriends would be
> solved if I were shorter. It is very hard for me to find
> a guy who is taller than or the same height as me.
> When I do, the guy is only a half inch taller so if we
> go out, I can't wear high heeled shoes, so I don't like
> to dress up at all! I have never had a friend who has
> been taller than me. (Brondino et al. 1988)

Changes in the amount and distribution of body fat
also occur at puberty. Soon after birth, babies begin to
accumulate fat just beneath the skin, which gives them
their plump appearance. By one year of age, most girls
have more baby fat than boys. From then until the age of
seven, many children may look thin and scrawny. Then
matters change once more, and most girls and many boys
begin accumulating fat again. This can lead to prepubes-
cent chubbiness and the beginning of weight self-
consciousness.

As girls begin their growth spurt, they begin to lose fat
again, particularly from their thighs and legs. Even so, girls
lose less fat than boys during this time and thus leave the
teen years with proportionately more fat beneath the skin
than is true for boys. For this reason girls have more
rounded contours than boys, who have more muscle. Boys
also appear more muscular because their bodies have less
fat to conceal bones and muscle.

Weight is an important component of body image and
body image is a potent concern of adolescents. Girls are
most satisfied with their bodies when they see themselves
as slightly underweight. In contrast, their body image is
very negative if they view themselves as overweight. In

general, young adolescent girls tend to be very critical of how they look, to believe themselves to be heavier than they really are, and to want to be thinner. While there is a decline in girls' tendency to overestimate their weight as they move through mid-adolescence, unhappiness with their body image continues to increase as they move into young adulthood (Phelps et al. 1993).

The culturally conditioned concern a majority of young women have with weight is evidenced in their behavior. It has been estimated that at least 75% of adolescent girls have at least one symptom of an eating disorder, most often fad dieting (Phelps et al. 1993). Weight tends to be less of a problem for teenage boys than for girls, but many young men are overweight largely because of poor eating habits. At least 30% of today's teenagers are overweight to some degree. However, obesity and the serious health problems associated with it are classified when body weight is 25–30% above what is regarded as normal. From the 1960s to the 1980s there has been a 40% increase in obesity among 12- to 17-year-olds (Bandini 1992). Obesity is most prevalent in the Northeast, followed by the Midwest, South, and West. Generally, it is more common in urban than in less populated rural areas. Perhaps not surprisingly, the incidence of obesity is greater in the winter and spring than in the summer and fall (Bandini 1992).

Although a variety of factors contribute to obesity in young people, poor eating habits are certainly one of the most important. Many young people simply consume too many calories for their body weight. Apparently, exercise and activity levels contribute less to a teenager's weight than does calorie intake. A number of studies fail to find meaningful differences between the activity levels of adolescents who are overweight and those who are not (Bandini 1992).

Dr. Judith J. Wurtman of the Department of Nutrition

at the Massachusetts Institute of Technology has suggested ways in which parents can help teenagers control their weight:

> Parents should make it easy for teens and younger children to lose weight or prevent rapid weight gain by not buying or making calorie-dense foods, serving meals that are not excessively high in fat, and by not keeping the refrigerator stocked with foods that are high in calories. Also, if parents exercise routinely—biking, long walks, swimming, badminton in the backyard—their children will view exercise as a normal part of life. (1981)

Breast Development

For girls, the first visible sign of approaching puberty is the growth of the breasts. This may begin between the ages of 8 and 13 and is usually completed between the ages of 13 and 18, the average being about age 15. Breast development occurs in stages, beginning with the elevation of the nipple and surrounding area (breast bud stage). Next the breast as a whole enlarges and the areola (colored area around the nipple) widens and deepens in color; then the areola develops and forms a secondary contour. Perhaps because of the breast fetish of American culture, aided and abetted by the media, teenage girls are extraordinarily sensitive about their breast development. It is one of the most worrisome perils of puberty for girls. The question of what to do about unsatisfactory breasts occurs regularly among adolescent girls. The following question is typical:

> I'm fourteen years old and I'm flat. I have less on my

top than any other girl in my whole class. I was wondering, is there any exercise I can do, or stuff I can
send for to make me bigger?
                    —Flat as a Board (Winship 1983)

In addition to worries about breast size, girls also anguish over the fact that their breasts may not be the same
size. It is quite normal for one breast to be larger than the
other initially; in almost all cases the other breast catches up
and the majority of girls end up with a matched pair. Dr.
Maryanne Collins, pediatrician and specialist in adolescent
medicine, has pointed this out: "When a young girl starts
to develop breasts, one side enlarges first. Invariably mothers and daughters get concerned because they do not realize that this is normal" (1981).

For some girls the perils of puberty are of a different
order. A girl who is well endowed may have to endure
jokes about being recognized before "she turns the corner."
She is also subject to bawdy remarks and stares of older
boys and men as well as to teasing and harassment from
other girls. The following excerpt from Judy Blume's book
Are You There God? It's Me, Margaret (1970) is an interchange
between two classmates, Laura and Margaret. Laura ma-
tured early and became the target of sexual rumor and innuendo among Margaret's friends:

"Don't you think I know about you and your
friends? Do you think it is fun to be the biggest kid
in the class?"
"I don't know," I said, "I never thought about it."
"Well, try thinking about it. Think about how
you would feel if you had to wear a bra in fourth
grade and how everybody laughed and how you always had to cross your arms in front of you. And

about how the boys called you dirty names just because of how you looked."

Body Hair

Soon after the first signs of breast development occur, another peril emerges: body hair. Like breast development, the appearance of body hair can have both positive and negative effects on how young women think about themselves. The first appearance of pubic hair may be taken as a sign of long-awaited maturity. On the other hand, if body hair growth is extensive on the arms, legs, and upper lip as well as in the pubic area and beneath the arms, girls can become alarmed at this "unattractive" feature. This attitude is clearly a reflection of our cultural values. The concern with body hair, for example, is not prevalent in many European countries where women do not shave their underarms or legs. The use of deodorants to counteract body odor (associated with the growth of body hair and the activity of oil-producing sweat glands) is also less common in European countries than in the United States. Nonetheless, in our society excessive body hair is looked upon as unattractive and girls who develop this trait often worry about it.

Menarche

Perhaps the most noted, or most notorious, peril of puberty for young women is menarche, the onset of menstruation. In some societies this is made a public event, but in our society it is a private family affair. It is often a later event, usually occurring about two years after breast development and after the peak period of the growth in height. At this time in the United States the average age of menarche is 12.7 years but the range is from 9 to 18 years (Ghai 1994).

Attitudes and perceptions of menarche are tied to social values and taboos, which vary over time. In an earlier era, menarche was described as "the curse" and was portrayed to young girls as a malady that had to be endured. This perspective often led to some embarrassing moments for young girls as it did for this fictional thirteen-year-old:

> It proved to be the curse, for the first time. I thought I was dying of tuberculosis, which in a vague way I knew caused hemorrhages. It must be a serious case because the hemorrhage had gone the wrong way. I wondered if they would find me dead in the car in the morning. I guess they must have told the porter to take special care of me because I'd rather die than call for help. Presently he asked me through the curtain if I was all right. I said, "I guess I'm sick." "What seems to be the trouble, lady?" To that I made no answer at all. I couldn't. With the intuition of a great gentleman, he must have guessed for soon after, a large black hand came through the curtain and handed me a package. (Morley 1939)

At the time this incident occurred (the turn of the century) menarche was very much a private matter, but behind the silence was a tacit understanding of the needs of the adolescent girl that could make the experience less difficult. The society that protected the teenager from premature adulthood also guided and paced her steps toward maturity. In America today there is no time or place for a gradual progression toward womanhood, and girls seem to be in open competition to get "it" as soon as, or before, their friends. For young adolescent girls today, menarche is a sign of belonging rather than of growth. Listen to Margaret in Judy Blume's *Are You There God? It's Me, Margaret* describe her feelings when her friends have started to menstruate and she is still waiting:

> Are you there God: It's me, Margaret. Gretchen my friend got her period. I'm so jealous. God, I hate myself for being so jealous, but I am. I wish you'd help just a little, Nancy's sure she's going to get it soon too. And if I'm last I don't know what I'll do. Oh please, God, I just want to be normal. (1970)

Although many girls like Margaret wish for menarche, in the event they often have mixed feelings about it, particularly the "hygienic hassles" that come with it. And, though Margaret may be eager to tell her friends that she has "got it," survey data suggest that many girls are reluctant to reveal their menstrual experiences right away. Most tell their mothers first and their friends only several months later. Interestingly, evidence for the mind-body connection comes from the finding that girls who tell their fathers, or who know that their mother has told their father, report fewer menstrual cramps and other discomfort (Brooks-Gunn and Roble 1983). Just knowing that her father is aware that she is menstruating, and that she has nothing to hide, may provide a teen with a more relaxed, less stressful familial climate.

Once girls have begun to menstruate and their breast development is noticeable, their attention turns to other facets of appearance. Now body shape, facial features, and acne become matters of concern. The anguish does not end there. In the middle and late teens, young women begin to worry about personality traits such as shyness, passivity, or temper. During this period, the perils of puberty are more psychological than physical. We will look at some of these psychological issues in the next chapter.

Perils for Boys

Puberty presents as many perils for boys as it does for girls. Boys worry about how tall they will get, about when they will have to shave, about the size of their penis, about spontaneous erections, about wet dreams and masturbation, and about acne. Boys, like girls, sometimes focus all of their worries on one particular physical feature, such as height or large feet (referred to in one family as the "British Fleet"). They become supersensitive about this issue because it represents all the other changes they are anticipating, changes they have no control over and about which they are extremely anxious. When parents or siblings touch upon this concern, the young man may often explode with angry words and a march out of the room, slamming the door behind him. Everyone is astounded because the reaction seems so out of proportion to the stimulus. This is, again, the *lightning rod effect*.

Height and Weight

An area of major concern for boys is height, which is considered to be the most important index of manhood and of attractiveness to women. While the "tall, dark, and handsome" label does not fit many of today's leading men, it nonetheless remains an image to which many young men aspire. Among boys, the growth spurt of adolescence usually begins at about age 12 or 13 (but can begin as early as age 10½, or as late as age 16), is most rapid during the fourteenth year (when some boys can gain from four to six inches in height), and ends at age 16 (but can end as early as age 13½, or as late as age 17½). Some additional growth in height can occur until the twentieth year in boys. But by the age of 16 most young men have attained some 98% of their total adult height.

The boy who grows tall during this period is compli-mented by almost everyone. Family friends remark on how tall he is getting. In addition, he feels taller emotionally. He can look down upon his mother and sometimes upon his father as well. Being able to look down on people during conversation may convey a sense of power and superiority. Being tall, however, is not an unmixed blessing and can bring problems for boys (as well as for girls):

> To this very day I haven't stopped growing an inch. I'm fifteen and 6'4". I don't like the idea of being so tall because everyone has to look up to me and when I'm at home I can't walk under the ceiling fan with-out seriously injuring myself. I'm outgrowing my bed every day. I have to ball up into a little ball so that my head and feet don't hang over the bed. Now if I was 5'11" I wouldn't mind at all because I could sleep better and walk in my house without hitting myself in the head. (Brondino et al. 1988)

There are other problems in being tall. Tall teenagers may be treated according to how old they look rather than how old they are. And they can be teased unmercifully with insensitive remarks like "How's the weather up there?" (Tall girls may hear, "Geez, the Amazons have arrived!") None-theless, in our society the boy who attains average height (5'9") or above finds more positive than negative effects from his height. This is not as true for girls who, as we saw earlier, may feel that undue height (above 5'7") limits their choices among young men and female friends. Generally, young men prefer young women who are shorter or at least not taller than they are, and the reverse holds true for girls.

For boys who attain average or above-average height, the most dangerous peril of puberty has probably been successfully passed. On the other hand, for those boys who do not reach at least 5'9", height becomes an unending cause of concern. This is what one young man wrote about his height:

> I'm real short and everyone in my class thinks I'm nothing but a clown. It's true, I'm apt to come up with a fast remark and usually can make kids laugh, but sometimes I wish they would treat me like a real person, not just a joke. (Winship 1983)

This adolescent developed one way to compensate for his short stature. Others may adopt a "short personality" with elements of Napoleonic assertiveness and acerbity. It sometimes helps to remind young people that attractive women sometimes marry men who are shorter than they are (e.g., Jackie Onassis, Sophia Loren Ponti, Nicole Kidman), and that shortness is no brake on brilliance (former Secretary of Labor Robert Reich is 4'10") or creativity (William Faulkner was 5'6" and John Cheever was 5'5"). Knowing that you are not alone in your shortness and that others have overcome any handicaps it presents, can help—if not totally remove—the young man's pain of being short.

Sexual Development

Changes in a boy's sexual apparatus begin between the ages of 10 and 13½ with the gradual enlargement of the testes. This enlargement continues for three or more years and can end anywhere from age 14½ to age 18. Pubic hair begins to appear at about the same time as the enlargement of the testes. As the boy matures, pubic hair continues to spread in area and to become darker, coarser, and curlier. By maturity, the triangular pubic hair pattern so common in women is less well defined in men. For adult males,

pubic hair may be continuous with the hair on the ab-
domen and chest.

Of perhaps greatest concern to boys is the growth in
the size of the penis. This organ grows rapidly about a year
after the enlargement of the testes and the appearance
of pubic hair, usually between the ages of 10½ to 13½.
This growth continues until between the ages of 13½ to 16½.
Average penis size is between four and six inches in the
flaccid state. Because there is so much erroneous (and myth-
ical) information about penis size, let me quote an authority on the subject:

> The size and the shape of the penis are not related to
> a man's physique, race, virility or ability to give or
> receive pleasure. Like an organ, penises differ in size,
> but the differences tend to diminish in the erect state.
> The penis neither atrophies with lack of use nor en-
> larges with frequent use. (Sperling 1981)

For many teenage men, this kind of legitimate information can be extremely important in easing their fears and
confusion. Nonetheless, even though we attempt to make
accurate information available to young people, the
mythologies about the size of the sexual organs and sexual
functioning persist. Consider this letter from a fifteen-year-
old young man:

> You may think I'm kidding but my penis is too big.
> It's nine inches in a relaxed state. The guys all call
> me names like Super Stud and worse, and they say I
> will never be able to marry a normal woman. Is this
> true? (Winship 1983)

The teasing by peers for any difference from the norm

is one of the perils of puberty.

By far the largest store of mythology about a boy's masculinity has to do with masturbation. Attitudes toward masturbation have become much more permissive than they were several decades ago and today 80% of adolescent males and almost as many adolescent females say they approve of the practice (Hyde 1990). Nonetheless, perhaps because it is done privately and in secret, many young men and women continue to feel guilty about the practice. This kind of guilt is vividly described by novelist Philip Roth in his novel, *Portnoy's Complaint*:

> It was the end of my freshman year of high school—
> and freshman year of masturbating—that I discovered on the underside of my penis, just where the shaft met the head, a little discolored dot that has since been diagnosed as a freckle. Cancer. I had given myself cancer. All that pulling and tugging at my own flesh, all that friction, had given me an incurable disease. And not yet fourteen! (1969)

Portnoy's fear and trembling over the consequences of masturbation has a long history. Consider the reminiscence from G. Stanley Hall, the "father" of modern adolescent psychology. Hall grew up during the middle of the nineteenth century and his account, although different in detail from Portnoy's, conveys the same sort of self-accusation and guilt:

> So great was my dread of natural phenomena that in the earliest moment I rigged an apparatus and applied bandages to prevent erethism while I slept which very likely augmented the trouble. If I yielded to any kind of experimentation on myself, I suffered

intense remorse and fear and sent up many a fervent prayer that I might never again break my resolve. At one time, I feared I was abnormal and found occasion to consult a physician in a neighboring town who did not know me. He examined me and took my dollar, and laughed at me, but also told me what consequences would ensue if I became unchaste. What an untold anguish should have been saved me if some one had told me that certain experiences while I slept were as normal for boys in their teens as are the monthly phenomena of girls. (1924)

Despite the guilt and self-punishment that often accompany masturbation, a large majority of adolescent boys engage in the practice. Most young people discover masturbation on their own. For boys there is a sharp increase in frequency of masturbation with the maturation of the sexual organs. From almost no masturbation at age 10, more than 85% of boys are masturbating at age 15. The increase in masturbation for girls is much more gradual and continues through the years of adulthood. While less than 20% of girls masturbate at age 15, more than 50% of women over age 40 engage in this activity (Hyde 1990).

The issue of masturbation confronts the adolescent with the question of self-control, the control over impulses. The issue thus has broader implications, for it serves as a measure of whether or not he or she will be able to control other impulses, such as those of overeating. If an adolescent feels that he or she has mastered an impulse in one domain, it is proof that impulses can be overcome in other domains as well. Unfortunately, the reverse is also true: if the adolescent feels at the mercy of sexual impulses, he or she may feel equally unable to cope with other unwelcome impulses. Gaining control over one's urges, sexual and otherwise, occurs gradually and involves struggle and effort as both Portnoy's and Hall's recollections suggest. Such struggle is part of growth and can contribute to a healthy sense of personal identity if, in the end, the young person feels in charge of his or her inner urges and desires.

Another issue of control associated with boys' sexual maturity is the unwanted erection. Once boys have experienced the spontaneous hardening of the penis and the resultant bulge in their pants, they become concerned about when and where this will happen. A common fantasy of this kind is found in Judy Blume's *Then Again, Maybe I Won't*:

> Just as I finished writing the figures on the board, I started to get hard. Mind over matter... mind over matter, I told myself. But still I went up. I kept my back to the class and prayed for it to go down.
>
> Miss Tobin said, "That's an interesting way to solve the problem, Tony."
>
> For a minute I thought she meant my real problem. But then I realized she was talking about the math problem.
>
> "Could you explain your reasoning to the class, Tony?"
>
> I started talking but I didn't turn around. I could just picture facing the class. Everybody would laugh and point at my pants. (1971)

This kind of experience is particularly embarrassing thanks to the young adolescent's belief in the imaginary audience. It is this belief that makes the young person sure that he is the center of everyone's attention and that they are all watching his pants.

Perils in General

The physical changes associated with puberty become perils precisely because adolescents have no way of knowing how things will turn out. Teenagers will have to wait several years before they can feel secure in their new body configurations. The worries that plague teenagers are nevertheless healthy because they are symptoms of integrative growth. They are evidence of adolescents' concerns about how much they are like and how much they are different from their peers. However stressful these worries might be, they help adolescents attain a strong sense of self that will enable them to deal effectively with stress when they reach adulthood. Before we go on to some more serious perils of puberty, here are some of the other worries of young men and women as they are amusingly presented by Delia Ephron in her book *Teenage Romance*:

Worry that there is a right way to neck and you don't know it.

Worry that your date will be able to tell you don't know it.

If you are a girl, worry that your breasts are too round. Worry that your breasts are too pointed. Worry that your nipples are the wrong color. Worry that your breasts point in different directions.

If you are a boy, worry that you will get breasts.

Worry that your nose is too fat. Worry that your nose is too long. Worry that your neck is too fat. Worry that your lips are too fat. Worry that your ass is too fat. Worry that your ears stick out. Worry that your eyes are too close together.

If you are a boy, worry that you will never be able to grow a moustache.

Worry that you won't like the food at other people's houses.

Worry that when you go to the bathroom people will hear.

Worry that the lock on the door doesn't work and that someone will come in.

Worry that everyone hates you.

Worry that everyone thinks you are stupid

Worry that you have ugly toes. (1981)

These are only some of the perils of puberty. With time and experience, most adolescents incorporate their various physical features into their sense of personal identity. And when these features are put in the context of the young person's other qualities—intelligence, loyalty, sense of humor, sympathy, and so on—they come to play a much less prominent part in the adolescent's self-evaluation. To be sure, the sensitivity and concern about physical attributes that teenagers experience in such an exquisitely painful way are never lost entirely. Nonetheless, they diminish in intensity and power as young people mature and construct a fuller and more elaborate self-definition.

Homosexuality

So far we have talked about puberty as it is experienced by the majority of young people. But there is a smaller group of young people—the size of this population is in dispute—who experience a different kind of peril. In early adolescence most of us go through a brief phase when we are attracted to members of the same sex. This attraction is not entirely sexual inasmuch as it derives, in part at least, from an early adolescent fear of the opposite sex and from admiration, and perhaps even envy of, someone of the same sex whom we regard as more attractive than we are. But for some teenagers, this is not a temporary but rather a permanent orientation. There are many theories about the origins of homosexuality, but the data strongly suggests that it is probably, to some degree, genetic in origin. Many of the young adolescents with whom I have talked about their homosexuality tell me that they were gay or lesbian when they were children. They did not, however, appreciate the full power of this orientation until they became adolescents.

The stigma of homosexuality is far less today than it has been in the past, and it is no longer listed as a perversion in the diagnostic manual of the American Psychiatric Association (DSM 1993, 3rd ed.). Massachusetts and Wisconsin have reelected homosexual congressmen. Issues such as homosexuals in the military, gay and lesbian parents, and spousal health and welfare benefits for gay couples have become public issues. Nonetheless, a socially negative attitude still prevails, and many adolescents still have to struggle with the awareness and acceptance of their homosexuality. The following personal reflections by teenage homosexuals will help convey the pain of this particular peril of puberty:

> I was thirteen and a freshman when I met my first lover, Carla. Before we were lovers we were really close friends. After a few months, the relationship began to get physical. It was about then, that I thought seriously about being gay. It wasn't until my sophomore year that I finally decided for sure that I was gay. . . .
>
> Being gay at an all-girl Catholic School is really hard. It is even harder when your lover goes to school with you and you can't do anything, because the slightest sign of affection labels you for four

years of school. Because Carla and I were so close, many people at school immediately guessed. That was really hard because people can be cruel when they don't understand. Some people just didn't talk to us. It got easier after Carla and I broke up junior year, because then I started dating people outside of school. (Heron 1983)

My name is Mike Friedman, and I would like to relate a few of the experiences that I have had over the last few months because I think they may be of use to people who are in the same position. Last summer I finally came to grips with the fact that I was gay. I had been having sex with a man since I was fourteen but thought it was just a phase that I was going through. I thought that I would grow out of it, but obviously I didn't. Last summer I decided that I should stop kidding myself. I was gay, and I should be happy with the way I am. (Heron 1983)

In my conversations with teenage homosexuals, they tell me that being truthful with their parents is the most difficult part of the whole process of accepting their sexual orientation. Parental reactions to a young person's "coming out" are somewhat predictable. Their immediate reaction is usually one of alienation that derives from their stereotype of the homosexual that is now projected onto their child. A second reaction, a product of the first, is usually that of failure and guilt—what did we do wrong (Strommen 1989)? Most families go through several stages in the awareness of a family member's homosexuality:

Subliminal awareness or suspicion of homosexuality.

Impact: the crises resulting from disclosure.

Adjustment: family attempts to get the young person to change orientation or to conceal it.

Resolution: the family mourns the loss of the heterosexual child.

Integration: the family accepts the young person's new role and may eventually accept lovers at family affairs. (Devine 1984)

Not all parents and families go through all of these stages, and some may get stuck at one or another of them. That is unfortunate. Teenagers do not become homosexual to punish their parents, nor is their homosexuality in any way the parent's fault. Freud was very clear in stating that homosexuality was not an illness or a sexual perversion but rather a different sexual orientation. What has to be remembered is that the large majority of homosexual individuals are responsible, productive members of society whose sexual preference is a matter of their private, not their public, life.

It is necessary, before closing this section, to mention some of the health and psychological risks associated with homosexuality in the teen years. Although a relatively small number (500) of adolescents 13 to 19 years of age have died of AIDS as of 1990, because of the long latency of the HIV virus, many young people who contract the disease in adolescence may not develop it until adulthood. In addition, male homosexuals in particular are at high risk for contracting a variety of sexually transmitted diseases. Finally, perhaps because of the stigma that is still attached to homosexuality, a disproportionate number of gay and lesbian adolescents take their own lives (30% of all teen suicides). Many of the negative risks associated with a homosexual orientation could be avoided or minimized if gay and lesbian teenagers had proper health care and psychological counseling (Sturdevant and Remafedi 1992).

Rape

Of all the perils of puberty, rape is surely the most destructive to the young woman's emerging sense of self. Rape of teenage boys is not unknown, but is not as common. In a 1985 survey of adolescent sexuality, 14% of the girls reported that they had been raped. The rapist in almost half of the cases was a boyfriend (Coles and Stokes 1985). Here is one case:

> Helen was fifteen. She had curly brown hair, amazingly blue eyes, and stood about 5'3" inches tall. She lived in a small farming town with about 5,000 people. She was a sophomore in high school and had a part time job working at a store. She liked the people she worked with. All of them were her friends.
>
> One afternoon after work, Henry, an eighteen-year-old high school senior, who also worked at the store, gave Helen a ride home. When he dropped her off at her house, he asked if could have something to drink. "Sure," said Helen. Henry was a friend, a pal; she trusted him.
>
> Helen's parents were both at work, so there was no one else in the house other than Henry and herself. She got both of them something to drink and then went into the living room to sit down to talk. That's when it started.
>
> Henry began to touch her. She was uncomfortable, and embarrassed. She wanted him to stop. She said, "No, Henry, don't." But he didn't stop. Henry was

much stronger than Helen and he was raping her.

Helen felt stunned. She couldn't believe this was happening to her—and in her own home. She was shocked that someone she thought was her friend was doing this to her. She was also scared, just plain terrified. She feared no one would come to make Henry stop and she feared her parents would come home and think she was to blame.

When Henry finished raping her, he got up, dressed, said, "Thanks, slut," and went back to his car. Helen just lay there on the floor awhile, feeling almost numb and wondering what to do now.

She didn't tell her parents what had happened—ever. Partly she kept quiet because she wanted to protect them from such horrible news, partly she didn't tell them because she feared they would not believe her.

Socially, Henry did a job on Helen after he raped her. He returned immediately to work and boasted that he and Helen had had sex. He said she had asked him into her house. She was "easy" said Henry. If Helen had thought about talking to someone at work about being raped, Henry had preempted that possibility. (Balk 1995)

A significant achievement of identity formation is the sense of *ownership* over one's body. Rape destroys that sense of ownership and creates a feeling of vulnerability to personal violation that can, and does, have long-lasting negative effects upon a young woman's sense of self and her relationships with others. Unfortunately, many adolescent girls who have been raped do not label it as such and do not report it. In addition to the intense sense of personal violation, girls feel intense rage, shame, guilt, depression, and self-blame. Many rape victims manifest one or more symptoms of *sexual dysfunction*, such as aversion to physical contact with males. Often rape victims have vivid *flashbacks*, intense visions of the rape scene. It is also likely that many rape victims suffer a kind of post-traumatic stress syndrome and suffer extreme depression years after the event (Koss 1988; Sorenson and Bowie 1994).

There is no excuse for rape and no complete cure for its victims. Unfortunately, in our postmodern world, where adolescents are regarded as sophisticated, there is a presumption that young women know how to take care of themselves. This puts the responsibility on the wrong shoulders. As adults we need to make sure we do not encourage rape by making opportunities available for it. Young teenagers in particular should not be allowed to go to unchaperoned parties, on single dates, or to stay home alone for extended periods of time. And as parents, health professionals, and educators, we also need to make sure that young men learn at an early age to respect women's rights. Rape is not a lark but a punishable crime.

CHAPTER 4

Peer Shock

We experience shock, a feeling of sudden and overwhelming anxiety, whenever we are confronted with something that is both unexpected and seemingly unmanageable. There are many different kinds of shock. For example, we are victims of *culture* shock if we move to a foreign country where the ways of thinking and behaving are far different from those to which we are accustomed. A number of years ago my family and I spent a year in French Switzerland and learned about culture shock firsthand. Over and above the language differences was a social etiquette very different from our own in America. For example, it is very important, when entering a French Swiss store or restaurant, to greet everyone. It is equally necessary to thank the proprietor and to say "good-bye" when leaving. On the other hand, you do not greet people whom you know on the street. If you don't follow these practices, you are regarded as badly brought up (*mal élevé*).

In many ways, moving from the culture of childhood to the culture of adolescence is like moving from one society to another. The abrupt change in the language as well as in the rules and expectations regarding conduct can lead to another variety of shock—*peer shock*. On entering the culture of adolescence the young person is thrust into a world of sexual innuendo, bias and prejudice, and intense competition and cruelty, as well as intense, but entirely new kinds of positive relationships. It is a world for which the games, the teasing, and the "dirty" words of childhood did not prepare the emerging adolescent.

The world of adolescence differs from that of childhood in three major respects. First of all, the structure of social relationships is different. Children come together mainly in play groups, and friendships are often determined primarily by who lives nearby. Who gets to play and who does not get to play will likely depend upon who gets there first or who has the toys or equipment. Among teenagers, in contrast, belonging to a group is determined by such qualities as social status and ethnic background. As a result of this tectonic shift in the basis for friendships, many young people who felt accepted by their peers when they were children experience the full force of social prejudice when they become adolescents. This produces one type of peer shock, namely, the shock of *exclusion*.

It is not just the structure of social relationships that changes from childhood to adolescence but the emotional tone and depth of the relationships as well. When children socialize, their interactions are generally cooperative and center around a common activity. Among teenagers the emotional involvement is much more complex and multi-layered. Friendships are initially based on mutual tastes and interests but increasingly are founded upon trust and loyalty. Because young adolescents are relatively inexperienced in these more intimate relationships, they often get hurt. They discover that some of the young men and women whom they regarded as trusted friends could turn on them or exploit the relationship. Such experiences constitute a second form of peer shock, namely, the shock of *betrayal*.

A third variety of peer shock results from a form of relationship that is relatively unknown in childhood: the romantic. During childhood, boys and girls are usually antagonistic to one another and close boy-girl friendships tend to be a rarity. With puberty, and the hormonal changes that accompany it, young men and women begin to find one another attractive, rather than repulsive. This is often a more abrupt turnaround for boys than it is for girls, who tend to be more socially oriented and more attuned to what the future will hold. This new romantic interest in members of the opposite sex, combined with a new ability to construct ideals, leads adolescents to form "crushes" on other teenagers who, for the time being, seem perfect in every way. But these crushes are short-lived. No one is perfect, and young teenagers eventually learn that their image of perfect beauty is human after all. The discovery that our romantic ideal has his or her own share of faults gives rise to the third variety of peer shock, that of *disillusionment*.

Adjusting to the culture of adolescence thus presents the young person with many potential stressors. Yet, like the stressors associated with thinking in a new key and with the perils of puberty, the different forms of peer shock can be healthy if they contribute to development by differentiation and integration. In many cases, young people can best use these stressors to grow in a healthy way if they have the support and sympathy of the significant adults in their lives.

Fads, Clubs, and Cliques: The Shock of Exclusion

Young people are brought together most loosely and most broadly by fads: a shared fascination with, and desire for, some fleeting icon of the popular culture of the time.

This may be a particular kind of clothing, musical group or style, or even language expression. Ownership of the icon identifies the adolescent as belonging to a privileged group. And the sense of belonging is what fads are all about. That is why the inability to possess the icon is so painful to those teenagers who must forgo it. Participation in fads also amounts to a kind of growth by substitution, an attempt to give the impression of social bonding by means of appearances. But true constructive growth comes from the inside out and not from the outside in.

In many ways fads provide a bridge between the culture of childhood and that of adolescence. Thanks to the mass media, children engage in fads generated by television programs. The popularity of Barney and the Power Rangers among contemporary children is an example of a fad that children all over the country engage in. In the past it was Cabbage Patch Dolls and Pet Rocks. Even children can experience a little of the shock of exclusion if, for whatever reason, they cannot have the Barney or Power Ranger toy. They feel momentarily excluded, unable to talk with or play with their friends, all of whom possess the treasured icon of the in-group of childhood.

Fads take on more power and significance in early adolescence when acceptance by peer groups becomes much more important than it was during childhood. Children draw their main strength and support from the family; even if they don't have the faddish item, this does not permanently undermine their sense of security and belonging. Young adolescents, in contrast, are trying to distance themselves from childhood and from childish things. One of these childish things is their dependence upon parents. Peer group acceptance becomes all important when you are rejecting your familial base of security and acceptance.

In early adolescence, therefore, ownership of fad icons

is very important to the young person's sense of being a member in good standing of the peer group. In the case of fads, however, it is often parents, not peers, who contribute to the young person's sense of exclusion. Some parents simply cannot tolerate a teenager wearing jeans torn at the knees, or dressed in preinhabited clothing purchased at a thrift shop. At this age, however, we have to be a little forgiving. Young adolescents need the support of the peer group as they assert their autonomy, and participation in fads is usually a relatively harmless way to do so. In addition, participation in fads eventually helps young people appreciate the difference between true growth and that which is just adornment.

A more serious experience of exclusion shock comes when young people are not admitted to clubs that they desire to join. Thanks to their new mental abilities, adolescents become sensitive to distinctions of social class, religion, race, and ethnic background that did not trouble them (or their parents) when they were children. As part of the self-differentiation process, teenagers tend to make friends among young people of the same background. In addition they often need to symbolize this affiliation and to make it public by the formation of a "club" with its own name, dues, rules of order, president, initiation rites, and so on. Teenagers who are members of the club emphasize their likenesses to one another; by excluding others from membership, they underline differences.

Clubs are, in effect, group efforts at self-differentiation and integration. And perhaps because they are group efforts, they can be extremely hurtful to those who are not members of the privileged elite. Writer Lynda Madaras recalled her own adolescent club when her daughter came home in tears about having been excluded from a slumber party:

Were we really that terrible? Then I remembered the Powder Puffs, a club my girl friends and I belonged to. Unlike Girl Scouts and the other adult sanctioned after-school clubs, the Powder Puffs had no formal meetings and no ostensible purpose—which is not to say the club did not have a purpose. It did. The membership cards, which were wondrously official looking since one girl's father had run them off in his print shop and which we carried about in the cloudy cellophane inserts of our identical vinyl leather wallets, certified us as members of this all-important Group. As if that weren't identification enough, we moved around in an inseparable herd, ate lunch together in our special territory of the playground, sat together giggling like a gaggle of geese in school assemblies, wrote each other's names on our scuffed tennis shoes, combed our hair the same way, dressed alike, and generally made life miserable for the girls who were not members of the group. (1991)

Writer Susan Allen Toth has a similar recollection of her early adolescent club called the Society Six:

I'm not sure on what grounds we admitted others as friends, how we made up the guest lists for slumber parties or valentines or birthdays, or how we knew whom to call to go to the movies. Most of us went on to college, but we certainly didn't base our friendships on intellectual merit. Most of us were moderately attractive, but one or two of us didn't date at all for years. Most of us were "popular" but I don't know exactly why. Perhaps we just defined ourselves in relation to the Society Six and to all the other girls below us, the loners, the stupid ones, the

fat ones. We had absorbed by sixth grade a set of
careful and cruel distinctions. (1981)

The "careful and cruel distinctions" amount to rules of
exclusion that can come as a terrible shock to teens such as
Pam who perhaps never thought of herself as different before. Exclusion is hurtful because it forces us to acknowledge that other people do not see us in the way we see
ourselves. The shock of exclusion can, with the help of
adult support and sympathy, help the young adolescent attain a more realistic view of self as seen by others.

More intimate than adolescent clubs are teenage
cliques. The clique is a small group of teenagers who do almost everything together. Although cliques tend to be very
exclusive there is a great deal of fluctuating allegiance:

> My daughter must have been nine or ten when it
> started—her first taste of the nasty world of play-
> ground politics and the cruel games young girls play
> with each other. She'd arrive home from school in
> tears, her former best friend was now someone else's
> best friend; she'd been excluded from the upcoming
> slumber party or was the victim of some other calcu-
> lated schoolgirl snub. She'd cry her eyes out, I didn't
> know what to say.
>
> "Well, if they're going to be like that, find some-
> one else to play with," I'd say.
>
> The tears flowed on. They got to be a weekly,
> then a twice weekly event. This went on for months
> and months. And then I finally began to realize that
> no sooner had she dried her tears than she was on
> the telephone, maliciously gossiping about some
> other little girl, a former friend, and cementing a
> new friendship by plotting to exclude this other girl.

> I was indignant, and I began to point out the incon-
> sistency in her behavior.
>
> "You don't understand," she'd yell, stomping off
> to her bedroom and slamming the door.
> (Madaras 1991)

Because of the intensity of the relationship, cliques
provide the most powerful learning experiences. Although
the twelve-year-old heroine of Carson McCullers's *The
Member of the Wedding* is not a member of a clique, she does
want to become part of the wedding couple:

> She wanted to speak to her brother and the bride, to
> talk to them and tell them of her plans, the three of
> them alone together, but they were never once alone;
> Jarvis was checking the car someone was lending
> them for the honeymoon while Janice dressed in the
> front bedroom among a crowd of beautiful grown
> girls. She wandered from one to the other of them,
> unable to explain. And once Janice put her arms
> about her, and said she was glad to have a little sis-
> ter—and when Janice kissed her, F. Jasmine felt an
> aching in her throat and could not speak. Jarvis,
> when she went to find him in the yard, lifted her up
> in a roughhouse way and said: Frankie the lankie the
> alaga fankie, the tee legged, toe legged, bow legged
> Frankie. And he gave her a dollar.
>
> She stood in the corner of the bride's room,
> wanted to say, "I love the two of you so much and
> you are the 'we of me.' Please take me with you from
> the wedding, for we belong together." (1946)

The longing of F. Jasmine (Frankie) to be part of the relationship between her brother and his bride, her discovery

of her need to be part of a group—the "we of me"—speaks movingly of the young adolescent's discovery of the need to belong as well as to the pain of exclusion.

Strategic Interactions: The Shock of Betrayal

We engage in strategic interactions whenever we try to withhold, obtain, or provide information in order to win some personal advantage (Goffman 1969). Perhaps the most straightforward example is that of a poker player's attempt to maintain a "poker" face. The player tries not to reveal, by facial expression, how good or how bad a hand has been dealt. Or the player may try to bluff and give the impression of a better hand than that actually held, or conversely, try and convey a poor hand when in fact it is strong. In any case, it is to the player's advantage not to give any clues to the other players regarding the strength or weakness of the hand. Success as a poker player, therefore, is a matter, in part at least, of the player's skill at strategic interactions.

We don't really observe such interactions in children. To engage in such interactions, we have to think about other people's thinking, and to do that we have to be able to conceptualize thought. Teenagers, thanks to their formal operations, are capable of engaging in strategic interactions and frequently employ them to conceal from their parents the fact that they have engaged in forbidden actions such as smoking. They may, for example, chew gum or use mouthwash to erase the smell of tobacco from their breath. Many adolescents are quite ingenious in the strategic interactions they invent to conceal the fact that they have skipped school.

Young people use strategic interactions in other ways as well. Much social interaction is strategic. For example, a young man learns that when he plans to ask a young woman for a date, he must first ask whether or not she is busy on a particular day or evening before he commits himself. This in turn gives the girl an opportunity to turn him down without rejecting his direct request. Similarly, many young people spend a great deal of time on the phone, not only talking but also giving the "busy signal" to prospective callers. The busy signal is a sign that the young person is popular and much in demand. Strategic interactions are also necessary for the employment of social tact, as in the avoidance of sensitive topics of conversation.

Although strategic interactions can be used to achieve positive ends, they can also be employed for less admirable purposes. When strategic interactions are used to get something to which the person employing the interaction is not entitled, we have *strategic manipulation*. The well-known "sting" of the con artist is an example. Stings take place when one party is operating on the basis of trust and cooperation while the other is being strategic. Consider a retired person befriended by a con artist. The retiree may behave according to the normal standards of friendship and might reveal his or her financial status as one might to a friend. The con artist might then talk about a lucrative investment—in turn apparently sharing information on the basis of friendship—that is sure to double or triple the money put into it in a short period of time. The retiree, still assuming that the other person is operating on the basis of a concerned friend, accepts the information as valid and proceeds to act upon it by giving the con artist money to invest. The con artist has strategically manipulated the retiree into investing money that will never be seen again.

Here is another, less hurtful, fictional example. A girl who has run away from home sees her picture in the newspaper. The paper is being read by a woman who has taken her in, befriended her, and given her a job. Rather than deny that the picture is of her, this is how she handles the situation strategically:

> Once I picked up the paper and looked hard at the picture. "Do you think she looks like me?" I asked Mrs. Peacock, and Mrs. Peacock leaned back and looked at me and then at the picture and then at me again and said, "No, if you wore your hair longer and curlier, and your face was maybe a little fuller, there might be a little resemblance, but then if you looked like a homicidal maniac I wouldn't ever of let you in my house."
>
> "I kinda think she looks like me," I said.
>
> "You get along to work and stop being vain," Mrs. Peacock said. (Jackson 1960)

In this story, the teenager gives out information as a way of concealing it. By making the comparison herself, she preempts Mrs. Peacock from doing so, and thus allays any suspicion that Mrs. Peacock might have that it is a picture of her. That is to say, the teenager strategizes that her benefactor will assume that if it were truly a picture of herself, that she would attempt to conceal, rather than make a point of, the resemblance.

Teenagers also employ strategic interactions when they steal. In so doing they violate the rules of honesty that presumably operate whenever we enter a store. When we approach a clerk with all of the items we wish to purchase, we are behaving according to the accepted rules of honesty. However, if we conceal one of the items we intend to take out of the store, we are engaging in a strategic manipulation. We are concealing information about the item from the clerk for our own benefit. Many teenagers who are honest and only use strategic interactions in games and in appropriate social situations are often appalled at friends who engage in strategic interactions for the purpose of stealing, as in the following fictional episode:

> One afternoon I needed some notebook paper so I stopped into the corner store next to Ben's Sweet Shop. Joel was with me. I decided as long as I was in the store, I needed a new ballpoint pen, too. My old one leaks on my fingers and smudges a lot. The pens were displayed in a mug, practically in front of the cash register. While I was deciding what color to buy, Joel picked two out of the jug and put them in his pocket. I think he took one ballpoint and one felt tip. They cost 49 cents. Joel didn't look at me, he just smiled his crooked smile and hummed a little tune.
>
> I was furious, just furious. I wanted to punch Joel in the nose. I wanted to mess up his angel face, to see the blood ooze out of his nostrils and trickle down his chin. I wanted to look him in the eye and say, "I've had it with you, Joel! You stink." (Blume 1971)

The narrator of the story was betrayed by a friend who not only violated the rules of conduct followed by honest people in a store, but also imposed that violation on a friend by making him an accessory to the act. Indeed the narrator was put in the awful position of being the "bad guy" no matter what he did. If he told on his friend, he broke the rule that you do not "rat" on a friend. If he did not tell, he was a partner to the theft. What the narrator learned was that we are sometimes confronted with moral dilemmas that are not of our own making but for which we have to suffer the consequences.

The shock of betrayal comes in many different forms,

but in every case the adolescent discovers that while he or she was operating according to one set of moral rules, say the free and honest sharing of information, the other person was operating according to another set of strategic rules, obtaining, concealing, or conveying information for personal advantage. Another shock of betrayal encountered by teenagers occurs when they are deliberately misled by someone of the opposite sex. Here again one person is operating strategically, giving information for his or her own benefit, while the other person assumes that moral rules, of honesty and truthfulness, are in play. In the following fictional account from a short story by Ann Muro entitled "Cecilia Rosas," a young man takes a woman's overtures seriously, only to find later that they were meant for her amusement and that of her friends:

> "Amadito," she whispered the way I had always dreamed she would.
>
> "Yes, Senorita Cecilia," I said expectantly.
>
> Her smile was warm and intimate. "Amadito, when are you going to take me to the movies?" she asked.
>
> Other salesladies watched us. They made me so nervous I couldn't answer.
>
> "Amadito, you haven't answered me," Miss Rosas said teasingly. "Either you are as bashful as a village sweetheart, or else you don't like me at all.". . .
>
> "Senorita Cecilia," I said, "I would love to take you to the movies any time."
>
> Miss Rosas smiled and patted my cheek. "Will you buy me candy and popcorn?" she said.
>
> I nodded, putting my hand on the warm imprint her warm palm had left on my face.
>
> "And hold my hand."

>   I said "yes" so enthusiastically it made her laugh.
> Other salesladies laughed too. Dazed and numb
> with happiness, I watched Miss Rosas walk away.

Later, when Amado prepares to serenade Miss Rosas, he
discovers that she was only toying with him:

>   "Ay, Amado, you're going to serenade your girl,"
> she said. I didn't reply right away. Then when I was
> getting ready to say, "Senorita Cecilia, I came to ser-
> enade you," I saw the American man sitting in the
> sports roadster at the curb.
>   "I'll be right there, Johnny," she said. "Have a
> nice time, darling."
>   I looked at her silken legs as she got into the car.
> Everything had happened so fast I was dazed. Bro-
> ken dreams made my head spin. The contrast be-
> tween myself and the poised American in the sports
> roadster was so cruel it made me wince.

Although Miss Rosas and the other salesladies may have
assumed that Amado knew that Miss Rosas was teasing
(being strategic), he did not, and experienced the shock of
betrayal. The experience leaves him sadder but wiser. As
he himself states, he was clearly different than the man she
preferred and so became unpleasantly aware of how he
compared to others. Here is how the episode ends:

>   Just about then Miss Rosas' father looked up from
> his newspaper. He asked the mariachis (whom
> Amado had hired to help him serenade Miss Rosas)
> if they knew how to sing "Canena Jail." They told
> him they did. Then they looked at me. I thought it
> over for a moment, then I nodded and started strum-

ming the brass strings of my guitar. What had happened made it only too plain that I could never trust
Miss Rosas again. So we serenaded her father instead. (Muro 1965)

Amado may have felt embarrassed, betrayed, and injured,
but ultimately he accepted what he saw of himself through
Miss Rosas' behavior and took another step toward self-
understanding and acceptance.

Another common strategic interaction occurs when a
young woman is operating according to the rules of romance (honesty, caring) while the young man is behaving
strategically. The result is predictable with the girl experiencing the shock of betrayal and the self-devaluation that
is its aftermath.

I had intercourse twice even though I didn't want to.
I was madly in love with this guy and he and his
friend picked me up one night in their car and we
drove around. Suddenly he stopped the car and told
me that if I ever wanted to see him again, I'd have to
have sex right now with him and his friend. I loved
him so much and didn't want to lose him so I did it.
God, I hated myself afterward. I don't see him anymore and I'll never have sex with anyone unless I
want to. Sex isn't a toy. It should be something very
special. (Norman and Harris 1981)

In this unfortunately all-too-common experience of
sexual exploitation, we see how adolescents can abuse the
ability to engage in strategic interactions. It is sad that some
young people, like this young woman, must learn about
themselves and other people through such a devaluing and
degrading experience.

It is important to say too, that there is absolutely no excuse for young men who behave like those described above. It would be wrong, a serious mistake, I believe, to explain away such brutish behavior as a consequence of bad upbringing or of a society that uses sex to sell everything from soap to cars. These factors are important, but at some point adolescents must be held accountable for their own actions. Teenagers are under more stress today than ever before, and they have less adult support and fewer resources for coping than did earlier generations—but despite the postmodern circumstances, such malevolence cannot be excused. There are some things that are morally wrong, and because we are human, and regardless of our background, we know that they are wrong.

Once adolescents become aware of strategic manipulation, they may become suspicious of other people's motives. This usually occurs in later adolescence, after young people have personally experienced the shock of betrayal. Sometimes, however, they can suspect a betrayal when it is not in fact intended. This was the tragic circumstance described by John Knowles in his classic novel, *A Separate Peace* (1960).

> My brain exploded. He minded, despised the possibility that I might be the head of the school. There was a swift chain of explosions in my brain one certainty after another blasted up like a detonation. Up went the idea of my best friend, up went affection and partnership and sticking by someone and relying on someone absolutely in the jungle of the boys' school, up went the hope that there was anyone in this school—in this world—whom I could trust.

This young man's feelings of betrayal had a tragic consequence. Consciously or unconsciously he contributed to his friend's crippling accident. Sometimes we are too ready to believe in strategic manipulation and attribute bad motives to those who wish us no harm. An important part of self-differentiation is learning whom we can trust and whom we cannot.

Romantic Attachments: The Shock of Disillusionment

Adolescents are romantic; they fall in love with love. Thinking in a new key allows them to imagine love in an idealistic and hence romantic way. They see only the good of romance, and if there is a struggle to win the girl or the boy of their dreams, they are nonetheless sure that they will live "happily ever after." In keeping with romantic inclination, adolescents tend to idealize the young person to whom they are romantically attracted. Inevitably, these idealizations and true experience come into conflict with enough force to produce a third form of peer shock, the shock of disillusionment.

We experience one variety of disillusionment when someone we care about expresses admiration for someone we dislike, for instance a political figure or movie star. Most of us take for granted that the people to whom we are attached share our tastes and it is a shock to discover that this is not always the case. Similarly, it may come as a blow to a younger brother or sister to discover the kind of people that their admired older sibling might be attracted to. Listen to this girl describe her moment of disillusionment with her older brother:

> My brother the basketball player invited his new girlfriend to a family dinner not long ago. My brother is terribly shy, and so very tall you wouldn't believe me if I told you his height. His girlfriend, on the other

hand, looks like a plump little gypsy, with jet black
curls and bangles up and down her chubby little
arms. She barely comes up to his waist and from the
moment she arrived, she never shut up. She babbled
and babbled and the next morning my mother
groused, "What is he doing with her? What is this
thing your brother has for short chatterboxes?"
(Anon. 1983)

Another, reverse kind of disillusionment occurs when
we discover that someone whom we like or are attracted to
does not have the same effect upon those whose opinions
we respect and value. When young people make a romantic choice, they expect that others will immediately see the
many reasons for this attraction. This is often not the case. It
often comes as a shock to adolescents when they discover
that others do not appreciate their romantic choices. They
must come to the painful recognition of our different preferences. As an article in *Young Miss* had to explain:

Regardless of the kind of guy you prefer, someone is
bound to find fault with your selection. Friends and
family members often have their own ideas about
who is right for you. And peer and parental pressures often can make it difficult to date a boy who
doesn't meet everyone's ideas of Mr. Right. (Weir
1983)

Although the discovery that other people do not share
our opinion of someone we are infatuated with can be hard
to take, it can be healthy. Love may be blind, but sometimes
friends and parents can help to restore our vision. It is part
of the slow process of learning that things are not always
the way we would like them to be. Even more disillusion-

ing is the discovery that someone to whom you are romantically attached does not share the same standards and values. According to one writer, Don Weir, "There is nothing more devastating for a shy, sensitive teenage boy than the sight of a girl he has a crush on, mooning over some superficial jerk" (1983). In the same way, there is nothing so disillusioning to a sensitive, intelligent young woman than the sight of the boy she is attracted to, drooling over some well-endowed, but empty-headed, flirt. Nonetheless, these shocks of disillusionment can be useful—if painful—learning experiences. They help adolescents differentiate between outward appearance and inner character.

Other shocks of disillusionment occur when adolescents find that someone they were attracted to, and who expressed attraction to them, was playing them for a fool. In the teenage romance novel *The Boyfriend War* (one of the Sweet Valley High series by Francine Pascal), Mick, a watersports instructor on a Caribbean island, is dating two girls, Jessica and Lila, and telling each one a quite different story. In the following scene they discover his duplicity:

> "I didn't mean to knock you into the water. But you should know better than to call me a dumb blonde. You know how I get when someone calls me that."
>
> "I didn't call you that," Lila said, treading water, "Mick did."
>
> "No he didn't," Jessica protested, "Mick wouldn't say something like that—certainly not to you. Why he told me himself that you're a mousy brunette and a stuck-up snob."
>
> "No he didn't," Lila said. "If he felt that way, he wouldn't be going out with me."
>
> "I told you, he only goes out with you because

he's afraid of annoying your uncle. He said so himself."

Lila put a wet hand on Jessica's arm. "Did he really?"

Jessica was confused by the strange tone in Lila's
voice. "Yes he did," she insisted, "And he called you
a stuck-up snob."

"Don't you get it Jess? Mick told me he didn't
want to go out with you. He said he was dating you
only because regular staff are supposed to be friendly
to the temporary counselors."

Jessica's eyes widened. "He said that?"

"Over and over again."

Jessica pulled herself onto the ladder at the end
of the pier and climbed up, with Lila following behind. They sat side by side with their legs dangling
over the edge.

"I smell something fishy," Jessica said finally,
"and it has nothing to do with the ocean."

"I can't believe he did this to us," Lila fumed,
pounding her fist against the pier. "Mick dated both
of us at the same time. We really liked him. And the
whole time he was lying to us both." (1994)

Sometimes teenagers experience the shock of disillusionment with their first encounter with someone who tries
to "get physical." "Getting physical" can be a dismal experience, particularly if one person has greatly overidealized
the other. What follows is a fictional passage about a young
teenager who has fantasized all winter about a lifeguard
whom she has known on summer vacations when she was
a child:

And above all Jim, sitting in his high chair, watching

and making the world small and safe.... When Jim comes, Nancy thought, then it will be all right, when Jim comes.

When summer does arrive, the family moves to the shore and Nancy finally encounters Jim at the beach:

> She was sharply aware of the slight pressure of his hand on her arm, of the naked upper half of his body so close to her own. "Don't you work any?" Her breath was coming in hard little gasps. "I mean don't you have a regular kind of a job?"
>
> "Don't need to," he said, "Got enough to eat on. Got a little shack up there, back a way. It's a good enough little place. I'll show it to you one day if you like."
>
> "No," she said nervously, "I mean, Mother wouldn't let me."
>
> "Mother wouldn't let me," he mimicked, and his teeth glistened whitely against the brown of his skin. "What a baby you are, Nancy."
>
> He was squeezing her arm. Glancing sideways, she watched a fat pink worm of a tongue crawl between his lips. She stood motionless an instant. Then, shaking her head frantically, she jerked away from his hand and darted forward, against an oncoming breaker, half fell, and stood up again, holding the thick wet rope with one hand.
>
> Looking back, she could see the beach, the mothers on their blankets, the children playing in the sand. Off to the left was her own mother, with the tiny blond girl, very close, still digging. She watched Jim climb to the top of his stand and sit, brown and still and watchful. It was for this that she had waited,

all through the winter. She turned away, and the ocean stretched vast and terrifying before her. "Mother," she said. And her lips sought and found an earlier name. "Mama, Mama." She hesitated briefly, her eyes burning with unshed tears. Taking a deep breath, she ducked under the rope that marked off the outermost limit for children. (Randall 1978)

As Nancy's experience illustrates, physical encounters are often not the romantic fireworks they were reputed to be. In reality, the shock of disillusionment can be so painful that the teenager may wish to return, as Nancy did, to the safety and protection of childhood. As a child there is no imperative to get physical, and parents provide a protective shield. Again, such hurtful disillusionment can be constructive in helping the young person differentiate between the ideal and the real. And each new discovery about others always occasions a new discovery about oneself that can be integrated into a more solid sense of self and identity.

Perhaps the event that teenagers fantasize about the most today is "doing it," or losing their virginity. Although the initiation of sexual activity is sometimes attributed to biological factors ("hormone attacks"), in fact the determinants are more social and cultural than they are biological. Over the last quarter of a century the number of young men and women who lose their virginity before leaving adolescence has steadily increased. Survey data indicate that the rate of sexual activity for girls ages 15 to 19 is the highest ever. Overall some 52% of girls in this age range reported having had sexual intercourse. For young men in this age range, 60% had engaged in coitus. Education seems to be a factor in whether or not teenagers become sexually active. High schools with high dropout rates had more sexually active teens than did high schools with low dropout rates (Morris 1992). Peer groups and communities also play a large role in the age at which young people engage in sexual intercourse (Howard 1992).

Young men and young women view the loss of virginity quite differently, and the way they may be disillusioned is therefore also different. Whether the reason is biological, psychological, or social, or, most probably, some combination of the three, boys have a different sexual orientation than do girls. Basically boys are more *erotic*, and girls are more *romantic*. This difference is nicely illustrated by the comments of an eleventh-grade boy and girl when asked to describe the three biggest problems facing teens:

> BOY: Every time a boy sees a girl, the first thing that pops into his head is sex, and not whether she's a nice girl or not. When guys are sitting in classrooms, girls distract the boys so that it's harder to concentrate.

> GIRL: A teenage girl, usually in fear of losing someone she loves, often turns toward the sexual relationship. And if this does not work out she will feel very lonely, empty, and confused. This will probably lead her right to an attempt at suicide. (Brondino et al. 1988)

The ways in which young women and men ruminate about intercourse are thus quite different. Girls tend to think about it as a romantic, loving relationship. At the same time they worry that if they go "all the way" they will lose their reputation. They are also concerned that if they do agree to intercourse, the boy will no longer respect them and look for a new girlfriend. Boys, on the other hand, think much less about the partner than they do about the act itself. Having intercourse becomes a rite of passage, an important step toward adulthood. Obviously there are wide individual differences; some boys are more romantic, and some girls are only out for a good time. But for the majority of adolescents, the portrayal given above is roughly accurate. It has not changed even with the dramatic increase in sexually active teens over the past quarter century.

The difference between the boy's and the girl's viewpoint on this matter is amusingly but realistically rendered in *Teenage Romance* by Delia Ephron (1981). The following is her version of the simultaneous thoughts of two teenagers out on a date together:

> BOY: You bet you do, you know it, you're going to get it. Hey, hey, hey, tonight's the night, you feel it in your bones. Bones? Not bad! That's where you feel it all right. Or, should you say bone? Check out your reflection in the glass of the ticket booth. Then on the way to join your date at the end of the ticket holder's line see if you know anyone the two of you could butt in front of, and call yourself an asshole, if you don't stop thinking about getting it, you'll jinx it. Stop thinking, I know it, I'm going to get it, and consider instead what you could say to your date that would really help you get it for sure like a compliment. As soon as you see her ask her if she did something to her hair, it looks different.

> GIRL: You know, you two really are a lot alike, it's amazing, it really is. Do you think he really likes you? Suppose he does. Think. Please God make him like me, make him like me really a lot. I really want him to. What if he said he loved you? Imagine it, he falls in love with you. Then imagine telling your best friend all about the date tomorrow. Oh God, tomor-

row! You don't want it to come. You don't want the
date to end. Oh, please don't end; don't end ever.

Our first sexual encounter is a very powerful experience. It is one of those events in our lives, like graduations,
marriages, and deaths of loved ones, that we will always
remember. For both young men and young women, the
loss of virginity is hard psychological evidence that they
are no longer children and that they have entered the adult
world. It is an experience we can never forget.

Because we invest so much in this first sexual encounter, it is bound to be disillusioning; it can never live up,
in either the bad or the good sense, to all that we imagined
it would be. Boys often have some fear of the experience
because their orientation toward competitive achievement
makes them worry about the adequacy of their performance. For young men, therefore, the experience can be
positive if they feel that they performed well. At the same
time it is a very self-centered experience, as the comments
below make clear:

> "It was like I had become a man, and I wanted to
> tell everyone about it."
>
> "I felt very relaxed, drained of all worries and
> cares. I was proud. A little warm all over. I really en-
> joyed myself. I felt I'd never be the same. I had taken
> a step on my way to manhood."
>
> "I felt like it was an accomplishment. I felt I was a
> big boy or a man. It gave me a sense of pride. It was
> like growing up." (Hess 1981)

For girls who want the sexual encounter to be embed-
ded in a fantasy of a caring relationship, a romantic setting
with tender words, the reality can often be bitterly disillu-

sioning. Below are some of the reactions of young women to their first sexual experience.

> "I felt guilty because I hardly knew the person I had intercourse with. The guy was older than I was and I thought he was something he was not. He sweet talked me, and being a young fourteen, I fell for it."
>
> "At first I was hurt because I felt I had lost the little girl in me."
>
> "I was really worried about it. I wanted to do it my first time with someone I really loved so it would be more like my giving it to someone. But unfortunately, that wasn't the way it was." (Hess 1981)

For boys, then, the first sexual encounter is more often a positive experience than a negative one. They feel that they achieved something they had serious doubts about achieving, even if they did not admit these doubts to themselves. For girls, the first sexual experience is more often a negative experience because it seldom lives up to the idyllic encounter that they had imagined. For both young men and women, however, the first sexual experience makes a lasting contribution to their sense of self and identity.

If the sexual experience comes at a time when the process of identity formation is well along (ages sixteen to nineteen) the event can contribute in a positive way, and is integrated with the young person's fuller appreciation and integration of their sexual self with their psychological self. But if it occurs early in the process of identity formation (ages twelve to fifteen), it cannot be easily integrated into a self that is only half-formed. As a consequence, it remains an isolated event, a powerful experience that is somehow foreign and apart from the rest of the personality. Early sexual experience thus contributes to a patchwork sense of self.

The peer shocks associated with moving into the culture of adolescence are a necessary and inevitable experience for young people in transition to adulthood. Although these shocks can be painful at the time they occur, by and large they help teenagers to clarify their feelings, values, and attitudes. Such clarification is an important part of constructing a healthy sense of self and identity. It should be emphasized, too, that adolescent socialization involves much more than peer shocks; many peer group activities are fun and enjoyable. Unfortunately, the pleasurable features of adolescent socialization blind adults to the very real stressors teenagers are also encountering.

It is also true, however, that the positive and enjoyable periods of adolescence are shrinking today. When the shocks associated with initiation into the culture of adolescence are combined with those originating from thinking in a new key, and those that are endemic to the perils of puberty, the adolescent is confronted with a formidable array of stressors. As we shall see in succeeding chapters, these normal and age-appropriate stressors are now compounded by the social stressors that derive from postmodern society. The new perception of adolescent sophistication has added to the demands upon teenagers for maturity without giving them the time and the space needed to attain this maturity. In the next chapters I will detail the ways in which society contributes to the stressors experienced by contemporary adolescents.

PART II

Given: A Premature Adulthood

CHAPTER 5

Vanishing Markers

The absence of a special place for teenagers in our society is evidenced by the erosion of the "markers" that once signaled their immature status. Markers are external signs of our progress along, in Kierkegaard's lovely phrase, "the stages of life's way" (Kierkegaard 1945). Markers may be as simple as the pencil lines on the kitchen wall that chronicle a child's growth in height from birthday to birthday, or as elaborate as a confirmation or bar or bat mitzvah. To the world, and to ourselves, markers proclaim our movement toward maturity.

We all have a "sense of becoming," of growing and changing as individuals. Markers confirm us in our sense of forward movement. This confirmation, however, must be social as well as personal. However personally gratifying the attainment of certain markers is, such attainments mean much more when they are accompanied by social recognition. Indeed, much of the gratification of reaching new goals comes from the public approval that accompanies such attainments. Graduation exercises, a driver's license, and similar markers reveal to everyone in the community that the teenager has taken big steps along life's way. The recognition of these steps by parents, friends, and teachers reinforces the adolescent's sense of progress and growth. For example, every four years I take on a group of entering university students as advisees. After four years, when they are ready to graduate, they appreciate having someone who was witness to their progress from "wet behind the ears" freshmen to "worldly and sophisticated" seniors.

Markers are not only signs of progress, they are often much more. Progress toward maturity entails new responsibilities and new restraints, as well as new freedoms. The teenager who turns sixteen, for example, can apply for a driver's license and a work permit. But driving a car means not only obeying traffic rules, but also taking responsibility for car maintenance. Holding a job requires that the young person be on time and perform the work that needs to be done. Young people are usually more than willing to accept these new restraints and responsibilities in return for the new freedoms and acknowledgments of maturity that go with them.

Nonetheless, markers are not an unmixed blessing. Progress to adulthood is not only a matter of gaining new freedoms, as well as responsibilities; it also means giving up "childish" things that were once enjoyed. Teenagers can no longer go "trick-or-treating" on Halloween, nor go sledding or swinging on playground swings. While there is a certain sadness in giving up these activities, and the sense of being a protected child that goes with them, there is a certain pride as well. There is a direct parallel between a child of seven or eight who says with pride, "I don't believe in the Easter Bunny anymore," and the car-driving sixteen-year-old who says, "I don't ride bikes anymore." In both instances the young person takes pride in a new accomplishment and a certain disdain (perhaps masking a bit of regret) for an earlier belief or skill that is now seen as a symptom of an outgrown immaturity.

If markers highlight where we are and where we have been, they also serve as beacons for the future, for where we are going. To college-bound high school students, getting into the college of their choice is a marker that they worked very hard to attain. Getting a good job, buying a new car rather than a jalopy, having one's own place, and eventually marrying and having children are goals that motivate many young people. Markers remain important to us throughout our lives, but only in adolescence is public recognition of these markers so crucial to our sense of having really attained them.

Given the importance of markers for our sense of becoming, we should be concerned at their disappearance. Not surprisingly, growth markers have disappeared in direct proportion to the rate at which the perception of adolescent sophistication has replaced the perception of adolescent immaturity. Why do young people need markers of approaching maturity when we view them as already quite knowledgeable about the world? First, markers help adults limit the demands for maturity, the stressors, that they place upon adolescents. Second, because they offer young people rules, limits, and prohibitions that they can internalize, markers are a source of stress-coping mechanisms. Internalized rules, limits, and prohibitions give young people the means to make age-appropriate decisions and choices.

Clothing Markers

Although it may seem like ancient history, it was not that long ago that children were dressed differently from teenagers. In the modern era, when I was growing up, I had to wear knickers. At that time, just after WWII, boys were not allowed to wear long pants until they reached the teen years. And I desperately wanted long pants. I remember having to wear corduroy knickers, which my mother said were warmer, that made a horrible noise when I walked. I eagerly looked forward to the day when I could walk back and forth to school without hearing that awful sound. At that time too, girls were not allowed to wear long stockings, high heels, or makeup until they reached the teen years. Wearing long pants or stockings was a sign that we, as young men and young women, had reached a new stage along life's way.

Today, in our postmodern world, even infants wear designer diaper covers, and by the age of two or three many children are dressed like miniature versions of their parents. Some girls of six or seven are now given expensive makeup kits and feel undressed if they go out of doors without lipstick and eye shadow. By the time girls are in their teen years, they are so adultlike in appearance that it is hard to guess their age. Teenage boys, too, are indistinguishable in dress from school-age boys and from young men. The ubiquity of blue jeans, T-shirts, and baseball caps for all ages and both sexes has all but eliminated clothing as a marker of anything other than conformity to the current fashions and fads.

For teenagers who are already confronting many postmodern stressors, the loss of clothing markers is significant. There was a great deal of pleasure in anticipating the day when you could wear long pants for the first time and display them to the "audience" as a sign of your newly attained maturity. Clothing markers also gave the newly enfranchised teenager a sense of superiority over "children" who still had to wear knickers and who could not wear makeup. Grown-up clothing and cosmetics were distinctive, positive, and something the adolescent could claim as a right. They were independent of all the anxieties about height, breast size, nose length, and so on. With the disappearance of clothing markers, teenagers lost an important symbol of having attained a new developmental level with its own demands and expectations.

Activity Markers

In the modern era, many activities were reserved for the teen years. Participation in organized team and individual sports, with uniforms, coaches, and intramural competition, was once the sole province of high school students. An adolescent entering high school could try out for the football, basketball, swimming, or track team. Those who were qualified would later compete while the whole school (or almost the whole school) watched and cheered them on. Those who were good enough to make first or second string might even win a letter. That letter, in turn, would be sewn on a sweater to be worn proudly, or, even more proudly, given to a sweetheart to wear.

In preparation for those glorious high school days, elementary and junior high school kids played sandlot games with ragtag equipment, uneven teams, and no adults anywhere in evidence. Some kids were much better than others. Some were invited to play; others were not. A kindly group of kids would let the uncoordinated play, a less kindly group would not. Partly the play was just for fun, but partly it was in preparation for "making the team" in high school. Going to high school and possibly making a team was a marker of status to be looked forward to. Today, by contrast, even young children are involved in competitive sports. Children as young as six or seven may be on a "traveling" soccer team that has its own uniforms, coach, and competitors. Programs like Little League, Pop Warner, and Pee Wee Hockey often have as much equipment, coaching, and scheduled competition as high school athletes. Another important marker of nearing adulthood— participation in team sports—has lost its symbolic value.

In part at least, the involvement of children in organized team sports is a reflection of our new postmodern perception of child competence. When children were regarded as innocent, it would have been unheard of to have them participate in potentially dangerous, but also clearly adolescent activities. Now that children are seen as competent, it is permissible to organize them for team sports. Unfortunately, this gives some parents a new outlet for meeting their own needs without sufficient regard for those of their children. Child psychiatrist Richard A. Gardner puts it this way:

> A father may become excessively involved in his son's Little League experiences, thereby trying to relive his own boyhood or compensate for early deprivation in this area. He may place great pressures on the child to win. It is not at all uncommon for the whole atmosphere of Little League games to be contaminated by parents who are excessively involved in the competition. The children, of course, are being used as pawns. (1973)

Competing in team and individual sports as a child, particularly when this is in response to parental pressure, may turn young people away from engaging in the same sports when they reach high school. The concept of sports burnout is getting increasing attention as a factor in the decline of students going out for high school athletics.

> While research suggests that in many cases children drop out [of sports] because they become interested

in other things, there is also concern that intense competitive pressures and too many sport demands may cause youngsters to drop out and abandon sports. . . . For example, a study of over 1,000 teenage swimmers indicated that too much pressure, conflict with coaches and insufficient success were among the reasons that swimmers reported their teammates dropped out of competition. (Smoll and Smith 1991)

Related to the loss of sports as a marker for young people is something equally important, a sense of spontaneity and a willingness to create games on one's own. A parent told me of an incident involving his son, who was nine and a member of a Little League team. They were to play on a Saturday morning. It was a lovely spring day, both teams were suited and ready, and all the necessary equipment was in place. But the coach did not show up. Afraid of losing and risking their chance of being in the "playoffs," the team decided not to play. For these youngsters, playing ball was not just getting together with friends to play a game. It was serious business. If the coach wasn't there, what's the point of playing? The game now belonged more to the adults involved than to the children who played.

Other activity markers have vanished as well. Given our new perception of child competence, we now have beauty contests for four- and eight-year-old girls. These youngsters are trained to walk, talk, and dress properly and to present themselves in the most attractive way possible. The motivation of at least some parents may be money, but for others, like those who place their children in organized sports, it may be an escape from an unhappy life. The number of these beauty contests and pageants appears to be growing—there are now even infant beauty contests!

The largest children's pageant is Miss Hemisphere, where more than one million contestants, starting at age three, (and even including boys ages three to eight), compete in all 50 states each year in preliminary, state, and national contests. The Dream Girl Pageant, an offshoot of Miss Hemisphere, holds separate competitions in 25 states, also leading to a "national" final. A growing pageant organization is "America's Stars of Tomorrow" which holds beauty contests for babies and also for little boys. (Whittemore 1982)

The tragic murder of six-year-old JonBenet Ramsey, a beauty contest winner, suggests that such age-inappropriate activities may also put young girls at risk.

Apparently there are no markers that escape being taken over by younger children. To illustrate, the martial arts used to be reserved for teenagers and adults, but no more:

Teenage males have been trying out for fighting ever since Bruce Lee flashed those furious fists 20 years ago. These days, however, they're being upstaged by boys and girls as young as three. At that tender age, Richard Dietrich started practicing the Tae Kwan Do at the Jhoon Rhee school in Alexandria, Va. Now a ripe old five, Richard has already earned a red belt (two notches below black) like his twelve-year-old brother, Michael. (Longway et al. 1983)

In still another, unlikely, realm—religious activities—markers have also begun to disappear. In some churches, well-intentioned clergy and parishioners allow children at any age to take communion. This means that the children no longer have to be of a particular age, or to have completed a specified course of instruction, before they can participate in this ritual. Yet before they attain formal operations, children cannot really understand the metaphorical significance of the wafer and the wine. Indeed, one clergyman told me of a rather embarrassing incident that arose as a result of this new bow to child competence. A three-year-old girl chose to take communion, but when she was given the wafer she took one bite and handed it back to the priest with the explanation, "I don't like it." He ate the remainder, but wondered about the wisdom of treating young children as competent enough to participate in communion.

As adults, we need to consider the impact of these infringements on teenage territory. Young people need a sense of "growing," of being in a process of transition. Birthdays are looked forward to as markers of increased maturity (not, as among adults, with dread as a sign of advancing age and infirmity). Children and adolescents operate on the basis of what I call an *age dynamism*: they want to be like the next older age group and not like the next younger age group. In the world of teenage romances, for example, the heroines are from fifteen to eighteen years of age, but the readers are thirteen or fourteen. Not being like the younger group and aspiring to be like the older group is a marker of place. But when adolescents finds younger children doing what they never did—competing in team sports, practicing Kung Fu—the age dynamism that is a reassuring marker of place is lost. What was once reserved for adolescence is now the province of children and even preschoolers. Teenagers are left with no activity entirely their own.

One consequence of vanishing activity markers is already clear. There has been a rapid decline, over the last decade, in the number of adolescents who are trying out for high school athletics. While other factors may be involved,

the loss of its marker quality may be one reason young people find high school sports less appealing today than was
true in the past.

Information Markers

As I have argued elsewhere, in the modern era children were seen as innocent and this perception was mirrored by society's protection of them from information
thought harmful to their tender sensibilities (Elkind 1994).
In the postmodern era, however, we have altered our perception of children from one of innocence to one of competence. This perception is, in turn, reflected in the fact that
we expose children to, rather than shield them from, the
seamier sides of human nature. Such exposure, it is believed, will give children the tough skin they will need to
deal with the postmodern world. In the same way, the
change from the modern perception of adolescent immaturity to that of adolescent sophistication has been accompanied by a sharp decline in adult efforts to shield teenagers
from violence and smut.

It is important to say that these changed perceptions
and practices have not come about because of any new, rev-
olutionary discoveries in our knowledge of child growth
and development. Such breakthroughs did occur a quarter
of a century ago with the work of famed Swiss psychologist
Jean Piaget (1950), who transformed the way we understand the growth of intelligence. If anything, however, his
work reinforced the perception of childhood innocence and
teenage immaturity. The shift from perceptions of childhood innocence and adolescent immaturity to those of
childhood competence and adolescent sophistication did
not correspond to any new discoveries in the field of child
and adolescent psychology. Rather, it was the direct result

of changes in society and in the family. In the postmodern world, where we can no longer shield and protect children and youth in the ways we once did, we need to believe that young people are competent and sophisticated. Otherwise, as parents and teachers, we would go mad with anxiety and worry.

It is important then, to distinguish between what we know from systematic observation and research about children and adolescents and the informal social perceptions of these age groups. For example, the attainment of concrete operations (which enable children to reason at the syllogistic level) at about the age of six or seven has been recognized since ancient times. The Jesuit dictum, "Give us a boy until the age of seven and he is ours forever," reflects this insight and the importance the Catholic church placed upon religious instruction during the early years of reasoning ability. Likewise, the bodily and mental transformations of adolescence were recognized and described by Aristotle:

> Young men have strong passions and tend to gratify them indiscriminately. Of the bodily desires, it is the sexual by which they are most swayed and in which they show absence of control. . . . They are changeable and fickle in their desires which are violent while they last, but quickly over: Their impulses are keen but not deep rooted. (1941)

Nonetheless, the socially determined perceptions of children and adolescents at any given time often override the time-honored constants of human development. That is what is happening today. Thanks to the notion of child competence, we now make an effort to prepare children for many dangers from which we once tried to shield them.

Child abuse is a case in point. A number of programs have been devised to teach children to protect themselves against those who might sexually abuse them. These programs come packaged in films, videotapes, and books. They attempt to teach children to make discriminations, for example, between "good" touching and "bad" touching and between "comfortable" and "uncomfortable."

Yet both clinical experience and research teach us that these are difficult, if not impossible, discriminations for young children to make. As psychologists Rappucci and Haugaard concluded after a comprehensive review of these programs:

> The complexity of the process that a child must go through to repel or to report abuse, the variety of abuse situations that a child may encounter, and the short duration of most prevention programs virtually ensure that a child cannot be assumed to be protected simply because of participation in a program. Adults must be encouraged to continue and to increase their protective efforts rather than be reassured that children are learning to be self protective. (1989)

It is certainly true, of course, that we can no longer protect children from stressful information in the way we once did. But trying to teach them skills that they cannot use, and creating anxieties that they have no way of warding off, is not beneficial to children. On the other hand if children are witness to, say, violence, then it is essential that we talk with them about it not once but many times. Likewise, if children witness something disturbing on television, we cannot assume that they will just shrug it off. We need to say something about the fact that it was frightening—"That was scary, wasn't it?"—to give them a chance to vent their feelings. But we shouldn't deliberately expose children to anxiety-provoking material in the vain hope that this will somehow inoculate them against its negative effects.

The media seem to have accepted the perception of childhood competence. Witness movies such as *Home Alone*, in which a boy is left behind when his parents go to Europe and he manages quite well, even outwitting two bungling burglars. Perhaps this also explains, in part anyway, the enormous amount of violence shown on television. And all this violence *is* having an effect. In my travels across the country I hear the same story: much more violent aggression on the playground. And this is not true just for older children but for the younger ones as well. The truth is that children may *not* be competent to handle all of the aggression, sexuality, and profanity that has become routine on television and in the movies. To be sure, disruptive family life contributes to this aggression, but television also plays a role.

Although it may not have seemed like much of a privilege to modern adolescents, shielding them from the baser sides of human nature until they reached the teen years did serve as a marker of maturity. Although there is some attempt to do this today with film, television, and music album ratings, these are much less than effective. Many theaters admit children to see films that are rated for adults (Greenberg, Brown, and Beurkel-Rothfuss 1986). And adolescents can easily rent X-rated videos. In truth, children have almost as ready access to adult-rated materials as do adolescents and adults. Accordingly, there is no longer any strictly "adult" information to which adolescents are given gradual access as a sign of growing maturity.

It is, however, not only the more lurid forms of adult information that have lost their marker quality. A few decades ago a family's finances were clearly none of the children's business. If they asked what a parent earned, what the house or car cost, and so on, they were given to understand that it was none of their affair. Today, in the postmodern permeable family, even young children know a lot about the family's income. If there is a separation or divorce, they probably know what the alimony and child support payments are—and whether or not they come on time. In one community, when their fathers were laid off work, several children tried to starve themselves because they did not want to be a financial burden. Financial information has, therefore, lost its marker quality.

The same is true for family information of an unpleasant sort. Children were once shielded from stories about the black sheep in the family or about those who were mentally ill or addicted—unless of course they lived with the family or the children saw them regularly. Only in adolescence were young people permitted into the discussion of troubled relatives. Today, however, parents make little effort to shield their children from this information. Parents have become lax in this regard, in part at least, because they know their children see so much of it on television anyway. This laxity also derives from the perception of childhood competence, which suggests that they can cope. Because children no longer have to wait until they are in their teens to be privy to such information, it has lost its value as a kind of initiation rite of adolescence.

Adolescence is the time when young people are best prepared to deal with less fortunate family members. In contrast to children, who are likely to imagine something far worse than the reality, adolescents are likely to make an effort to achieve a sympathetic understanding of troubled relatives. Sometimes parents can, however, be overprotective and not share this information even when their child is approaching adulthood. When this happens, they not only deprive the young person of a significant marker, but also prevent the adolescent from reaching out to the person in difficulty. This happened to Brenda, an eighteen-year-old who wrote:

> There was a secret about my cousin who had been in a mental hospital for three or four years. I knew she had run away from home, but I didn't know she was in an institution. She had tried to commit suicide. I just found out about it. I've seen her since then and I think if I had know about her problem, I might have been able to help her. I wish my parents had said something, that really bothers me. (Norman and Harris 1981)

By not sharing this information with Brenda when she became an adolescent, her parents not only deprived her of an important symbol of growing maturity, but also an opportunity to form a relationship with her cousin. Too much shielding and protection can be as harmful as too little.

Other information markers have disappeared as well. Sexual information is now readily available even to young children. Up until the sixties there was a form of censorship of the media. Nudity, foul language, and explicitly sexual activity were simply not allowed. There was no *Playboy* or *Penthouse* on the newsstands, no songs with titles such as "I Want Your Sex," and no soft-porn movies available on cable television or at video rental stores. The gradual introduction to the world of sexuality that was the marker of adolescence in the modern world is no longer possible. Because television is in the home, and because parents are not always there to monitor it, even young adolescents are witness to considerable sexual material. In a survey of 15- to 16- year-olds in three Michigan cities more than half had seen the most popular R-rated movies either in theaters or on videocassette (Greenberg, Brown, and Beurkel-Rothfuss 1993).

The amount of sexual material in the media is not only large, it is growing. Between 1983 and 1993 content studies of sex in soap operas and on prime time programs indicate that references to all forms of sexual behavior increased. Sexual behavior occurs on the average of three times per hour during prime time. Other media add to this exposure. About 75% of popular song lyrics refer to love and sex. Some 60–70% of music videos also have characters who express sexual feeling or who engage in sexually suggestive behavior. Popular songs such as "(When I Think About You) I Touch Myself," "Damn, I Wish I Was Your Lover," and "Let's Get Sexual" deal with masturbation, lust, and sexual intercourse (1993).

Inasmuch as children are exposed to much of this material before they become teenagers, they are familiar with nudity and sexual language long before they enter the teen years. Freedom to access sexual information is no longer a marker of having reached adolescence. When school-age children talk knowingly about sexual body parts, when they giggle about "making out" and "getting some," it is hard for the teenager to feel that he or she is privy to information not available to children. Unfortunately, children and adolescents are exposed to a media sexuality that is often without the qualities of caring, kindness, and sensitivity that make it a human rather than an animal activity.

Violence is another kind of information from which children were once largely shielded and learned about only as adolescents. All that has changed with television. American television is the most violent in the world. It is estimated that the average American child or teenager views 1,000 murders, rapes, and aggravated assaults per year on television alone (Comstock and Strassburger 1993). As Alfred Hitchcock is reputed to have said, "Television has brought murder into the home, where it belongs." Hitchcock of course was referring to the fact that murder is often between family members. But one has to question whether it belongs in homes where there are young children.

After the media attention given Susan Smith, the mother who drowned her two children in 1995, I had a number of phone calls from parents. These parents reported that their young children had, after seeing this news on television, asked questions to the effect of, "Mommy are you going to kill me?" Other children, who inadvertently saw on television bodies being dragged down the streets of a city in Somalia, suffered nightmares.

Perhaps in order to keep up with television, films have become, if not more violent than television at least more explicit and more gory:

> The trouble with most of the horror films made now is that there is no serious content. They reflect no myths, they have no center. They are just pure sensation but that is a reflection of our times because so many adults are living lives of pure sensation. Horror films aren't bad for kids, they have a good scare, especially when they go with friends and it is a group experience. (Stein 1982)

The issue from the perspective of this book, however, is not whether watching violence and horror damages children (at the very least it is likely to "numb" them emotionally). Rather the issue is what children's exposure to so much horror and violence does to this kind of information's usefulness as a marker of increased maturity. When only teenagers were permitted to see horror films and violent programs, such viewing could be used as an index of mature status. It was part of what teenagers could do now that they were grown, or partially grown, and it was something younger children could not do. Admission to the ranks of those who could watch such material was a rite of passage and contributed to adolescents' growing sense of themselves as "older people" who would not be rattled by such material. Now that even young children are on a regular diet of horror and violence, freedom to view this material has lost its value as an index of a maturing personality.

Image Markers

The images of teenagers provided by the media have changed dramatically over the last quarter century. The manner in which adolescents are portrayed on the radio, in film, on television, in books, and in song lyrics are signs of their place within the larger society. Such images give preteens an idea of what it will be like to be a teenager; they give teenagers a sense of where they are, and they provide young adults with reminders of where they have been. At one time adolescents were portrayed as rather flighty, impulsive, and given to rash schemes and overambitious projects in need of adult restraint, common sense, and good judgment. In the media today, however, that kind of portrayal of adolescents is largely absent.

The new realism that insists upon portraying young people as full-fledged adults means they are confronted with every conceivable adult problem—from sex, drugs, and AIDS to concerns about global warming and degradation of the environment. Certainly, we cannot and should not protect young people from knowing about all of the threats and dangers of the world in which they live. It is unfortunate that adolescents in the media are portrayed as *fully* competent to deal with these complex issues. Teenagers who identify with these media characters are dissuaded from seeking the adult support, guidance, and reassurance they so badly need to cope effectively with stressful choices. At the same time, teenagers are deprived of those images of adolescent awkwardness and insecurity that make their own feelings of perplexity and helplessness more bearable. Without signs of the boundaries of their protected world, and with images that suggest that their powers are limitless, teenagers may never seek the guidance and support they need, and may expose themselves to stresses for which they are totally unprepared.

Authority Markers

Another important marker of the teenager's place in the social order is his or her place vis-à-vis authority. True authority is based upon superior competence, wisdom, and experience. Power, in contrast, is based upon superior force. A number of recent changes in our society have undermined the authority of both parents and teachers, the two categories of adults with whom teenagers interact the most. When these adults lose their authority—their claim to superior knowledge, values, and skills—teenagers lose an all-important marker of their place in the social order.

The next two chapters deal with the contemporary decline in the authority of both parents and teachers. Those chapters, however, are concerned with the specific disruptive effects of declining adult authority in the contemporary family and school. Here we need to identify authority's marker quality and demonstrate how it can be looked at as another way in which society as a whole is becoming more homogenized with respect to age and authority. Such homogenization deprives teenagers of still another important marker of their once special status.

Consider for a moment what divorce does to adolescents' sense of parental wisdom, competence, and values. This event not only confronts adolescents with difficult problems of self-definition, but it also changes their perception of adult authority. Many teenagers think, for example, that because their parents have messed up their own lives, they have nothing to teach the young adolescent about life and love. And when, in some single-parent homes, teenagers are treated as total equals to the remaining parent, this also contributes to the decline of parental authority. (Such equal treatment is particularly perilous in early adolescence, when young people badly need the guidance and limit-setting of a more knowledgeable adult.)

The media is a more pervasive contributor to the decline of parental authority than divorce. Although the impact of television on children has been widely debated, perhaps its most serious impact has been overlooked. More than anything else, television has contributed to the decline of parental authority. Television is much too pervasive for parents to monitor and to control. Unlike television in most foreign countries, where it is closely monitored and only on for a portion of the day, we have an unceasing diet of television programming. At any hour of the day or night, there are programs on the television screen. And, in this country there is at least one television set, and often more, for every family. Except by being with young people every waking moment, it is impossible to effectively monitor television viewing.

This parental impotence with respect to television has quickly spread to films, books, audio tapes, "rock video" tapes, and most recently the Internet. Advertisers have been quick to sense the new feeling of parental impotence in face of the all-pervasive media. As a consequence, we have advertising campaigns directed at teenagers who have become a "niche" market (and who have a large proportion of disposable income because they are not usually asked to contribute to family finances). Much of this advertising uses sexual innuendo to motivate young people to purchase products. The more such advertising permeates the media, the more powerless parents feel to combat it, and the process feeds upon itself.

In addition to advertising, parents have lost their authority to monitor what adolescents watch on cable channels and on videocassette rentals. And the content of these films and videocassettes is frequently cruel, exploitative, and sexist:

> The predominant form of sexually violent behavior is individual or gang rape, followed by exploitative/coercive sex in which the male dominates the female. Approximately 80% of the nude scenes in these films depict female nudity without male nudity; in fact, instances of female nudity exceed those of male nudity by a factor of 4 to 1. Full frontal nudity is more common for females than for males. Similarly, music videos frequently portray female nudity apart from male nudity and present images that suggest female bondage or present a single female as the object of desire for more than one male. A cut from the Choice's rap album entitled, "One Just Ain't Enough," for example, describes a woman's experience of "awakening in a near stranger's bed," walking into a potential gang rape in the living room—and being aroused. (Brown, Greenberg, and Beurkel-Rothfuss 1993)

Because young people watch so much of this material, and because parents are often unaware of its content, it be-

comes the authority for young people in matters sexual.
One fifteen-year-old girl wrote the following in her journal
in an effort to understand the two conflicting messages
about sexual activity she had heard from the authority of
two different popular songs:

> This song was about sex. The song was saying basi-
> cally "come over to my house so we can do it!" This
> represents sex as being o.k. Later I heard "Let's Wait
> Awhile" by Janet Jackson. Which basically says,
> "Let's not rush into it. It's kind of hard as a teenager
> to decide which is right. The guy who was talking
> about it as being good seemed happy with a carefree
> sound. Janet sounded sad and depressed. Even
> though I know it's better to "wait awhile" the other
> song was more appealing. It seemed harmless. They
> talk about it like "come over and have ice
> cream...." I really know which is the right way, but
> sometimes the way the media talks about it you re-
> ally begin to wonder. (Brown, Greenberg, and
> Beurkel-Rothfuss 1993)

Although this young woman knows "which is right,"
presumably from values instilled by her parents, she also
gives evidence of looking to media figures and song lyrics
for guidance in her behavior. Adolescents are not helped in
this search for guidance by the frequent use of sexual innuendo in advertisements appearing in venues targeted to
young people:

> In one issue of *Rolling Stone* (February 4, 1993) an
> advertisement for Swatch watches proclaimed, "We
> do it deeper"; an advertisement for Obsession per-
> fume contained a photograph of a nude man and

woman, lower bodies pressed together while standing on a moving swing; and an advertisement for
Guess jeans consisted solely of a busty blonde
woman in a wet and revealing dress. (Brown, Greenberg, and Beurkel-Rothfuss 1993)

At the very least, therefore, parents now share their authority with the media.

It is not only parents whose authority has declined in recent years. The authority of teachers has diminished as well.

Relations between the lay public and the teaching
profession . . . changed in significant ways. In the
1940s, few teachers belonged to a union, strikes were
uncommon, administrators were powerful within
their school building or their district and in hiring,
promoting and assigning teachers. Though their pay
was low, teachers had more education than did the
parents of their students and commanded the respect that went with the authority they wielded.
Teaching attracted a number of gifted women, for
whom career opportunities were limited. In some
communities, there were substantial restrictions
placed on teachers' behavior; as models for community's youth, teachers were expected not to smoke or
drink or otherwise set a bad example. (Ravitch 1983)

The new technologies, particularly computers, have
added to the decline of teacher authority. As young people
are increasingly able to access information of all kinds on
their own, the authority of the teacher as a purveyor of information has declined. Teacher authority has declined
from another direction as well. Many questions are now
asked about the content of curricula; about historical, eth-

nic, racial, and gender bias. These challenges to the content of the curricula make teachers a little less sure of the material they once taught without much of a critical eye. Young people sense this lack of confidence and hesitation and it can erode the teacher's authority.

The importance of adult authority for teenagers' growth by differentiation and integration can hardly be overstated. When teenagers interact with adults whose authority they respect, they can have productive if painful battles over ideas and actions. Such adults provide healthy opponents against whom to test their own opinions and values. But when adults' authority is undermined or lost, so too is their value as foils of healthy development. The generations have become homogenized and the special status of being a teenager has been lost, and with that loss, an important opportunity for developmentally productive growth.

Vanishing markers, then, give ample evidence that there is no special place for teenagers in today's society. Markers such as clothing, activities, innocence, media image, and adult authority have all but disappeared as providers of information heralding teenagers' special place within society. The disappearance of these markers starves young people of those experiences they require to nourish their growing sense of an integrated sense of self and identity. As we shall see later, the absence of markers also confronts teenagers with stressful new freedoms. We need to look now at another phenomenon of today's society that also impairs identity formation while adding stress to teenagers' lives: family permutations.

CHAPTER 6

The Postmodern Permeable Family

The family can be defined as a set of sentiments, values, and perceptions that determine the relationships of family members to one another and to the larger society. Starting from this definition, I attempted, in Chapter 1, to show how the sentiments, values, and perceptions of the modern nuclear family have been reconfigured into those of the postmodern permeable family. Within the permeable family, which includes two-working-parent families, divorced families, single-parent families, adoptive families, and remarried families, children and adolescents often lose their defined place within the kinship structure. In a remarried family, for example, an oldest child might suddenly become a middle child. Likewise, in a single-parent family, the absence of one parent alters the young person's role and place within the family.

Before we look at some of the permeable family varieties and how these affect young people's struggle to define themselves, we need to appreciate the extent to which the permeable family has replaced the nuclear family. In 1970 about 12% of children and adolescents lived with only one parent; in 1989 the figure was about 25%. It is estimated that by the time they reach the age of 18, at least 50% of young people will have spent some time in a single-parent home. Divorce and separation are the major reasons for single-parent families. The United States has the highest divorce rate in the world. Although there is some evidence that the divorce rate is declining, it is still predicted that about one in every two marriages will end in divorce (U.S. Department of Commerce: Bureau of the Census 1996).

The other major cause of single-parent families is unwed mothers. Since the 1950s the age of marriage for young people has steadily risen. Today, on the average, young women marry at 25 and young men at 27. This contributes to the increasing separation between marriage and childbearing. Statistics tell the tale. Whereas in 1960 only 5% of all births were to unwed mothers, the figure had increased to 25% by 1988. Currently, about a million babies each year are born to unmarried women and teenagers. Adolescents are more likely than are older women to have children out of wedlock (Bureau of the Census 1990).

The number of two-working-parent families, another permeable family variation, has also increased significantly since the 1970s. There are many different reasons for this. For one thing, the women's movement opened up many educational and vocational options that were previously closed to females. Also contributing to the number of women in the work force is the fact that we have become part of a global economy, wages have stagnated, and it now often takes two wage earners to maintain a standard of living that could once be provided by the employment of a single family member. Finally, the permeable family sentiment of *shared parenting* has made it more socially acceptable for mothers to work. For all of these reasons, the percentage of women with children ages 6 to 17 who were working full or part time outside of the home rose from about 47% in 1970 to about 75% in 1990 (Bureau of Labor Statistics 1990).

The new and varied kinship structures of the permeable family have had many different consequences. We have already seen how the new perception of teenage sophistication has changed the social expectations for maturity made upon teenagers. When adolescents live in one or another permeable family kinship structure, the perception of sophistication places additional stressors on young people. First, because adolescents are now expected to be mature and sophisticated, the emotional hardships they experience in adapting to these new living arrangements may go unnoticed or unaddressed. Second, the changed roles and expectations accompanying these new living arrangements complicate the task of identity formation. They force adolescents to rework elements of their identity that seemed firm and well in place. Teenagers must in effect start over at a time when the task of identity construction is already well underway.

Separation and Divorce

We need to distinguish between separation and divorce as a one-time event and the ongoing experience of living in a single-parent or remarried-family household. In this section we will be mainly concerned with the *event* of divorce, and how this affects the young person's efforts toward identity formation. In later sections we will deal with the *consequences* of divorce as these are played out in single-parent and remarried-family households.

The effect of separation and divorce upon adolescents differs from their effect upon children. Teenagers, thanks to their ability to think in a new key, can appreciate the full impact of divorce—its emotional, personal, social, and financial repercussions. By contrast, children are protected from these long-term concerns by their limited ability to think far into the future. When there is a divorce, children know that there is something terribly wrong, they suffer from the acrimony and from the absence of a parent, but they do not and cannot anticipate all the future consequences of the breakup. Moreover, children—and teenagers to a lesser extent—hold on to the half-belief, half-hope, that the parents will reunite.

It is not simply because adolescents can imagine all of the ramifications of divorce that divorce is perhaps harder on them than upon their younger siblings. In addition, their new readiness to find fault with their parents is mightily reinforced if the parents separate. Young people seem to say to themselves, "You see, I knew it, I knew he or she was like that." An adolescent's obligatory negative appraisal of parents, which normally dissipates with time, is strongly reinforced when the parents separate. Not surprisingly, the results of one study of 421 undergraduate students concluded that "parents from families broken by divorce were consistently more negatively evaluated than were parents from either intact families, or families where the father or mother had died. These findings held whether or not the mother had remarried and regardless of the sex of the students doing the evaluations" (Spanier and Slick 1981).

Other research suggests that it is marital conflict within the family, rather than divorce per se, that stresses young people. A three year longitudinal study of over 1,000 seventh, ninth, and eleventh graders found that levels of conflict within the home, not divorce itself, was associated with measures of depression and anxiety and with physical symptoms in the children. Adolescents from intact homes with high levels of conflict scored higher on all measures of stress than did adolescents who came from low-conflict divorce families. Twenty-five percent of the adolescents reported that their parents' divorce was a change for the better (Mechanic and Hansell 1989).

In general, divorce is harder on younger adolescents than those who are approaching adulthood and for whom the identity construction process is largely complete. But for younger adolescents, still in the process of identity formation, the divorce can be enormously disruptive. To appreciate the extent of this disturbance, we can listen to how a couple of teenagers talked about the news that their parents were about to divorce:

> JANIE, 14: When my parents told me about their divorce plans, I couldn't believe it! I kept thinking that they really didn't have to do it. Sure they didn't get along, but couldn't we all learn to live with it? I couldn't really face the idea of how things, my life, I mean, would change.
>
> GENE, 15: My reaction to my parents' divorce was to go to my room. Partly I was hiding out and partly sulking. I didn't come out for more than a day. I just kept comparing my family to my friends whose parents were staying together. Why couldn't we be happy like that? I really blamed my parents for the trouble they were going to cause me. (Jackson and Jackson 1981)

Divorce is particularly painful for young adolescents because at that time the imaginary audience and the personal fable are at their most powerful. Young people are sure everyone knows that their parents are divorcing and that they are either pitying them, or feeling superior to them, because their own families are intact. Divorce also forces young people to revise an important clause in their personal fable: "Other kids' parents will divorce but not mine." In addition to dealing with these new feelings and reassessments, young people must reevaluate themselves as well as their parents. What seemed secure and familiar components of an identity, are suddenly changed, foreign, and alien.

The impact of separation and divorce upon teenagers is compounded by the understandable but regrettable tendency of some parents to deny the problem or to avoid discussing it with their offspring. Yet open discussion with parents can often help adolescents cope more effectively with difficult emotional problems. Such discussions give teenagers an opportunity to express their feelings and to begin to make the emotional and intellectual adjustments required by the new addition to their identity—namely, "Now I am a child of divorce"—and to face the anxiety of communicating this fact to friends and to teachers.

Unfortunately, many parents are too engrossed in their own emotional turmoil to attend to the adolescent's anxieties and fears. Sometimes, parents handle the problem by not informing the adolescent until after the fact. But this merely postpones and does not really address the problem. Consider this description of how a sixteen-year-old girl learned about her parents' impending divorce:

> I don't disapprove of the divorce but I believe that parents shouldn't just spring it on their kids. I had to find out from my grandmother when my parents got divorced. We came up from Florida when I was eleven. Mom was just settling into the house and we

spent a lot of time with my grandmother. She told us.
I thought my parents were just spending some time
away from each other. (Norman and Harris 1981)

This young woman was given no help in dealing with the
momentous changes occurring in her life. However troubled and emotionally drained parents are, they really must
provide some kind of support or forum for the adolescent
to voice anxieties and concerns.

There are as many different divorce stories as there are
families undergoing the change. Each family and each story
is unique. Nonetheless, even in the most accommodating of
divorces, the probability is very high that divorce will be an
unsettling experience for the adolescent. For whether the
divorce is amicable (rare) or bitter (usual) there is at least
one common consequence: teenagers lose their privileged
status of belonging to an intact family. Every adolescent
who experiences divorce must also confront new, unexpected problems of differentiation and integration. If parents fail to provide the care and mentoring the young
person needs in order to deal with these new challenges, it
may limit the adolescent's ability to construct a sense of
personal identity.

The frequency of divorce in America has not made the
experience any easier for adolescents to bear. It doesn't really help if a friend's parents are divorced too, no more
than a friend's broken leg reduces the pain of one's own
fractured limb. Nor does the commonness of divorce remove any of the new challenges to identity formation that
divorce inevitably brings with it. The high incidence of separation and divorce means only that many more teenagers
than in the past are struggling with stressors engendered
by family disruption. And the new perception of adolescent

sophistication means that fewer adolescents are getting the parental support and reassurance they so badly need.

Single-Parent Households

Not surprisingly, immediately after a divorce, parenting is less effective. Mothers (about 90% of mothers retain custody) become more inconsistent. Sometimes they ignore the teenager's rule-breaking and sometimes they overreact and impose penalties that are much more severe than what is warranted by the offense. Likewise, fathers are likely to become more permissive, perhaps out of guilt, perhaps out of a desire not to spoil the limited time they have with their children (Hetherington, Cox, and Cox 1982). Most families return to some sort of equilibrium after two or three years. Eventually family members regain their emotional stability and are able to be there for one another in a way that was perhaps not possible when parents were battling one another in court.

Research suggests that the best indicators of an adolescent's success in adapting to single-parent family life are the closeness they feel with the parent with whom they are living, and the extent to which that parent monitors their activities. Adolescents do best when their parents know where they are, how they spend their money, and who their friends are (Buchanan, Maccoby, and Dornbusch 1992). The reverse, unfortunately, is also true. Those teenagers who fare most poorly are those who do not feel close to the parent with whom they are living and whose activities are monitored little if at all. Such young people feel abandoned and often look to their peer group for moral support and guidance. When teenagers are asked why they join gangs, a frequent response is that the gang represents "the family they never had" (Hamburg 1992).

The permeable family sentiments of shared parenting, the value of autonomy, and the perception of teenage sophistication contribute to single parents leaving their teenagers on their own. Likewise, giving adolescents too much freedom is encouraged by a society that treats adolescents as sophisticated rather than immature. And while teenagers are indeed more knowledgeable and urbane than they were given credit for being in the modern era, they are less sophisticated than we might wish them to be today. So, while the research evidence supports adolescents' needs for closeness and monitoring, the media present a picture of young people who have little to gain, emotionally or intellectually, from adults.

Even more destructive than lack of parental closeness or monitoring are those single mothers or fathers who use the teenager to meet their own needs. While this is very understandable, because the parent is alone and has no one to share with or to confide in, it often gives the adolescent a feeling of equality and premature adulthood that may cause him or her to bypass the difficult process of differentiation and integration. For example, one mother consulted me about her fifteen-year-old son who felt free to give her his assessment of each of the men she was dating and who told her at what time he thought she should be home. Yet she had encouraged just this behavior by treating him as the "man of the house" and by sharing with him her feelings for the men whom she was dating.

For young adolescent girls who live with their mothers, the problems often become even more complicated. Some single mothers become so needy that they may "fall in love" with someone who is totally inappropriate for them and who has quite a different background from their own and from their former husband's. Perhaps this is what makes these men so attractive. In any case, what happens

is that the mothers engage in behaviors that shock and em-
barrass their daughters. Yet these mothers often demand,
"be happy for me," without any awareness of the unhappiness they are causing for their offspring. Such parents put
their teenagers in an untenable position—asking them to
approve of behavior that they themselves once denounced
as cheap and wrong. The following case study from my
files is not untypical and will make this type of family dis-
aster more concrete. (I have disguised the information to
protect the people involved.)

> Mrs. K. is an attractive woman in her middle to late
> thirties. She recently divorced her physician hus-
> band (who was carrying on with his young nurse)
> and retained custody of her teenage daughter. As
> part of the settlement, she also kept the family home,
> a large house in an exclusive suburb. The daughter
> came in for counseling in connection with her fre-
> quent running away from home, often to be with
> older men. She told me that her mother had a young
> "ski bum" boyfriend who swaggers about flexing his
> muscles because he thinks he looks like actor
> Sylvester Stallone in the movie *Rocky*. The daughter
> also said that he makes passes at her whenever the
> mother is not around. To make matters worse, the
> mother and her boyfriend have wild parties that dis-
> turb the neighbors and embarrass the daughter. She
> will no longer bring her friends home.

In this family scenario, as in many similar ones, the
mother wanted her daughter to condone and approve her
behavior, to serve as an approving conscience. This put the
daughter in an impossible situation. At a time when she
was trying to deal with her own sexuality, and needed a

model of restraint and good judgment, she was given a parental example of impulse and wild abandon. At a time when she needed parental limits and standards, she was presented with unrestricted freedom and no standards. In the event, she was given very little to help her gain a healthy, differentiated, and integrated sense of her sexual identity. Before we were able to remove the daughter from this home, she ran away again. When she returned, she was already three months pregnant. She had just turned fifteen.

The extent of problem behavior exhibited by teenagers living in single-parent families is then often directly related to hurt and conflict engendered by the parents' seemingly bizarre behavior. I see many examples of parents who engage in the most extraordinary actions that are totally out of keeping with their upbringing and personality. Another example is a divorced mother who became pregnant and, because of religious convictions, decided to have the baby. She had broken up with the baby's father, one of a series of lovers she had taken after the divorce. She now expected her teenage daughter and son to accept their new half-brother without question. Indeed, she expected her children to support her in her decision and to condone her actions. Not surprisingly, both teenagers eventually ended up as wards of the court: the daughter for sexual delinquency and vagrancy, the son for alcoholism.

Sometimes the consequences can be delayed, akin to the post-traumatic stress disorders that we are seeing in other situations. In one case that I dealt with, the mother had two children out of wedlock after she divorced her husband. The children were by different fathers, neither of whom was in evidence. Her oldest daughter, who had graduated high school and was working at the time her mother became pregnant with the first illegitimate child, became very responsible. She helped support the family and looked after her two half-brothers. When she was thirty-two, however, she deliberately got pregnant without any prospects of marriage. Despite her outward appearance of maturity and responsibility, the model set by her mother clearly affected her own sense of self in a very fundamental way.

Fathers who have custody may also engage in behaviors that impair their adolescents' efforts at identity formation through differentiation and integration. Many teenagers find themselves in a difficult situation when their fathers marry women who are closer to them in age and generational orientation than to their fathers. When there is a physical attraction between the teenage son and his father's new wife, or when the teenage daughter bitterly resents a rival for the attention of her boyfriends, the situation can become explosive. In one home of this sort, the teenage daughter attacked her youthful stepmother and had to be put in a detention center. Much of the constructive work she had done toward identity formation was undermined by this experience and by being labeled a delinquent.

To be sure, these are cases that came to the attention of the courts and may be extreme. But I have seen many similar cases outside of my work with the courts. In truth, the variety of family forms encourages parents to engage in behaviors that can work against adolescents' efforts at identity construction. And the perception of adolescent sophistication further complicates the problem by making it easier for parents to ignore the needs of their adolescent children. For most teenagers, the teen years represent a time of exploring safely the intricacies of personal relationships with friends and non-parental supporting adults. When parents act like adolescents, they make it very difficult for young people to differentiate appropriate from inappropriate adult behavior and thus hamper the young person's efforts at growth by differentiation and integration.

It should also be said, however, that many single parents do a superb job of raising their teenage children. And many teenagers find that living in a peaceful single-parent home can be healthier and happier than living in a conflictual two-parent home. The endlessly battling two-parent home can bring unbearable pain and confusion to the children and teenagers involved. Joanne, age fifteen, explained:

> Now that my Mom and I are alone together, it's really peaceful. I don't have two parents telling me what to do all the time. I don't have to wait for my mother to consult with my father or vice versa. They never agreed anyway! Now when I ask my mother a question, she answers. It's a lot easier now. (Norman and Harris 1981)

A seventeen-year-old girl writes:

> The only difference I can see living with my mom alone is that my sister, who's nine, tends to be more affectionate toward guys. I think she misses my father more than I do. But, then, she never knew what he did to my mother. She only remembers the good times because she was always asleep when they argued and hit. (Norman and Harris 1981)

For these two girls, and many others, living in a single-parent home meant the end of a problem and a new quality of life.

In general, the single-parent home can bring new responsibilities—when appropriate and not overpowering—that can contribute to the adolescent's sense of growth, of competence and of self-confidence. Allen, age sixteen, provides an example of a young person whose experience of living in a single-parent home was, to some extent, very productive and constructive:

> I've got a lot more freedom now and my mother says that I am the man of the house. There's nobody that can tell me what to do, either physically or verbally, and you feel a lot more sense of yourself. My brother feels the same way. I don't think he really liked having my dad around either. (Norman and Harris 1981)

Although this young man may be a bit too cocky about his freedom, he does appear to have used his father's absence to assume responsibility and to further his growth toward independence. In this case, as in others, the perception of adolescent sophistication may lead the parent to see the male adolescent as too adult, as the "man in the house."

Living in a single-parent home is often more difficult for the young teenager than it is for the older adolescent. The young teenager is so concerned with imaginary audience approval that any deviation from what they perceive as normal family life may lead to embarrassment and self-consciousness about the family. Even though we have moved into the postmodern era, and even though permeable families outnumber nuclear ones, the nuclear family persists as the idealized norm. Fortunately, as young people mature and become more experienced, the "audience" loses its power. John, sixteen years old, expressed this diminished concern quite well:

> I miss my father, but I know my parents were unhappy together so I guess it was the best thing that

they split. It's no big deal living with my mom. I
didn't like it as much when I was younger because
the other kids would talk about their fathers and I
couldn't. But now a lot of kids I know have parents
who are divorced. (Norman and Harris 1981)

We are adaptable creatures and most young people
eventually are reconciled to the new living arrangements of
the single-parent home. Nevertheless, adapting to a new
lifestyle and to a new social status complicates the task of
identity formation; it can lessen the available time and take
away some of the support needed for the task. Yet, as some
of the preceding comments by adolescents suggest, the reverse can sometimes also be true. In families torn by daily
conflict, particularly when there is addiction and/or abuse,
divorce may give the adolescent more, rather than less,
time to work on self-definition. Living in a single-parent
home may also help the young person attain a better sense
of himself or herself and of the parents than might be possible in a conflictual environment. As long as parents recognize that the adolescent, however sophisticated, is still in
need of caring, limit-setting, and monitoring, living in a single-parent home need not be a major barrier to attaining a
healthy sense of personal identity.

This is an important fact to remember. Some studies
and research reports target the single-parent home as the
main culprit when young people exhibit problem behavior. But this is an oversimplified interpretation of the data.
The increase in problem behavior of young people today
cannot be attributed to any single cause. Single parenting,
for example, is often closely associated with poverty so
that poverty, rather than the number of parents, can be the
significant factor in adolescent turmoil. As I have argued
elsewhere (Elkind 1994), all of the institutions that relate to

young people—schools, media, legal systems, and even the helping professions—contribute to the new morbidity. It is not single-parent families per se, but rather, the lack of social support for such families that does the harm (Ellsworth 1988).

Blended Families

The stressful effects of divorce and separation, and of living with a single parent, can be followed by an even more stressful experience—becoming a member of a step-family. Stepfamilies are among the fastest growing varieties of the permeable family in America today. More than 50% of first marriages now end in divorce and the majority of those who divorce eventually remarry. Accordingly, many of the 50% of young people who spend some time in a single-parent household also spend time in a two-parent household. Almost one in every five families in America is a stepfamily and the projection is that this number will rise to 50% by the year 2000 (Glick 1989).

When remarriage means less loneliness, more financial security, less conflict with a former spouse, and more support for household organization and decision making, it eventually benefits children as well as parents. Nonetheless, while the newlywed parents are often very happy, their children seldom are. Children and adolescents are forced to relate in a positive way to strangers who are, at the same time, grandparents, uncles, aunts, and stepsiblings—most of whom they would not have chosen on their own (Coleman and Ganong 1991).

Blended families create identity problems for all of the parties involved, but teenagers are the most vulnerable. To put their problem in perspective, we have to acknowledge that stepparenting is far from easy for either the stepfather or the stepmother. For example, the stepmother must fight against the stereotype of the "wicked stepmother" that children have acquired from such fairy tales as "Snow White," "Cinderella," and "Hansel and Gretel." Fictional stepmothers are always cruel to their stepchildren and favor their own children. Research seems to support the view that the real stepmothers have serious difficulties with stepchildren. In one study of 2,000 Florida teenagers, one-fourth of the respondents living in intact nuclear families reported "significant stress" at home. In permeable families with a stepfather or a single parent, this proportion rose to one-third. But in permeable families with a stepmother, the number of adolescents who reported significant stress rose to one-half (Kleen 1982).

These statistics may reflect the fact that many custodial stepmothers are not happy with their roles. Several different factors probably account for this circumstance. For one thing the custodial stepmother usually spends more time in childrearing than does the custodial stepfather. She thus spends more time raising another woman's child or children. As a consequence she is more likely to be the target of the children's resentment of the divorce and of the reconfigured family. Moreover, stepmothers are often considerably younger than their husbands. The husband's children are thus likely to be older, and the age gap may be too small to enable the mother to exert effective discipline. For example, I counseled a family in which the father was forty-eight and the wife was thirty-one. She was totally unable to exert any authority with his three children aged twelve, fifteen, and seventeen.

Although stepfathers are not burdened by negative stereotypes or by being too close in age to their new wives' children, they face other problems. Since the mother usually retains not only custody of the children but of the family home as well, the stepfather often moves into his new wife's home—a well-established household. The stepfather may thus be seen as an intruder or interloper. In addition, if he has children of his own who have remained with his former wife, he may feel guilty about giving more fatherly attention to his stepchildren than to his own offspring. Finally, if the stepfather attempts to move in and play the disciplinarian too quickly, he may encourage the reaction, "You're not my Dad, I don't have to listen to you."

Perhaps because of these difficulties, second marriages are even less enduring than first marriages with some 60% of these marriages ending in divorce (Pill 1990). More important, from the perspective of this book, is the fact that second marriages are more likely to dissolve if there are children involved and if the children are older than nine years of age (Visher and Visher 1988). In many of these divorces the problem is not so much between husband and wife, but rather conflict over children.

Becoming a member of a blended family, therefore, is stressful for everyone involved. Each family member—parent and child—has his or her own particular problems with this new living arrangement. The real difficulty is, of course, that no one comes to the situation fresh, as it were. Each adult, adolescent and child comes from a well-defined place in an earlier living arrangement. Because the place in the stepfamily feels new and uncomfortable, the old place in retrospect looks even better than perhaps it really was. Nonetheless, despite the many problems, a new family is constructed.

In the process of building a blended family, it is often the teenagers who have the hardest time adjusting. Children are not seeking identity as much as security, and most new stepparents are able to provide that. Most stepfamilies are more financially secure and can afford more in the way of clothing, lessons, and vacations than is usually true for single-parent families. Likewise, even though the step-parents have to accommodate to some changes in their role and their self-definition, they usually do so on the basis of a well-established sense of identity and with the ongoing support of a new mate.

For the teenager, however, the blended family presents special problems. As Florida State University researcher Kay Kolvan says, "Adolescents are going through so many changes of their own that they have a special need for stability at home, and a parent's remarriage always upsets that at first" (Kleen 1982). Becoming a member of a blended family may shake up some of the adolescent's established elements of his or her identity. A young man, for example, who has been told he is the man in the family will certainly feel betrayed when his mother remarries and the stepfather usurps his role. Likewise, a young woman who has run her father's household may feel displaced and unnecessary if the father remarries and the new wife assumes the home-making responsibilities.

There are many other land mines in the terrain of blended families that need to be avoided or handled with care. Suppose a boy is the oldest in the family and is accustomed to assuming a leadership role with respect to his younger siblings. His parents divorce and his mother, who has custody, remarries. If there are children older than he is in the blended family, he may lose his position as the oldest, as well as his leadership status. His siblings may now look up to their new stepbrother and sisters for guidance. Such an eventuality forces the adolescent to reevaluate himself and the loyalty of his siblings that he had taken for granted. The respect and admiration of his siblings had been a source of pride and the loss of this privileged position in their eyes may become a source of shame and unhappiness—undoing a lot of identity work that had already been accomplished.

In addition, the overt affection between the natural parent and the stepparent can raise unexpected problems. Adolescents retain their attachment to the biological father or mother, and witnessing displays of affection between the parent and what amounts to a stranger can be upsetting— particularly because many teenagers maintain the fantasy that their parents will reunite. Such displays raise questions in adolescents' minds regarding the lastingness of relationships, about loyalty, and about values. Stepparents have to be attuned to these concerns and perhaps, at least initially, be somewhat reserved in their open demonstrations of affection. Otherwise, it might be taken as an indirect swipe at the absent parent. When stepparents are not sensitive to teenagers' concerns, they may bring on issues that need not have arisen. A typical complaint is this one by a teenage girl:

> John, my stepfather, goes around introducing me to his friends as "my daughter." I've asked him to stop, but he doesn't listen. I have a real father who loves me, so what is John trying to prove? I think John's a terribly insensitive person and an intruder. I'll never forgive him. (Wood 1982)

This young woman does not want to feel that she is losing her relationship with her natural father; she has made his role in her life a clear part of her identity, and this has to be recognized, not dismissed and denied as this stepfather apparently chose to do. Research suggests that stepfathers who move slowly and gradually into the parental role are the most successful.

Here is another complaint, this time against a stepmother:

> My stepmother Francine is a real cold fish. The only
> time she kisses or hugs me is when she's trying to
> get me to bad-mouth my sister Jill (and vice versa).
> Jill and I used to go along with it, until we figured
> out that it was dumb to sacrifice our good, close re-
> lationship for Francine's fake affection.
>
> Francine also talks about the house where we
> lived when my mom was alive in a really mean way.
> She refers to it as "stupid" and "tacky" and says
> mom's old furniture is "not worth saving."
>
> Jill and I wanted Dad to remarry, because we
> were hoping for a new mom. But why did he have to
> fall for her—she's nothing but an old icicle heart.
> (Wood 1982)

This marriage seems especially unfortunate since both
daughters were prepared to accept a new maternal figure.
A cardinal rule in remarriages is never attack or criticize the
absent parent. They cannot defend themselves and quite
naturally their children resent such criticism. Some stepparents, however, seem unable to help themselves in this
regard. In my clinical practice I sometimes encounter people who actively try to turn their spouse against his or her
own children. Such parents have deep-seated feelings of insecurity and inadequacy and feel unloved and rejected if
the spouse remains attached to children of a former marriage. Fortunately, such stepparents are the exception rather
than the rule.

Although adjusting to a stepfamily is difficult for
everyone, with goodwill and effort the problems can be re-

solved with positive benefits for all involved. But it does take time, usually two to four years, says psychologist Judith Wallerstein:

> I've had people tell me about a "miraculous trans-formation" in their relations between them and their stepchildren—how indifference or hostility sud-denly turns to liking and even love. I have to tell them it isn't miraculous, that it happens all of the time. If the parents in a stepfamily recognize from the outset that everything isn't going to go smoothly and show patience with one another and the kids when upsets occur, they usually manage to work things out. (Kleen 1982)

The experience of being a member of a stepfamily, like the experience of living in a single-parent household, places special demands upon teenagers. Nonetheless, most ado-lescents can handle these demands and get on with the task of defining themselves as individuals. If, prior to the di-vorce and remarriage, young people have been well-parented with caring, limitations, and support, they will be able to adjust to the new family configuration. On the other hand, young people who have had a conflictual childhood are likely to have the most difficult adjustment to blended-family living as adolescents.

Teenage Mothers

Another permeable family variation that has always been with us but that has become more prevalent since the 1970s is the unwed teenage mother. The increased number of teenage mothers is a direct reflection of the second sex-ual revolution that made premarital sex socially acceptable among unmarried adults. Inasmuch as adolescents model adult behavior, the acceptability of premarital sex has become an adolescent norm as well. In the 1990s, more than half of the unmarried women age 15 to 19 have engaged in sexual intercourse at least once. By the time they reach age 19, three-quarters of unmarried women and 86% of unmarried men are sexually active (National Commission on Children 1991).

The most obvious consequence of these trends is an increase in teenage pregnancy and childbearing. Roughly one million young women under the age of 21 become pregnant each year, and almost half of these women choose to carry their infants to term. About one-fifth of teenage girls will have one or more babies by the time they reach age 20. When a young mother chooses to give birth, whether she plans to rear the child or to give it up for adoption, there are serious health risks for the child as well as significant psychological, educational, and vocational risks for herself. All of these risks are greater than if childbearing had been delayed to a later age.

With respect to infant health risks in this country, fetal and infant death rates are higher among adolescents than among any other age group (Voydanoff and Donnelly 1991). Six percent of the babies born to mothers under 15 years of age die in their first year of life, many from sudden infant death syndrome (Voydanoff & Donnelly 1991). Children born to young mothers are more likely than babies born to older mothers to be mentally retarded and to have learning disabilities (Dreyer 1982; Voydanoff and Donnelly 1991). Studies also report that because infants born to teenagers are often premature, they are also more vulnerable to neurological problems such as epilepsy and cerebral palsy.

Young mothers are at risk as well. In general, teenage

mothers are less likely to complete high school than young women who delay childrearing until their twenties. Teenage mothers are twice as likely to drop out of school than are older mothers. Once out of school, few teenage mothers ever return. This is true regardless of the economic circumstances of the girl's family or her ethnic background. It has been found that from one-half to two-thirds of the girls who drop out of high school give pregnancy or marriage as the main reason for terminating their education (Trussel 1976).

Because of these potential problems, a number of programs for pregnant teenagers and for teenage parents have been undertaken to reduce some of these risks. These programs, such as Project Redirection, begun in the 1980s in four cities—Boston, New York, Phoenix, and Riverside, California (Quint 1991)—and the Hull House project in Chicago (Marsh and Wirick 1991), have had some positive health outcomes. Nonetheless, the results have been less satisfactory with regard to high school graduation and reduction of repeat pregnancies. Lack of education and vocational skills often dooms the teenage mother to a life of poverty and dependence upon welfare. Close to 60% of families who receive Aid to Families with Dependent Children are headed by young women who were teenagers when they had their first child (National Commission on Children 1991).

All of these consideration have important consequences for the teenage mother's emerging sense of personal identity. She must begin to deal with and incorporate a whole new set of evaluations and role definitions. There is still a social stigma to having a baby outside of marriage that the young woman's own family may share. This is evident in the following letter to Ann Landers' advice column from a new grandfather:

Dear Ann Landers:

Please do not congratulate me on becoming a grandfather. My daughter who had the baby is not married and you know it. The girl gave up her chance for an education, a good future and the respect of her friends and relatives for a no-good bum. . . .

The only reason I have permitted our daughter and her bastard brat to live under our roof is because my soft hearted wife begged and pleaded with me not to throw them out on the street. I have no use for this weak, stupid girl who has denied me the joy of walking her down the aisle and giving her in marriage to a decent man I could be proud of.

To put it bluntly, Congratulations are not in order. Our daughter is a tramp. (Landers 1983)

Although this father and grandfather seems particularly insensitive and self centered (most concerned with polishing his own image and meeting his own needs), his attitude is not that unusual. Although it would be wrong to excuse the teenage mother from any and all responsibility, some compassion is in order. The young woman is struggling to reconfigure her sense of self to incorporate society's new attitudes toward her as well as her new roles and attitudes toward herself. Because teenage pregnancy is often regarded as the result of careless, impulsive behavior, the young woman is looked upon as emotionally immature and unprepared for the responsibilities of parenthood. If she drops out of school, she abandons her role as a student and is immediately excluded from her peer group and the normal and healthy influences of those social interactions.

The young woman described in the letter will have an even harder time achieving any kind of an integrated concept of self if even those aspects of identity she might hope would still be in place (beloved, admired, and supported daughter) are suddenly withdrawn by her father. Further, whatever issues led to her early pregnancy will remain unresolved while she struggles to deal with all the social stigma, the loss of friends, the enormity of being a school dropout, and the demands of mothering an infant.

We know much less about teenage fathers than we do about teenage mothers. Recent surveys suggest, however, that in the majority of cases the young men who impregnate teenage women are not teenage boys but rather older adolescents and young men in their twenties. In many cases these men abandon the young mother. A new emphasis should be placed on the legal responsibilities of fatherhood for young men.

The permeable family form of the unmarried teenage mother is an unhappy one for all concerned. For the young mother, and sometimes the young father, it is a disruptive experience that seriously impairs their efforts to develop a differentiated and integrated sense of personal identity. To parent an infant while remaining, in many respects, a child; to be required to nurture when one's own needs for nurturing are unduly strong—this makes the formation of a consistent, whole, and meaningful definition of self difficult if not impossible to attain. Unfortunately, the social and cultural conditions that encourage teenage pregnancy are not easily remedied. This is particularly true today when so many supports for sexual restraint are missing and when there is enormous peer group pressure to become sexually active. Health education will not really help the situation as long as every other avenue of information geared to the teenage audience (books, movies, television, song lyrics, and advertising) depict adolescents who have discovered the "joy of sex."

We have now looked at some of the variations of the

postmodern permeable family that are becoming the norm of contemporary American life. We have also seen that such variations in family form work the most hardship on adolescents. The family is in flux just when the young person is trying to discover what it means to be a man or woman, husband, wife, father, or mother. When the people who have filled these roles in the past and who have been the primary models for them suddenly change their behavior and allegiances, the basic foundation upon which adolescents construct their identity is badly shaken. If parents consider the needs of their teenagers, as well as their own needs, some of the stresses of permeable family life can be lessened if not avoided.

CHAPTER 7

Schools for Scandal

A school for Scandal! tell me, I beseech you
Needs there a school this modish art to teach you?
No need of lessons now, the knowing think:
We might as well be taught to eat and drink.

Richard Brinsley Sheridan's play *The School for Scandal*, first produced in 1777, was a comedy of manners and a light satire on the time and energy the upper classes of the era spent on gossip and innuendo. In our day, the American high school has become a school for scandal in a literal sense. The problems of American high schools were brought to national attention by the publication of *A Nation at Risk* (Gardner and Larsen 1983), which was the final report of the Committee on Educational Excellence, an eighteen-member panel of educators and government officials who had been appointed two years earlier by the Secretary of Education. This report, like a number of others (e.g., Boyer 1983), gave evidence that contemporary high school students were not only doing more poorly academically than students of the past, but also that their academic performance was inferior to that of students in many other Western and Asian countries.

Sadly, although the reports of the eighties ushered in some of the most radical reform efforts in the last 100 years, many of these efforts have failed (Gibboney 1994; Wilson and Davis 1994). In my opinion the educational reforms of the eighties misfired because they were still looking at education from a modern rather than from a postmodern perspective. That is to say, they were focused upon the academic aspects of education and ignored all of the social changes that have occurred in the family and in the perceptions of children and adolescents. For example, adolescents who now regard themselves as sophisticated see the high school as not acknowledging their new postmodern status and as continuing to treat them as modern, immature teenagers.

Because, in my view, the schools have failed to address the broader social functions of the postmodern school, the narrow emphasis upon academic reform has had little success. Statistics from the 1991 annual report of the National Educational Goals Panel—a council of governors, members of Congress, and U.S. Department of Education officials—highlight the continuing educational deficiencies of students. Although the number of students graduating from high school in 1990 was larger than ever before, and a higher percentage of these were showing more minimal competencies than in the past, the overall results were not encouraging. The report's authors noted, "Scores on existing national tests have declined or stagnated during the past several years."

Some of the findings tell the dismal tale. A third of the eighth-grade mathematics students were unable to figure the price of a restaurant meal from the menu; a third of the high school juniors could not write a coherent paragraph about themselves. There were declines between 1984 and 1990 in eighth graders' ability to write effectively. The picture is even more bleak for minorities. While the overall rate, in 1990, of high school dropouts was 12.2%, the rate was 13.2% among blacks and 32.4% among Hispanics. Despite the momentous efforts at reform instigated by *A Nation at Risk*, a decade later the schools have not improved, and in some cases are doing even worse than a decade ago.

The other, less-publicized scandal of our high schools is their failure to provide a protected place for adolescents to socialize and to get on with the task of constructing a sense of who and what they are. During the modern era (roughly the late nineteenth century to the middle of the twentieth) the high school was a special place for adolescents; it was their place. It was an arena where they could devote their energies to the task of personal, social, and occupational growth without pressure from the "real world" outside. It was a place where the adolescent could be safe. It was, as Ernest Boyer (1983) wrote, "The one institution where it was all right to be young."

It is no longer all right to be young, or immature, in today's schools, where the prevalence of drugs, sex, and violence makes youthful vulnerability a handicap. As one writer describes it:

> Drugs, for an enormous number of kids, are not merely a weekend enterprise; many of them get high or drunk during the day, during class. High school teachers, even in comfortable suburban school districts, often describe their work as being more like that of a traffic cop than an educator: "I keep them in line until the three o'clock bell." One former student of mine recently told me, "A good day is one in which nobody gets freaky." (Jackson and Jackson 1983)

The transformation of the high school from a safe haven for socialization and learning to a forum for drugs, sex, and violence is a postmodern phenomenon. It is, in part, a reflection of the changes in our society and in the family that have accelerated since mid-century. It is also, however, a reflection of the schools' reluctance or inability to adapt to the demands of the postmodern world. The relative lack of success of most school reform over the last few decades has been amply documented (e.g., Gibboney 1994), and is directly attributable to the reformists' failure to recognize that schools have changed quite independently of their efforts, and are more in keeping with changes inside the family and society at large. Modern reforms are ineffective for postmodern schools but that fact still eludes many contemporary reform movements. We can look at schools, at the curriculum, and at teachers to illustrate why our junior and senior high schools are no longer a meaningful place for large numbers of adolescents.

The Schools

The failure of most reform movements is traceable to the fact that schools always lag behind societal changes and still exemplify many modern ideas of schooling. One of these outdated modern ideas is that "bigger is better." In keeping with this idea, school systems and schools, particularly the "comprehensive high school," shrunk in number and grew in size. But the failure is also due to economic pressures that have led to increased class size. Both large schools and large classes not only have negative academic impact, they also provide an inhospitable environment for young people who are struggling to construct a sense of self and identity.

School Size

A major problem with our junior high schools, middle schools, and high schools is their overall size. American schools started out as rather small enterprises, but during the modern period the trend was toward bigness in everything. Large schools, unfortunately, make it more difficult for young people to find meaningful relationships with mentors, a necessary condition for constructing a healthy sense of identity. The change in size of American schools is vividly described by Diane Ravitch in *The Troubled Crusade*:

> Beyond the obvious gains and losses that had been registered in the course of thirty-five years was a change in climate so basic and yet so elusive that it was difficult to measure or even describe. Although some few big high schools were vast educational factories in 1945, most schools, colleges and even universities were small compared to what was to come. In some communities teachers "boarded" with families, not because of choice but because of low pay; not a situation they might have chosen, but one that assured intimate familiarity with the community and the children. Even where teachers had independent lives, they were expected to spend after school hours as supervisors of extracurricular activities and to know their students; they in turn could count on parents to support and reinforce demands made by the school. Colleges and universities never questioned their role *in loco parentis*: they were responsible for the young men and women in their care, as if the institution itself were their parents. Alcohol was seldom permitted on campus, drugs were unheard of, and even the social lives of students were regu-

lated; infractions of the rules of behavior might be
punished by suspension or expulsion. (1983)

The large size of schools and the roles of teachers
clearly reflected the modern perception of adolescents, and
even of young adults, as immature and in need of adult
guidance and direction. With the postmodern shift to the
perception of adolescents as sophisticated, the schools un-
derwent a dramatic transformation. Again, Diane Ravitch
cogently describes the alteration:

> Much had changed by 1980. The drive to consolidate
> small schools and small school districts had largely
> succeeded, helped along by the vast expansion of
> enrollments in the 1950s and 1960s. Big schools be-
> came the rule, not the exception. In a society where
> bigger was considered better, small districts and
> small schools were described as backward and inef-
> ficient. The number of school districts shrank dra-
> matically, from one hundred thousand at war's end
> [WWII] to sixteen thousand in 1980. Growth had
> many benefits: efficiency of scale, diversity of cur-
> riculum, differentiation of types of students and
> teachers. Enlargement meant exposure to a more
> varied setting and interaction with a broader variety
> of ideas and people than was possible in a small
> school or college. (Ravitch 1983)

Although bigness has certain economic and adminis-
trative advantages, its disadvantages for schools are
only now beginning to be recognized. Ravitch highlights
the negatives:

> The trade off, of course, was that bigness meant im-

personality, bureaucratization, diminished contact between faculty and students, formalization of relationships among colleagues, a weakening of the bonds of community. Colleges and universities withdrew from the *in loco parentis* role they had previously exercised. No longer part of a community of values shared with students and parents, teachers and administrators found it difficult to administer discipline, or even to establish rules that everyone found acceptable. Teachers and professors defended themselves against the new anonymity by joining unions. Students complaining that no one knew their names, wrote them vividly in the bathrooms and hallways of their schools. The invasion of drugs, first in college in the 1960s and then in the high schools and even junior high in the 1970s dulled students' senses and insulated a portion of the student body from adult standards. The lingering influence of the counterculture, that remnant of the 1960s youth rebellion, left many adults wondering whether there were any standards of learning or effort or behavior worth defending. (Ravitch 1983)

From a small, orderly world of knowns, certainties, and reasonable expectations, students have entered a world of unknowns, uncertainties, confusion, and often danger.

Class Size

Another powerful impediment to effective instruction is the large class size of all too many secondary classrooms. It is well established that the effectiveness of education is directly related to the amount of one-on-one time between student and teacher. The larger the class, the less one-on-one time. And the larger the class, the less time the teacher has to respond in a meaningful way to homework assignments. In many high schools, classes run between twenty-five and thirty students. A teacher with five classes may see well over a hundred students each day. As Theodore Sizer suggests, even good teachers compromise the quality of their teaching by spending less time grading papers and in preparation than they would with smaller classes (Sizer 1984).

Closely related to the problem of large classes, and in many cases dictated by it, is the practice of tracking—grouping young people according to ability. Many high schools have advanced placement (AP) courses for which students may get college credit. More often than not such classes are small and taught by the best teachers. In this way the rich get richer and the poorer students get stranded in larger classes with the less dynamic teachers. Programs for students with learning disabilities, funded by Title 1 and begun in 1975, have really not been very effective and many of these young people are receiving, despite the government subsidy, substandard education (Gibboney 1994).

In addition, there is little social support for what has been called the *forgotten half*, the 50% of high school students who do not go on to college. We are so focused upon the academic that we do not value the skills and abilities of those people whom we rely upon in our everyday lives: the plumbers, electricians, carpenters, painters, and auto mechanics, not to mention the service people in stores, restaurants, and offices. In many European countries, these jobs are looked upon as professions; waiters, for example, are highly trained, and are well regarded and respected. In our society, high school students who are not on the academic track may feel that they are second-rate citizens and if they are in a vocational school may be called, derisively, "vokies."

What do large school size and large class size mean

from the standpoint of the adolescent's efforts at self-definition? One clear consequence is the loss of what has been
called mentoring. In the autobiographies of many men and
women who became successful despite adversity, there is
almost always a significant person who recognized their
special gifts and devoted time, energy, and skill to helping
them realize their talents and abilities. More often than not,
the significant person was a teacher or a coach whom the
successful person encountered in school. Studies of individuals who have attained eminence before the age of forty
reveal that the most important mentor was not someone
who taught them the skills of their discipline or craft, but
rather someone with tremendous enthusiasm for his or her
field (Cox, Daniel, and Boston 1985).

What these gifted and talented people took from this
first mentor was a sense of excitement, an intense commitment, and a deep involvement with what was to be their
life's work. Teachers with large classes, burdened with end-
less bureaucratic busywork, often lose enthusiasm for the
subject they love and have little time for mentoring. Many
gifted and talented students fail to realize their potential
because today's crowded classes and schools militate
against the mentoring of such students by individual faculty members.

School size affects teenagers' efforts to define themselves in still other ways. Self-definition, for example, is fa-
cilitated by being with people who know us well and who
give us useful information about ourselves. Sociologist G.
H. Mead (1934) wrote of the *looking glass self* and argued
that our self-conception is, in large measure, the "reflected
appraisal of others." Accordingly, the more people who
know us well, the more likely we are to get a balanced picture of ourselves inasmuch as the biases of one person are
likely to cancel out those of another. In large schools ado-

lescents know, and are known by, fewer people than would be the case in small schools.

The difference between the two types of schools is a little like the difference between a small town and a big one. In a small town everyone is likely to know everyone else and this serves as a constraint against untoward behavior. In a big town most people are strangers to one another and have more freedom to behave as they choose. For adults, who have attained a well-defined sense of self, the anonymity of a large city may be welcome since it allows individuals to live their lives in their own way. But for young people, who are in the process of constructing a sense of self, the control exercised by living in a place where you are known to everyone is an important contributor to a solidly established sense of internal control and a well-grounded sense of identity. Within a large circle of friends and acquaintances, teenagers come to understand how they are both alike and different from other young people. In a large school, adolescents are deprived of this variety of input about themselves.

It is also true, as Ravitch suggested in a passage cited earlier, that larger size contributes to the prevalence of substance abuse, theft, vandalism, and violence in high schools. Social controls are weaker in large schools than in small schools, just as they are weaker in large cities than in small cities. The importance of social controls is demonstrated by the behavior of conventioneers in a strange city. When they are in a city where they are not known, some people will engage in activities they would never do at home. The same is true for students in large high schools, regardless of where the high school is located. The large comprehensive high school that may draw students from a number of surrounding small towns may create a big-city atmosphere. In such schools, adolescents may feel free to do things they would never dare to do in their home communities. The result is that the rural comprehensive high school leads to the same problems as those that prevail in large urban high schools.

We should not, however, make the mistake of assuming that, like conventioneers, teenagers want the opportunity to act in an environment free of the usual constraints. For young people in the process of constructing a conception of themselves and the world, the lawlessness of the large school can be alarming. Seeing other young people breaking the rules with impunity forces adolescents to question the rules they have been taught, as well as their own system of personal values. As an illustration, here are the remarks of a twelfth grader attending an inner city high school who was asked to give a reason for hating school:

> There are only one or two reasons why I hate school. One of them is because of all the racial incidents in our school system. For example, in our last school year one student was walking down the third floor corridor. He was the only one of his color who was on the floor at the time.
>
> He was beaten very badly.... Nothing was heard of this. I'm sure someone took the blame for it but no one ever heard about it. When no one knows if or if not the students were punished they automatically think they can do it and get away with it ... something must be done. (Barnicle 1982)

As we listen to the student, we hear more than that he disapproved of the racist attack; his sense of personal justice was offended. He expected the adults in charge of the school to find the culprits, announce the proper punishment, and carry it out. Clearly, this is not what happened, and it upset the teenager's value system, his belief in justice, and his trust that adults would uphold the rules. The questioning brought on by events such as these may be healthy for those young people who already have a strong sense of who and what they are. For identity-attained adolescents, such experiences reinforce their sense of alienation from the kind of hoodlum who would engage in such attacks. In addition, the failure of the school authorities to act appropriately only confirms their acceptance of the fact that it is not a perfect world and that injustice is often as common as justice.

On the other hand, for teenagers who have not yet attained a strong sense of themselves, this kind of experience can have the opposite effect. For adolescents who are still struggling to make sense out of themselves and their world, such an experience can lead to the conviction that "anything goes" and that you can get away with the most heinous actions if you are clever and if the adults in the system lack backbone. They do not learn the difference between right and wrong, just and unjust, but what you can get away with and what you cannot. This amounts to growth by substitution, because they learn to look to the particular situation for guides to action rather than to fixed inner standards that enable them to judge actions by their intentions not by their consequences.

The Smorgasbord Curriculum

To fully appreciate the disruptive effects of much of contemporary curricula, a little history is in order. Modern junior and senior high schools are relatively recent inventions, first introduced in the middle of the last century. They were set up to prepare young people not only to be responsible citizens of a democracy but also to live in the new world created by the industrial revolution. In such a world, John Dewey recognized, the classical education devoted to the learning of Greek and Latin, designed for the children of the leisure classes, was inappropriate. Dewey argued that education should prepare young people for the life they will lead and that learning should be practical rather than abstract—that young people should learn through doing (1938). Unfortunately, the Dewey philosophy of progressive education became distorted and perverted and was all but abandoned in the 1950s and 1960s.

The challenge of the Sputnik (the first manmade satellite, launched by Russia in 1958) brought much criticism on our educational system for letting Russia get such a scientific advance. A massive curriculum reform initiative was undertaken, emphasizing science, math, and language; it was relatively compartmentalized and undid the integrated curriculum advocated by Dewey and the progressive educators. The fragmentation of the curriculum accelerated after 1965 when the federal government put educational policy on a national level. Following federal mandates, the schools developed special programs for disadvantaged, handicapped, bilingual, and gifted and talented young people. In addition, the antiauthoritarian and student-activist sixties gave rise to many nonacademic courses, from rock music to surfing. In the last two decades new courses in drug and sex education, as well as programs in character education and values clarification, have been added at both the junior and senior high school levels.

While this dendritic expansion of the curriculum is a bow to the postmodern values of diversity, modern methods of teaching and assessment are still being used. Too many high school classes, like too many college classes, continue to be taught in a lecture format with students learning only what they need to learn to pass a test, most of which they promptly forget once the test is taken. More-over, subjects are still taught in isolation from one another, and students are given no clues as to the application of the material to their everyday lives.

The postmodern emphasis upon diversity, unhappily coupled with modern ideas of instruction, was reinforced in the 1980s with the introduction of a host of different curric-ular and instructional initiatives that further fragmented the educational process. Programs to improve thinking skills such as DeBono's CoRT (1988) and Costa's program for De-veloping Minds (1985) were adopted by some school sys-tems. Other school districts subscribed to programs based on research on effective schooling popularized by Madeline Hunter (1984). Still other communities adopted Mastery Learning (Bloom 1981) and its derivative Outcome Based Instruction—the idea that schools had to decide what stu-dents were to learn and to design curricula and school rou-tines to ensure these outcomes (O'Neil 1994). So, added to the diversity of curriculum content ushered in during the 1960s and 1970s were the variegated patchwork of instruc-tional and assessment programs promulgated in the 1980s.

A Postmodern Critique

Although our society is very diversified and effective educational practice must speak to that diversity, this is not what has happened. There is a blinding mismatch between the ethnic, racial, cultural, and ability differences young peo-ple bring to school and the diversity of curriculum content and teaching practices they find once they get there. Perhaps the most important reason for this disparity is that so many of these "innovations" are built upon the modern concep-tions of progress, universality, and regularity described in the first chapter. Without a change in these foundation conceptions, any innovation is bound to be cosmetic, a change in appearance without any real change in substance.

Progress

As an illustration, let's begin with the Mastery Learning and Outcome Based Instruction programs. Both initiatives are founded upon the modern conception of progress. They start from the image of an educational ladder and the idea that the academic learning experience is essentially the progressive accumulation of knowledge, skills, and values. The problem is that individual growth and learning are not uniformly progressive. In 1950 Jean Piaget, who was in some respects quite postmodern, argued that the attainment of knowledge is not a stepwise progression. Rather, he contended, it is more like an expanding spiral where the child has, at each stage of development, to unlearn lower-level understandings of concepts such as space, time, and number and to relearn them at a higher, more abstract, level.

In fact, the schools actually do educate in this way but without acknowledging the fact. The elementary curriculum, for example, is geared toward *making the unfamiliar, familiar.* Children learn many facts about the physical and social world of which they were previously unaware. They learn that light objects float and that dense objects sink; they learn about distant places and peoples, like the desert and the Eskimos. At the secondary level, however, the curriculum is aimed at making the familiar, unfamiliar. Adolescents learn that water is a liquid made from two gases, that *Alice in Wonderland* and *Gulliver's Travels* are not just wonderfully entertaining stories but also political satires or allegories. From a developmental perspective, unlearning and relearning are as important as new learning. Yet Mastery Learning and Outcome Based Instruction presuppose a straightforward progression of learning, albeit at different rates.

Universality

Many of the educational reforms of the 1980s are also based upon the modern belief in universality. To illustrate, DeBono's thinking skills program CoRT (1988) is designed to be simple and practical, to be independent of the learner's prior knowledge, to be translatable to the thinking skills required by life experiences, and to be useful across a wide range of ages from six to sixty. Likewise, the effective teaching model promoted by the late Madeline Hunter is based upon seven presumably universal principles of teaching:

1. Anticipatory set—develop a mental set to focus learning attention on the lesson.
2. Objective and purpose—state explicitly what is to be learned.
3. Input—analyze the task (break down the content into small steps).
4. Modeling—show the learner what is to be learned or how something is to be done.
5. Checking for understanding—find out if the students know what they are to do and have the skills to do it.
6. Guided practice—practice the skill and drill that is to be learned under teacher supervision.
7. Independent practice—learner practices lesson after the teacher is sure that the student will not make serious errors. (Hunter 1984)

From the perspective of this critique, the reason that these two programs have not been successful is that they are built upon the modern belief in universal learning and thinking processes that can be acquired by all children (Gibboney 1994). While there are certainly biologically linked universals—such as the Piagetian stages—there are

probably no acquired universals. Yet the postmodern appreciation of psychological diversity—say in the recognition of different learning styles—seems to be constantly
subordinated to a belief in learned universals that ignore
the particularity of learning.

For adolescents, the insistence upon acquired universals is particularly disruptive. The reason why adolescents
dye their hair, wear earrings, ink on tattoos, and wear what
might generously be called "odd" clothing is to assert their
individuality. Large schools, large classes, and a curriculum
that presumes acquired universals tries to homogenize adolescents who are striving to express their uniqueness. To
succeed in such an environment young people need to
smother their individuality. As Carol Gilligan and her colleagues have demonstrated, this is particularly true for
young women. These investigators found that young
women needed to subordinate their individuality in order
to be socially accepted and eventually attain a sense of self
and identity. Teachers, however unconsciously, reinforce
this form of self-abdication in young women. The process
of identity formation as it is played out in schools is not the
same for young women as it is for young men.

Regularity

Finally, many of the educational reform initiatives of
the 1980s presupposed a regularity or lawfulness of the
teaching-learning process. The emphasis upon "accountability" reflects this belief that teaching and learning are related in a lawful manner and that poor learning necessarily
reflects poor teaching. Yet there is no evidence of a one-to-
one relation between teaching and learning. For example,
the best algebra teacher in the world will not be able to
teach a pre-formal operational adolescent how to solve si-

multaneous equations in two unknowns. Contrariwise, bright students often learn *despite* bad teaching. The assumption of a lawful relation between teaching and learning ignores the many factors that mediate this relationship, including the teacher's personality and the student's developmental level.

Moreover, what many educational innovators fail to recognize is that the relation between learning and instruction is as chaotic as it is regular and lawful. Every classroom meeting is a *nonreplicable* event. Students and teachers come to each meeting changed in significant ways from the previous session. The problem with much educational reform and a great deal of educational research is that it takes for granted the lawfulness of the learning/instruction relationship. Yet when we talk of teaching as an art, which indeed it is, the idea that it is creative and original can hardly be reconciled with the idea that teaching and learning are lawfully connected. Teacher accountability can be assessed, but not by learner outcomes.

If schools do not acknowledge the chaotic nature of the educational process, adolescents surely do. Indeed, it is because adolescents are aware that learning is an irregular process that they demand an encompassing moral and social order. Where schools and teachers need to provide progress, universality, and regularity are in the social and moral rules—which are universally recognized by all religions and peoples—that govern the school. In fact, just the reverse often occurs—the social and moral rules are assumed to be irregular and particular while instruction and learning are regarded as progressive, universal, and regular. Not surprisingly, postmodern teenagers feel that the school is not a place where they can be young, where their needs for limits, values, guidance, and mentoring can be met.

The Chore of Teaching

Teachers are important role models for students. When teachers are no longer excited about what they are teaching and have lost their commitment to young people, their effectiveness as role models is diminished or lost. Although there were always some teachers who were in education for the wrong reasons, there were always a majority of dedicated teachers who were able to provide most students with someone they could look up to, admire, and emulate. When this relationship obtains, much healthy self-differentiation and identity formation can occur within the context of a teacher-student relationship. Yet the climate necessary to foster good teaching in many contemporary public high schools has virtually disappeared. Even dedicated teachers are becoming discouraged, as this one explains:

> I'm not receiving the same positive response from my students. In the past, I felt more like a coach to my students, helping them achieve the highest level of skills they're capable of. But I've felt more in an adversarial position recently and I don't know why. It's almost as if they say, "I defy you to teach me." I had one class of students last year with a dozen chronic behavior problems. It affected my whole life. (Boyer 1983)

Theodore Sizer's book *Horace's Compromise* (1984) gave a vivid portrayal of the struggles of a gifted and committed teacher trying to accommodate the demands of today's students, administrators, and parents. Even though Horace taught in a relatively affluent school, the compromises he had to make to his own standards were enormous. More recently, in *Horace's School* (1992), Sizer has offered a model that he has implemented in his Coalition for Effective Schools. In this most recent book, Horace muses about today's middle-class students:

> Sure, they rack up lists of "extracurriculars" to dazzle university admissions officers, but even when they show a dash of substance, too many of them lack style, that gossamer quality which separates the interesting person from the conventional one. They get top grades on the English Advanced Placement exams, but never read a serious piece of fiction outside of school. They score high on the social studies tests, but later will vote for political candidates on impulse, if they vote at all.
>
> The kids play a game with school, making deals with us, striking bargains. What will be on the test, Mr. Smith? Will this count in the grade, Mr. Smith? When do we have to read this by, Mr. Smith? If we do this, will you ease up on that? They all ought to be ambassadors, Horace thinks, wheeler dealers striking bargains and making treaties. However, the treaties will be ones to lessen work, lessen the pain of thinking anew, lessen anything that may get in the way of having a happy time after school. Treaties protect the Good Life. Horace snorts to himself: What a cynic I am. Aren't we adults that way too, excessively so? What are all of us coming to?
>
> Many of Horace's colleagues find his criticism harsh, but he persists. We do not know the half of what these kids can do, he contends. But his friends retort, can one school turn them around? The whole society is soft. The kids culture is defined by MTV and cravings created by national merchandisers.

Even their parents do not want the school to change much. Get Susie into a good college, they say. And if we do, they love us. If they do not, they blame us. But style? Come on, Horace.

What has taken the joy out of teaching and made it such a chore? The causes are as many and as varied as they are familiar. Thanks to the family permutations and vanishing markers of our postmodern society, many more students than in the past are troubled, unhappy, and difficult to teach. In addition the diversity of curricula, the plethora of educational reform initiatives, and demands for accountability have all sapped time and energy that once went into teaching and mentoring. Salaries have not kept pace with the rate of inflation. For example, the average annual salaries for teachers in public schools (unadjusted for inflation) was $30,054 in 1982–83 and was only $35,019 a decade later in 1992–93 (National Center for Education Statistics).

Although there remain pockets of excellence in both public and private schools around the country, overall the situation for teachers and students is not encouraging. Educators Wilson and Davis argue, as I have here, that true educational reforms must be based on postmodern rather modern conceptions:

> Our decade-long effort to reform U.S. education has failed. It has failed because it has not let go of an educational vision that is neither workable nor appropriate to today's needs. Until traditional assumptions about the nature and meaning of education are upset (and new paradigms replace old ones), good ideas will languish regardless of their appropriateness. Reforms that seek to correct symptoms without first addressing causes are doomed. Just as no

amount of bailing could have kept the *Titanic* afloat,
no amount of improved content can save our crum-
bling educational structure. (1994)

In many ways students are the real victims of the failure of the reform movements of the 1980s, just as they were
of similar reform initiatives of earlier decades. While teachers struggle to learn new methods and approaches, there is
less time for students. Students may often feel like guinea
pigs who are being experimented upon without their permission or consent. At a time in their lives when they need
adults who at least give the impression that they know
what they are doing and why they are doing it, many
teachers are forced to undertake new unproven practices
that make them appear as novices to their students.

As Wilson and Davis make clear, however, true educational reform will come about only when teachers and administrators change the ways in which they think about
students, learning, curricula, and, indeed, the aims of education. When that happens, there will be a much better
match between the needs of young people and what schools
provide—so wonderfully described by Erik Erikson:

The evidence in young lives of the search for something and somebody to be true to can even be seen in
a variety of pursuits more or less sanctioned by society. It is often hidden in a bewildering combination
of shifting devotion and sudden perversity, sometimes more devotedly perverse, sometimes more
perversely devoted. Yet in all youth's seeming shifti-
ness, a seeking after some durability in change can
be detected, whether in the accuracy of scientific and
technical method or in the sincerity of obedience; in
the veracity of historical and fictional accounts or the

fairness of rules of the game; in the authenticity of artistic production and the high fidelity of reproduction; or in the genuineness of convictions and the reliability of commitments. (1968)

Teachers pummeled by the demands of educational reform, accountability, wheeling-and-dealing students, and score-minded parents have difficulty providing the kind of authenticity, fairness, veracity, and genuineness of conviction that are so important to give young people who are trying to acquire such traits for themselves. In an age when many parents have less time to devote to their children, teachers too are preoccupied with many things other than their students and the students' need for identity formation.

Needed Reforms

In summary, high schools are no longer a protected place for young people to find authenticity and commitment and an opportunity to construct an identity by differentiation and integration. Most schools are too large, and most curricula and technology too dated to meet the developmental needs of postmodern youth. True educational reform will have to take place at many levels and from different perspectives. Many large educational systems are too top heavy with administrators who overburden teachers with busywork. School boards may often include individuals who have only a small commitment to education but a large commitment to their own political fortunes. Educational funding should be shifted to a more equitable basis than property taxes.

The preceding issues deal with the structural aspects of American education, but conceptual changes are needed as well. As I have suggested, schools are still operating on

the basis of modern conceptions that impede effective ped-
agogy. The modern departmentalization of the curriculum,
for example, makes it difficult for students to integrate their
knowledge and to see relations between what they read in
literature and what they learn, say, in political science. Likewise, the training of teachers often occurs without any
training in child and adolescent development. Such training is critical for successfully adapting curricular material
to the intellectual ability of students.

In this regard, it has to be said that teaching is not a
profession. Unlike medicine, law, dentistry, optometry, and
so on, there is no agreed-upon body of knowledge, skills,
and values that all teachers are required to learn in order to
become a teacher. Most of what teachers learn about teaching they learn on their own in the classroom or through a
master-teacher mentor. Yet education *can* become a profession. Child and adolescent development is the most solid
and substantial basis upon which to build curricular, assessment, and teaching skills. If teachers were trained in
child and adolescent development, this would make them
child development specialists. With child development as
a common core of training, teaching could become a true
profession.

PART III

Result:
Stress and Its
Aftermath

CHAPTER 8

Stress, Identity, and the Patchwork Self

Stress is a constant in our postmodern lives. How we learn to deal with it in childhood and adolescence determines how well we will handle it in our later years. How does stress work? What are its energy dynamics? How does an integrated sense of identity enable us to manage stress effectively? These are questions we have to answer before we can understand why a patchwork self, in its many different forms, does the opposite—mismanages stress.

The Stress Reaction

In the broadest sense, stress is our response to demands for adjustment. As living organisms, we must constantly respond to inner and outer demands for adaptation, or *stressors*. Some of these inner and outer demands are biological and specific, such as hunger, thirst, and the need to find warmth in freezing temperatures. Other inner and outer demands are psychological but equally specific, such as our need for mental challenge or to respond to an inquiry for, say, directions. Our reactions to these demands are well matched. We eat when we are hungry, drink when thirsty, and add clothing when the temperature drops. Our reactions to particular psychological demands are also in keeping with the challenge. We read or engage in dialogue with friends if we feel the need for mental stimulation, and we usually respond with the appropriate information when we have it. In the broadest sense then, stress is coincident with life, and there is no life without stress.

In the narrower sense, however—the sense in which we usually use the term—stress is our response to an *extraordinary* demand for adaptation. If we are exposed to extreme cold or to extreme heat or if we are forced to go without food or water for a long period of time, habitual reactions will not suffice for this stressor. Similarly, many psychological events can also make extraordinary demands for adaptation. If we lose our job, or get passed over for a coveted promotion, or win a much-acclaimed honor, the demands for adjustment are much greater than usual.

Unlike our very specific reactions to everyday stressors, our response to extraordinary stressors is always the same. The discovery of this general response to extraordinary demands for adaptation was the discovery of Hans Selye, who devoted his long life to the elucidation of this concept. Selye was led to the discovery of the general stress response when, as a young physician in Prague, he was struck by a particular phenomena. He was intrigued by the observation that patients suffering from many different illnesses all showed symptoms in common. Conventional medical wisdom ignored these general symptoms and insisted that they were secondary to the unique primary symptoms that differentiated each illness. That is to say, traditional medicine looked at illnesses as separate and distinct without appreciating that they could still all share a common clinical syndrome, a general condition that Selye described as "just being sick." He officially labeled this condition the General Adaptation Syndrome (GAS) (1976).

According to Selye, the GAS response has two stages. The first is the shock stage, reflecting our initial reaction to an intense, unexpected demand for action. Signs of distress appear: heartbeat is irregular, blood pressure falls, muscle tone is lost, and body temperature drops. Then, in the second, countershock stage, the body reactions are reversed and prepare us for defense. The adrenal cortex is mobilized and enlarged, and the production of corticoid hormones is stimulated. Now heart rate and blood pressure increase, as does body temperature. Muscle tone is restored and we are prepared for "fight-or-flight."

Our psychological response to stressors follows a parallel course. When we first hear bad news or good news, we are stunned, not really able to take in the information that has been given to us. After the initial shock of disbelief, the defense reaction follows. If we failed to get a much-desired promotion, we may rationalize that it would entail too much work anyway, or deny that we really wanted it, or blame the decision on politics and the successful candidate's strategy of playing "yes-man or -woman" to the manager. If we do indeed get the promotion, we now view ourselves and the manager in a new and more favorable light. In victory we may even be gracious to the unsuccessful candidate.

The way in which our bodies and our minds mobilize for action in response to excessive demands of any kind is clearly a carryover from when our ancient ancestors were hunters and gatherers living in the wild. Such mobilization was essential if human beings were to survive in a world where most of the dangers to life and limb came from wild animals and hostile tribes. Living in such a world required constant vigilance and preparedness. In today's postmodern world, however, the excessive demands for adaptation are much more likely to come from psychological rather than from physical events and threats. Although we cannot anticipate all the psychological stressors we will encounter, in many instances (like taking an exam) we are in a position to know in advance that extraordinary demands will be made upon us. On such occasions we have the opportunity to prepare for and to manage the stress.

Stress management is very important. In modern society we can rarely take refuge in the physical action that the stress response prepares us for. If we have not learned to manage stress, the mobilized energy may be discharged through one or more of our body organs and we can experience stress symptoms like headache, stomachache, and indigestion. If the stress continues and we have no other way of dealing with it, chronic stress diseases such as migraine, ulcers, or colitis may result.

Unmanaged psychological stress can affect our quality of life as well as our physical well-being. The quality of our lives depends upon how much energy we have to devote to the various types of activities that add up to a satisfying lifestyle. If much of our available energy is burned up in stress reactions, there will be less for other activities. If we are always dealing with crises, our leisure will be spent recuperating, with no time to take genuine pleasure in life. Stress burns energy, and to see how it affects our lives we have to look at its energy dynamics.

Stress Dynamics

As biological organisms, we might be said to run on two different, but related, kinds of energy. One of these might be called *clock* energy. This is the energy that we burn up in any twenty-four-hour period that is replenishable with food and rest. It is the energy we use for our daily activities. A second type of energy might be called *calendar* energy. Unlike clock energy, calendar energy comes to us in more or less fixed amounts, is largely determined by our genetic endowment and is not replenishable. Calendar energy is generally used for growth and development. Although our daily fund of clock energy tends to decline when we begin to age, the decline is usually gradual and can be offset by more efficient use of time and effort. Calendar energy, because it is concerned with growth, is apportioned unequally at different stages of the life cycle. Children and adolescents use proportionately more energy for growing than adults. While growth occurs at every stage of life, at least at the level of cell replenishment, far more growth occurs at the early stages of life; therefore, more calendar energy is required during those years. Making so much of the calendar energy available to us when we are children and teenagers may be nature's way of supporting the laborious process of growth, including the process of constructing an integrated sense of self and identity. But, as we shall see, when this energy is well invested, it pays rich dividends later.

To better understand the relationship between the two kinds of energy, a simple analogy may be helpful. We can think of clock energy as the money we have in our checking account and of calendar energy as the money in our savings account. In general, we try to meet our recurring weekly and monthly expenses out of our checking account, which we regularly renew with deposits from our weekly or monthly salary, or the earnings from our business or profession. Our savings account is, in contrast, is usually reserved for major purchases such as a house, a car, our children's college education, and, eventually, retirement.

How we manage our checking and savings accounts

reflects on our style of life. If we repeatedly overspend our checking account—by buying expensive clothing, stereo equipment, or other luxury items that we really cannot afford—we eventually have to draw upon our savings account. As a consequence we jeopardize our long-term goals for short-term pleasures. On the other hand, if we are so concerned with putting away money that we are reluctant to indulge in luxuries—even to the extent of not going out to dinner on occasion or once in a while buying something we like but could do without—that quality of our daily life suffers at the expense of long-range plans. The goal we all work toward is to have an enjoyable life day to day while still putting enough away so that our future needs will be comfortably looked after.

In the same way, how we manage our energy reserves also reflects upon the quality of our lives. Suppose, for example, that our everyday lives are full of stress. We work with and for people whom we neither like nor respect, and this makes demands upon us over and above those imposed by our work. If, in addition, we have a stressful home life, we will necessarily overextend our clock energy and be forced to draw upon our calendar energy reserves.

The consequences are twofold. Biologically, the continual mobilization of the body for fight-or-flight can produce diseases related to chronic stress and will accelerate aging. Psychologically, the drain on our long-term energy reserves reduces the amount of calendar energy that we will have available to meet the demands of our later growth phases, such as the midlife crisis. If we do not have the energy necessary to deal with these later periods, we may succumb to disease or to psychological arrest. An example of the latter eventuality is the person who, five years after getting a divorce, still insists that things are as they were with his or her former spouse. Such a person is psychologically stalled and cannot get on with his or her life.

It is important to recognize that the stress that saps one's reserves may come from within as well as from without. The person who did not complete the process of constructing a sense of self and identity as an adolescent may persist in this quest as an adult. For this type of individual, energy that might be spent in the joys of everyday life, in the pleasures of family, friends, work, and recreation, is spent instead upon what seems an unending quest for self-definition. These people are the neurotics of our time. Totally self-centered, they look at each new situation as an opportunity to learn something about themselves. Sometimes charming, sometimes annoying, always demanding of attention and acclaim, they are at best tolerated by friends and family. Their lack of development leaves them isolated and completely out of phase with those who have successfully completed the process.

The goal we need to strive for in managing our energy budget is the same goal that guides the management of our financial one. That is to say, we need to budget in such a way that we can live an enjoyable daily life and still have abundant energy for further personal growth and development. How, then, does an integrated sense of self and identity move us toward this goal?

Stress and Identity

Most situations that produce psychological stress involve some sort of conflict between self and society. Whenever we satisfy a social demand at the expense of a personal need, or satisfy a personal need in defiance of social approval, we create new claims for our time and attention. If, for example, our work requires us to spend long hours, or even days, away from our family, our spouse and children will be unhappy and ask that we spend more time with them. Contrariwise, if we stay home from work in order to care for a sick child or spouse, our employer may well become unhappy and demand that the work be made up, even if it requires longer hours. If we don't manage our energy budgets well, we may create unnecessary stress for ourselves.

The major task of psychological stress management is to find ways to balance and coordinate the demands that come from within and those that come from without. It is at this point that a healthy sense of self and identity plays a major role. An integrated sense of identity, as we have seen, means bringing together into a working whole a set of attitudes, values, and habits that can serve both self and society. The attainment of such a sense of identity is accompanied by a feeling of self-esteem, of liking and respecting oneself, and of being liked and respected by others.

More than anything else, the attainment of a healthy sense of identity and a feeling of self-esteem gives young people a perspective, a way of looking at themselves and others, which enables them to manage the majority of stress situations. Young people with a healthy sense of themselves look at situations from the perspective of others as well as from their own. The person who has to work long hours makes it a point to call home often and to set aside time to spend with spouse and family when this is possible. Similarly, the person who has to care for a sick relative can try to arrange something with his or her employer so that at least some of the work can be done, either by someone else or by the worker at home. In taking the other person's perspective in advance, the individual with a good sense of self avoids unnecessary conflict and angry confrontations.

To be sure, some conflict is unavoidable, and those are the ones for which we need to save our energies.

The Three Stress Situations

There are three major types of stress situation that all of us encounter. One of these occurs when the potential stress is both foreseeable and avoidable. This is a *Type A* stress situation. If we are thinking about going on a roller coaster or seeing a horror movie, the stressor is both foreseeable and avoidable. We may choose to expose ourselves to the stress if we find such controlled-danger situations exciting or stimulating. Likewise, if we know that a particular neighborhood or park is dangerous at night, the danger is foreseeable and avoidable and we avoid it, unless we are looking for trouble. It should be said that some people—skydivers, mountain climbers, car racers, and so on—thrive on Type A stress. The thrill may come, in part at least, because the threat and danger are under their own control.

The situation becomes more complicated when the foreseeable and avoidable danger is one for which there is much social approval and support, even though the individual may not personally engage in the activity. Becoming a soldier in times of war is an example of this more complicated Type A stress situation. Young people who enlist win social approval at the risk of physical harm. On the other hand, young people who avoid becoming soldiers protect themselves from physical danger at the cost of social disapproval.

Adolescents are often caught in this more difficult type of stress situation. If their peers are using alcohol or other drugs, there is considerable pressure on them to participate. Yet such participation puts teenagers at risk for social disapproval and loss of respect from parents and teachers, and, often, from themselves. They may not like the image of themselves as drinkers or drug abusers. It is at this juncture that a strong sense of identity and a healthy feeling of self-esteem play their parts in stress management

Young people with a good sense of self will weigh the danger to their hard-won feeling of self-worth against the feelings associated with the loss of peer approval. When teenagers look at the situation from this perspective, the choice is easy to make. By weighing the laboriously arrived-at integrated sense of personal identity against the momentary approval of a transient peer group, young people are usually able to avoid a dangerous situation. In my clinical experience I have found that adolescents who have been well parented, and who think well of themselves, choose peers who share the same values and beliefs as they do. They never put themselves in the situation of having to go along with an alienating peer group in the first place. The peer group has no intrinsic power; it exercises power only when it fills a parental vacuum and when the teenager lacks a healthy sense of personal identity.

A second type of stress situation involves those demands that are neither foreseeable nor avoidable. These are *Type B* stressors. Accidents are the best example of a Type B stressor. Teenagers who get shot when they are unknowingly in the midst of a gang fight are becoming increasingly common victims of a Type B stressor. Young people who witness violence on the streets provide another example of an extraordinary unforeseeable and unavoidable demand for adaptation. The sudden death of a loved one or the divorce of one's parents are other examples of stressors that cannot be predicted or avoided.

Type B stressors usually make the heaviest demands on young people's energy reserves. As we noted in the discussion of parental divorce, this event forces young people to deal with attitudes of friends and teachers at the same time that they are struggling to deal with their own unhappiness and depression. Likewise, a young person who has witnessed a violent crime may suffer from nightmares, and the sleepless nights tax energy reserves. One young man who lived through a terribly destructive hurricane became terrified every time he saw a dark cloud in the sky. Even young people with an integrated sense of identity and a healthy sense of self may require psychological counseling to deal with severe Type B stressors.

Nonetheless, adolescents who have an integrated sense of self and identity have the best chance of managing these stressors as well as they can be managed. In the case of divorce, for example, adolescents who are capable of seeing their parents' point of view may be more accepting of the separation than if they look at it only from their own, personal perspective. For example, one young man, who went on to win honors at an Ivy League school, told his father when he and the boy's mother divorced, "You are entitled to live your own life and find happiness too."

This ability to see situations from different perspectives also helps adolescents deal with the death of a loved one. If an elderly grandparent was suffering great pain and could not enjoy any of the activities that he or she formerly enjoyed, the young person may appreciate that death can sometimes be a blessing. As one teenager told me with regard to his grandfather who had just died, "He was in such pain, he was so doped up, he couldn't really recognize me. I loved him so much I just couldn't stand to see him that way." By enabling adolescents to see death from the perspective of the person who is dying, as well as from their own sense of loss, young people are able to mourn the death but are also able to get on with their own lives.

The third type of stress situation is one in which the

stressful event is foreseeable yet not avoidable—death and taxes come to mind. These are *Type C* stressors. Other, less extreme examples of foreseeable but unavoidable stressors are visits to the dentist, examinations, and having to spend time with people whom we cannot stand. What makes many Type C stressors so painful is the anticipation. These situations force us to look forward to an unhappy event and the thought may be as painful as the experience itself.

For young people who have attained an integrated sense of self, most foreseeable and unavoidable situations are manageable if not enjoyable. Again, the ability to cope with this type of stress comes from young people's ability to de-center from their own way of looking at things, to see the situation in other ways. Going to the dentist may not be fun, but it is better than having to go for surgery or having a chronic illness. When we look at a painful situation from the standpoint of those who have it much worse, we get a more realistic appraisal of the stress we are confronting. If we were sitting around a table with a group of people and we all wrote our troubles on a piece of paper and exchanged them, most of us would choose our own problems over those of the other people.

Another strategy for dealing with Type C stressors is preparation. Young people who have a good sense of themselves prepare for the exam rather than worry about it. The motivation to study for an exam also comes from de-centering and self-regard. Adolescents who have a good sense of self feel that other people have a good opinion of them as well. Many young people spend time preparing for exams to reinforce their own, and other people's, self-evaluations. Feeling prepared for an examination has the added benefit of reducing some of the stress associated with the taking of the exam itself.

It is important to say, too, that integrated teenagers

come in any and all personality types. Some are introverted and shy, others are extroverted and fun loving. Some are preoccupied with intellectual concerns, others primarily with matters of the heart, and still others with sports and physical activity. Despite their diversity, they all share the healthy characteristics of the integrated teenager: a set of attitudes, values, beliefs, and habits that enables these young people to meet their own needs as well as those which society places upon them.

To be sure, life is complex and full of the unexpected. Even the most integrated teenager, of whatever personality type, may occasionally be so overwhelmed by stress that he or she loses the integrative perspective and suffers bouts of self-doubt and low self-esteem. We are all human. Sometimes, no matter how well put together we are, we say the wrong thing or do something stupid that is hurtful to others. At such times it is appropriate and healthy to feel a little guilty and a little angry at ourselves. We cannot and should not always feel upbeat. The important thing is that our positive sense of self and identity far outweigh the negative. The negative is important to keep us humble and to avoid any grandiose sense of self and identity. Healthy stress management does not mean that we always feel good about ourselves.

Stress and the Patchwork-Self Personality Types

A patchwork self is the end result of personality growth by substitution. A teenager with a patchwork self has acquired a set of attitudes, values, beliefs, and habits that are more or less unconnected. Often these attitudes, values, beliefs, and habits are not in keeping with one another. Indeed, teenagers with a patchwork self often behave as if they always had to choose between giving in to others and looking out for themselves. In addition, they have chronic low self-esteem because they are angry at themselves if they give in to others but are equally angry at themselves if they stand up to them.

The teenager with a patchwork self mismanages stress because he or she brings inner conflicts to the stressors, thus making the energy demands so overwhelming that the adolescent seeks merely to escape. Teenagers with a patchwork self, like integrated teenagers, come in many different personality types. Some of these patchwork-self personality types are more likely to succumb to one type of stress situation than to another. Accordingly, in our discussion of how patchwork-self adolescents mismanage stress, we can look at how the three types of stress affect different patchwork-self personality types.

Type A Stressors

Type A stressors are most often damaging to two types of patchwork-self teenagers: the *anxious* teenager and the *conforming* teenager. Some young people, when confronted with foreseeable and avoidable dangers, proceed to worry and stew over their decisions. Because they lack a strong sense of self, they cannot decide whether to avoid the situation or to give in. Many arrive at an alternative solution: they get sick. Anxious teenagers often develop bodily complaints when they are confronted with Type A stressors.

> A thirteen-year-old white male is referred for evaluation of his headaches. They are frontal, have occurred nearly daily for the past six months and are not associated with vomiting, auras, or neurological symptoms.... After the initial visit, he is asked to keep a headache diary for a month. When he returns, the frequency of headaches are noted to be ap-

proximately three or four times a week, occurring most often during the week, especially on mornings when he has either gym or history (with a disliked teacher). His physical and neurological exams remain normal. Four additional sessions of counseling are set up incorporating the parents into the process as well. After a month, the parents have a better understanding of normal adolescence, the teenager's academic schedule has been reorganized, a new best friend has appeared and the headaches have disappeared. (Strassburger and Reeve 1991)

In this case, the young man was just beginning the process of identity formation and his difficulty came from not yet having constructed a strong sense of self that would have enabled him to deal with the foreseeable and avoidable stress in a more positive way.

Sometimes a patchwork self is the product of growing up in two cultures with conflicting values and customs. Adolescents growing up in this environment of dual cultures have difficulty putting together an integrated sense of self and often resort to illness when confronted with foreseeable and avoidable stressors. For example, Dr. Merilee Oaks observes that headaches are particularly common among a group of teenage girls she is encountering in Los Angeles.

I'm seeing a group of teenage girls of Latin origin and they have a lot of psychosomatic symptoms in connection with anger and depression. These girls are caught in a culture conflict. They are growing up in the freedom of the American culture while living in families with repressive Old World parents and grandparents. These girls don't know how to fight back or to express themselves because their cultural mores say that you must not argue with elders. I've seen daily migraine headaches among these girls. (McCoy 1982)

In my own small practice I have seen a number of Japanese and Indian teenagers who are in the same dilemma and who not only have headaches but who seem particularly susceptible to colds and flu.

Other anxious teenagers confronted with foreseeable and avoidable dangers develop boredom or fatigue. "I've had a number of teenagers come in to see me complaining of fatigue and excessive sleeping," says Dr. Charles Wibbelsman, a specialist in adolescent medicine. "They often come in saying, 'I think I have "mono,"' or, 'I must be anemic or something.' That could be. But often these teenagers don't have an underlying medical problem. Yet they are tired all of the time and sleep twelve or fourteen hours a day. When a physical disease is not present, this fatigue could well be a sign of anxiety and depression" (McCoy 1982).

Still other anxious teenagers experience stomach pains and disorders. "The gastrointestinal tract, most notably the stomach and the intestines, is quite easily affected by the emotions," says Dr. Wibbelsman. "It may take a stomachache, diarrhea, or more alarming symptoms to point out to the parent just how tense, depressed, frightened, or angry the teenager is feeling" (McCoy 1982).

In all of these cases, we can see the underlying characteristics of the patchwork self. Anxious teenagers have a low opinion of themselves and an unconnected, often conflicting set of beliefs, values, attitudes, and habits. Confronted with a foreseeable and avoidable risky option, their conflicting values pull them in multiple directions. Their solution is to avoid the decision making by getting sick. Often the particular response to stress was learned in childhood and never given up. Lacking more mature stress-management strategies, the anxious adolescent reverts back to earlier, more infantile, stress-reduction measures.

Conforming teenagers with a patchwork self behave differently when confronted with Type A stressors. Because they lack self-acceptance and support, and do not get this at home, they seek it from their peer group. When confronted with a foreseeable and avoidable danger, they may often engage in the risky activity in order to win peer group approval.

> I would never have taken acid if it wasn't offered or if the kid hadn't said, "It's such a good time." If the kid said, "We don't know what's in this and it might be dangerous, it would mess up my hormones," I don't think I would have taken it. When I took the Quaaludes, everyone else was taking them, so I did it too. It was the same thing with cigarettes. I started because everybody else was smoking them. It wasn't just one or two people, it was everybody I know, I'd go to a party and the whole place would be an ashtray. (Jackson and Jackson 1983)

It is important to reemphasize here that the peer group has no power in and of itself. The peer group gains its influence only from the neediness of those teenagers who look to it for support and guidance. Anxious teenagers find the risky behaviors advocated by the peer group too threatening but do not wish to appear afraid or daunted. By getting sick, they have an excuse for not engaging in the risky behavior—but at the price of resorting to childish and immature stress-reduction strategies. Conforming adolescents really want to grow up and get an integrated sense of self, but do not know how to go about it and engage in risky behaviors to win peer group approval. Yet such behaviors are often in conflict with the young person's best interests and so create further anxiety and stress.

Type B Stressors

Teenagers with a patchwork self also have a different perception of Type B stressors, those that are both unforeseeable and unavoidable. As noted earlier, such stressors include accidents, divorce, and death. Other Type B stressors are such experiences as moving to another state, starting junior or senior high school, breaking up with a boyfriend or girlfriend, getting raped, or being mugged, beaten up, or robbed. Clearly, coping with such stressors is difficult for even the most mature and integrated adult, much less a teenager. Experiences of this sort violate our deepest sense of ourselves and our identity. For young people in the process of constructing an identity, or for those who have acquired only a patchwork sense of self, Type B stressors can be devastating because they strike at an already weak and fragile sense of self.

Most damaged by Type B stressors are two varieties of internalizing teenagers. Both groups are likely to perceive such events, not as chance occurrences that could happen to anyone, but rather as evils visited on them because of their fate or bad luck. One group of young people try to *deny* or *isolate* the negative experience so that it will not further reinforce their sense of vulnerability and susceptibility to misfortune. In the following case a young teenager, traumatized by his grandmother's death, refused to deal with it. As a result, the stress reaction was converted into bodily symptoms.

A 15-year-old white male is admitted by his physician for abdominal pain of three weeks' duration.

The pain is sharp, intermittent, and is located in the right lower quadrant. He denies nausea, vomiting, fever, weight loss and diarrhea. . . . Only after six weeks of counseling did the complete story emerge: the patient had been raised by his mother and maternal grandmother. When talking about the latter he became very quiet and maintained poor eye contact. At age 12, he returned home from school to witness his grandmother have a fatal myocardial infarction. He was the only one home at the time and was terrified. On reflection, his mother stated that he had refused to go to the funeral and had never really mourned the loss. His first hospitalization for abdominal pain occurred three weeks after the grandmother's death, and he was readmitted to hospital three years later, near the anniversary of her death.

After this information was revealed, the patient went home and talked at length about his grandmother, weeping frequently. His abdominal pains subsided during the next six weeks of counseling and did not recur during the subsequent four years of follow up. (Strassburger and Reeve 1991)

With counseling this young man was able to integrate the reality of his grandmother's death into his view of himself and the world. When powerful experiences are not integrated into our sense of self and identity, they continue to draw upon our energy reserves and reduce our capacity to deal with the stress in our lives. Denial and isolation are not effective stress-management techniques and always come back to haunt us later.

The other group of teenagers for whom Type B stressors are particularly damaging are those with *self-punishing* tendencies. Such adolescents are already convinced that

they are the only ones who ever experience disappoint-
ments, failure, accidents, and injury. It is this lack of perspective that makes them believe that there is nothing to be
done, that they are helpless and accursed. When young
people think about themselves this way, the stage is set for
self-punishing behavior in the face of Type B stressors.
Below is the poem written by a fifteen-year-old boy, two
years before he committed suicide. It reflects, among many
other things, his struggles to integrate conflicting feelings
about love and academic achievement:

To Santa Claus and Little Sisters

Once . . . he wrote a poem
and called it "Chops."
Because that was the name of
　　his dog, and what it was
　　about.
And the teacher gave him an "A"
And a gold star.
And his mother hung it on
　　the kitchen door, and read it to
　　all his aunts.
Once . . . he wrote another
　　poem.
And he called it "Question Marked Innocence."
Because that was the name of
　　his grief and that's what it
　　was all about.
And the professor gave him an "A"
And a strange steady look.
And his mother never hung it
　　on the kitchen door, because
　　he never let her see it . . .

Once, at 3 A.M. . . . he tried
　　another poem.
And he called it absolutely nothing, because that's
　　what it's about.
And he gave himself an "A"
And a slash on each damp wrist,
and hung it on the bathroom
　　door because he couldn't reach
the kitchen. (Cobb 1995)

In case studies of young people who have taken their own lives, there is routinely a history of family conflict and turmoil that makes it difficult or impossible for the young person to construct a strong sense of self and identity (Peck, Farberow, and Litman 1985). Such events also conspire to instill a sense of helplessness and hopelessness. The ongoing life experiences that block healthy development are the predisposing (background) causes of adolescent suicide and suicide attempts. Type B stressors—unforeseeable and unavoidable events—often serve only as the precipitating (immediate) cause of the self-destructive action.

Both the denying/isolating and self-punishing teenagers show two characteristics that mark a patchwork self; low self-evaluation and unconnected, often conflicting, attitudes, values, beliefs, and habits. Once more we encounter the debilitating duality of this form of self. Such adolescents feel that the odds are against them and that there is nothing that they can do to change the odds. Fortunately, as in the case of the first example, if the syndrome is picked up early, many young people can be helped with counseling and psychotherapy. Indeed, there is a growing societal awareness that *all* children and adolescents who experience disasters of the Type B variety can benefit significantly from crisis counseling.

Type C Stressors

Type C stressors, those that are foreseeable and un-avoidable, have damaging effects on other types of patch-work-self teenagers. In these young people, the personality type is both a reflection of and a reaction to their life experiences. One type of personality most affected by Type C stressors is the *angry* adolescent. What integrated teenagers perceive as necessary and unavoidable demands, angry teenagers perceive as unnecessary restraints and unacceptable exertions of authority by adults. For angry teenagers, every Type C stressor becomes a battle over power and control. Whether it is doing chores, keeping their room clean, or doing homework, nothing is done without a struggle. And, more often than not, nothing gets done.

It is important to say at this point that some negativistic behavior of this kind is fairly typical of even the most well-integrated teenager. But it has a different source. Many integrated teenagers often resist parental requests and commands when they feel the issues in question are more appropriate to children rather than to those of their advanced maturity. That is to say, integrated teenagers may resist adult authority when they feel that their integrated status is not recognized or appreciated. In contrast, with angry teenagers it is not the content at issue, but rather adult authority itself. These young people feel that they have not been well parented and that their parents have not earned the right to boss them around.

With the angry teenager, the constant of the patchwork self—low self-worth—is denied or explained away. Such young people refuse to take responsibility for their actions or for their failures to act. Other people, events, or situations always take the blame. Such teenagers appear insulted if they are taken to task for not doing their share of chores or their homework. Too often they use foul language in their rejection of legitimate demands and stomp out of the house, slamming the door behind them. Not surprisingly, these angry teenagers have the power to provoke a lot of reciprocal anger in their parents, and often their teachers as well.

> Dennis and Roland's parents are watching television in the family room of the Brockton, Massachusetts split level home. As usual, Roland's stereo is blasting through the house. Dad can no longer stand the noise so he marches upstairs and yells "Turn that damn thing down." Eighteen-year-old Roland responds immediately by screaming, "F... you," and he begins smashing the walls of his room with a baseball bat. Sixteen-year-old Dennis charges into the hallway hollering at his father, "What the hell are you doing to my brother? Why don't you leave him alone?" (York and York 1982)

Sadly, this is not an isolated example; similar scenes occur all too frequently in homes all over the country. In our postmodern society many young people are growing up without clear limits and rule setting that they can internalize to make their own. What they have is a patchwork set of rules with no inner coherence or force. Without their own internalized and integrated rule system, adolescents can neither appreciate nor abide by rules laid down by others. When such adolescents do conform to rules, they do so out of expedience with no guarantee that they will abide by the same rules in the future. For this reason angry teenagers both lie and steal with impunity. There may be rules, but they are for other people, not for them.

Angry teenagers have the characteristic low self-evaluation and mixed bag of values, attitudes, habits, and beliefs that are the trademark of the patchwork personality. What sets this group of young people apart is their projection of their anger and resentment at themselves onto others, namely, parents and teachers. It is a reflection of the patchwork value system that, while they will not take responsibility for their own actions, they demand total accountability from others.

Another variety of patchwork-self personality that is undone by Type C stressors is the *frightened* teenager. These young people perceive foreseeable and unavoidable demands as threatening. With respect to school, for example, whereas the angry teenager is truant, the frightened teenager may display *school phobia*. As one parent wrote of her daughter's fear:

> It just got worse and worse. She was so afraid of this nun who yelled at students if they gave the wrong answers or asked questions. She didn't dare ask questions. Her fear got in the way of her understanding the class material and she wasn't doing well. She was so afraid of being yelled at for making a mistake, she avoided going to school whenever possible. Which meant she got farther and farther behind. (Weiner 1992)

In some teenagers, the fear of school masks a fear of separation from their parents. Some adolescents believe, for example, that if their parents are left alone, they will fight and decide to get a divorce. In such instances the fear of school is really a screen for a more deep-seated fear of family dissolution.

We see a different variety of frightened teenager in families where a parent is alcoholic, abusive, rejecting, or some combination of these. This situation is clearly foreseeable and many young people regard it as unavoidable as well. As a consequence, many teenagers living in homes with addictive parents become what has been called *co-dependent* (Whitfield 1991). In alcoholic families, for example, the adolescent may be forced into an identity as a caretaker who assumes responsibility for the others in the family. Such identity-assumption enables the alcoholic to continue his or her dysfunctional behavior and to deny the addiction. Adolescents forced to adopt this type of patchwork identity often show a variety of symptoms, including psychosomatic illness, overachievement or underachievement, martyrdom, addiction, and compulsive behaviors (Whitfield 1991).

In co-dependent teenagers the pattern of disrupted identity formation is more visible than in most other situations. Clearly the adults abrogate their responsibilities insofar as caring, rule and limit setting, and protection. The adolescent has to assume these functions, but because they are acquired simply by substitution, rather than by integration, they lack authenticity and cause the young person no end of problems. Likewise, the trademarks of the patchwork self—low self-evaluation and conflicting attitudes, beliefs, habits, and values—are particularly striking in these young people.

As I have suggested in a number of these case illustrations, a patchwork self is treatable. With counseling and or therapy for these adolescents and their families, many adolescents can construct an integrated sense of self and identity and go on to lead happy and productive lives. Unfortunately, all too many teenagers never get the kind of help they need to move them forward along life's way. With only a patchwork self, they have no strategies for avoiding, coping with, or preparing for stress. In addition, they often unnecessarily expose themselves to stressors of

CHAPTER 9

Teenage Reactions to Postmodern Stressors

On every measure that we have—physical, psychological, and academic—young people today are doing worse than their counterparts did half a century ago. In the postmodern world, adolescents have to cope with psychological stressors that could never have been imagined by adolescents growing up before mid-century. To make matters worse, a large proportion of today's teenagers have some type of patchwork self, which renders them vulnerable to stressors of all kinds. This lethal combination of increased psychological stressors and a growing number of teenagers who are vulnerable to them has contributed to the many psychological dysfunctions and to the new morbidity among contemporary youth.

Psychological Stressors

It is not surprising that the same social changes that undermine the teenager's ability to cope with stress also impose their own new, and powerful, demands for adjustment. Vanishing markers not only deprive teenagers of important opportunities for growth by integration, but also present them with demands for a premature adulthood. The major stressors upon young people today—freedom, loss, and failure—are not new to this generation, but their intensity and the age at which the young person must cope with them are unique to the postmodern era. These three types of stressors correspond to the three types of situational demands described in the previous chapter. Freedom is a Type A stressor that presents teenagers with a foreseeable, yet avoidable, risky behavior. Loss is a stressor that demands of adolescents that they come to grips with an event that is unforeseeable and unavoidable. Finally, failure is a stressor that requires adolescents to prepare for events that are foreseeable and unavoidable.

Because these stressors come early and because young people are less well prepared to deal with them than was true in the past, dysfunctional reactions are both more common and more severe than in the modern era. In this chapter I will describe some of the more severe reactions to these formidable demands for adaptation.

Stress Reactions to Freedom (Type A Stressors)

Today's youth have many freedoms not available to earlier adolescent generations. They can choose whether or not to become sexually active, to abuse drugs, or to look at pornography—freedoms largely unheard of in earlier generations. Nonetheless, many young people are unprepared to exercise sound judgment in deciding whether or not to engage in these activities. Among anxious adolescents, the postmodern freedoms are responsible, in part at least, for a horrendous increase in psychosomatic illnesses and eating disorders. For conforming adolescents, there has been a very large increase in substance abuse, particularly alcohol.

Anxious Teenagers

Psychiatrist Erich Fromm, in his book *Escape from Freedom* (1969), took as his thesis the idea that freedom can be frightening and anxiety inducing. Freedom forces us to make, and take responsibility for, difficult life choices. The new freedoms available to postmodern teenagers do make many of them frightened and anxious. If adolescents choose to use their new options to, say, smoke pot or become sexually active, they must take responsibility for their actions and may have to face angry and disappointed parents and teachers. One young woman, who had cut classes to go to the mall, was caught and waited with dread for her father to come home:

> It was a school night and Renee was sitting in her room. She felt as if she would explode, because she knew what would happen to her later in the evening. Her hands were cold and clammy and her stomach was in knots. She was only seventeen years old and already was failing in the world.
>
> Her heart jumped to her throat as she heard the front door open, then slam shut. Dad was home and she was in for it. Her mother had called him at work and told him what happened—he was not very pleased with what he had heard. Now Renee heard his bellowing voice as he called for her to come out of her room. (Brondino et al. 1988)

Postmodern freedoms often place anxious teenagers in the proverbial position between a rock and a hard place. If they don't go along with their peers, they get rejected and ostracized. But if they do engage in risky behaviors, they invite angry confrontations with parents. Many adolescents in this situation develop physical symptoms such as headaches and stomachaches. Surveys of pediatricians suggest that from 5–25% of adolescents who come to their offices do so complaining of chronic headaches or of recurring abdominal pain (Brown 1992).

While a young person's physical complaints may be psychological in origin, they are no less painful or debilitating than those associated with organic pathology. Moreover, the process by which stress gets transformed into organic symptoms is unconscious and involuntary, it is not feigned: "I cringe when I hear someone say, 'It's just a psychosomatic pain,'" says Dr. Marilyn Mehr, a specialist in adolescent medicine. "The implication is that if it's psychosomatic, it isn't real, either emotionally or physically" (McCoy 1982).

Eating disorders are another dysfunctional reaction to the new freedoms encountered by postmodern adolescents. In part at least, eating disorders are often a reaction, *not* to the freedom to eat an unlimited amount of food, but rather to the opportunity to break away from parents and to become sexually active. *Anorexia nervosa* is a syndrome that involves an intense fear of gaining weight and of becoming fat. The young person refuses to maintain the minimal body weight for his or her height and build. *Bulimia* is a syndrome in which the adolescent has recurrent episodes of binge eating (rapid consumption of large amounts of food in a short period of time). Such binges are usually followed by either self-induced vomiting or the ingestion of laxatives or diuretics, strict dieting or fasting, and vigorous exercise to avoid weight gain.

Currently, it is estimated that about .5% of adolescent and young adult women meet the criteria for anorexia nervosa and about 1.3% meet the criteria for bulimia. In addition, an increasing number of teenage girls and young women are manifesting one or more less severe symptoms of an eating disorder. Most commonly this is dieting; not from a plan offered by a physician, but rather from diets offered in books and magazines. Although eating disorders are found predominantly among females, some 5–10% of young people with eating disorders are male. While it was once thought that eating disorders were a middle-class phenomena, such dysfunctions are now observed in teenagers from all backgrounds and with a wide variety of personality types (Fisher 1992).

Although the patterns and experiences that lead to anorexia and bulimia are extremely varied, these problems are often precipitated by a particular incident that seems to trigger a whole set of anxieties and concerns that then lead to the eating disorder behavior:

> Judy, a fifteen-year-old anorexic, was shopping with her mother for a new pair of jeans when her mother remarked that Judy's stomach was really beginning to stick out unattractively.... In response, Judy sucked in her stomach and took a long look at herself in the mirror. At that moment, her stomach appeared enormous to her. She decided that she didn't like the jeans she had on or any of the other pairs she tried on subsequently. Judy left the store without making any purchases. That evening she began a strict diet that led to anorexia nervosa. (Landau 1983)

Anorexics and bulimics are extremely anxious over loss of control of their impulses. Their dysfunctional behavior is an attempt to gain control over themselves and others (they often create concern about their health and appearance in their parents as a manipulative device). Many female anorexics and bulimics become amenorrheic (fail to menstruate) and end up arresting the growth of secondary sex characteristics including breast growth. By appearing childlike, these young women preclude sexual overtures, and no longer need to deal with the freedom of becoming sexually active. The rapid increase in the number of eating disorders among adolescents speaks both to the increased number of young people with patchwork selves and also to the powerful stress of postmodern freedoms.

Conforming Teenagers

Other teenagers, often of the conforming type, give in to peer pressure—most often to join their peers in drinking to excess. Young people abuse alcohol for the same reasons that adults do—to reduce stress. Alcohol is the intoxicant of choice among teenagers. The extent of teenage drinking gives some idea of the number of vulnerable young people as well as the power of the stressors they are experiencing. The National High School Survey in 1991 found that 33% of high school seniors, 24% of tenth graders, and 13% of eighth graders admitted to getting drunk (drinking five or more drinks) every two weeks (Johnston and O'Malley 1991).

The health risks of abusing alcohol are much less well known than are those for abusing other drugs. For example, the same 1991 youth survey found that fewer than 50% of high school seniors believe that drinking five or more drinks carries with it a significant health risk. The facts tell a different story. Alcohol abuse by teenagers is a major contributor to the new morbidity. Alcohol-related homicides, suicides, and unintentional injuries associated with car accidents, account for about 80% of teenage deaths. The results of many different studies give evidence that from 45–50% of teenage victims of violent death had been drinking alcohol before their death, as evidenced by their postmortem blood alcohol concentration. Some 2,500 teenagers die each year in automobile accidents and more than half of these are attributable to drunk drivers. Rodgers and Adger (1993) contend that alcohol abuse is the cause of more teenage deaths than cancer and leukemia combined.

Teenage drinking is not a new phenomenon, and certainly alcohol was not unknown to adolescents of the modern era. Nonetheless, the percentage of young people who are drinking today is greater than ever before. In part this is a reflection of our postmodern perception of adolescents as sophisticated and the acceptance of this perception by the larger society. Perhaps because of this perception, the liquor industry now targets young people as a profitable market. The introduction of sweet wine coolers was clearly directed at the young adolescent. Wine coolers made alcohol palatable to younger age groups. As a result, wine coolers are now an entry-level drink for young adolescents before they move on to beer and hard liquor. The increased alcohol consumption of contemporary youth is also a reflection of our affluent society. Alcoholic beverages are expensive, and only in an affluent society such as ours do young people have enough disposable income to buy them regularly.

Peer pressure, the perception of adolescents as sophisticated, and the relative affluence of our society are perhaps the most immediate causes of the alarming extent of teenager drinking. There are background causes as well. Some of these are the hardest for parents to deal with. As the following observations by some teenagers make clear, parental example plays an important part in a teenager's approach to the use of alcohol:

> RAY: I'd like to drink like my mother. She knows when to quit and she never drinks too much. She can hold it. That's the way I'd like to drink. I don't always. Usually she drinks at home. When I drink, I like to do it at home too, I don't like to go out, it's more comfortable.
>
> CHRIS: My folks are probably the most accomplished

social drinkers in town. Every night, promptly at 5:30, the booze comes out and they party. Dancing at the club. Dancing here and there, running all over. I really love their lifestyle. They get high enough so that everyone's having a good time. Not squashed. (Cross 1979)

In many cases it is a combination of parental example and environmental stressors that pushes young people into depression and serious alcohol abuse. The following case study is not an atypical example:

When she was 15 years old, Paula completed the ninth grade at a middle school and began tenth grade at a high school located in a different neighborhood. She had a difficult time making friends in her new surrounds and felt lonely and isolated. Her mother was "tired and irritable most of the time," according to Paula and "couldn't pay attention to my problems." Her brother was living at home but "never understood me," and her sister was married and into "problems of her own." Paula's loneliness on top of her previous anxieties gradually mounted, her grades plummeted from the B average she had proudly maintained in the past, and her self-esteem likewise went into a tailspin. To ease her psychological pain, she began to drink whenever she had the opportunity. A road to substance abuse had been well paved by her family. Paula's father was a recovered alcoholic, her sister had drug-related problems while at high school and her brother was currently having difficulty controlling alcohol and drug use. (Weiner 1992)

Adolescents can, and do, become alcoholics. It is now well established that there is an inherited predisposition to alcoholism particularly from fathers to sons. For young men so disposed, the earlier they begin to drink, the earlier the symptoms of alcohol addiction will make their appearance. These symptoms include: continuous or periodic impaired control over drinking; preoccupation with obtaining sufficient supplies of the drug; use of alcohol despite adverse consequences; and distortions of thinking, most notably denial (Rogers and Adger 1993). It is estimated that more than 400,000 young people under the age of 18 are alcoholic and in need of treatment (Adger 1991). Although genetics play a role in alcohol addiction, the social and familial factors that impair identity formation are also important in the history of this dysfunction.

A combination of social and familial contributors is also operative in those young people who abuse illicit drugs such as marijuana and cocaine. Up until recently there was some good news about illicit drug use. After reaching a peak in 1979 when 54% of high school seniors reported using them, only 29% of the class of 1991 reported such use. This decline is due largely to the media campaigns publicizing the physical and psychological harm associated with the use of these drugs. As this media campaign has waned, however, the use of marijuana is once again on the rise—presumably because the current crop of young people do not believe it has harmful effects. Overall, the fact that almost a third of high school seniors continue to experiment with illicit drugs is an unsettling statistic. As is true for alcohol, a higher percentage of young men than young women use illicit substances. There are, however, exceptions to this generalization. Teenage girls are more likely than teenage boys to use amphetamines, barbiturates, and tranquilizers. They are also more likely than boys to use over-the-counter diet pills (O'Malley, Johnston, and Bachman 1993).

There are many reasons why teenagers use drugs, but the most immediate cause is, in most cases, peer pressure. Doing drugs is a risky undertaking. From the standpoint of an integrated personality, it is a foreseeable and avoidable hazard. Although many adolescents with an integrated sense of self may try drugs once, much as they might try a roller coaster ride once, drug use remains a danger that can be avoided. Such teenagers will resist peer pressure to indulge further. But when adolescents are hit all at once with stressors of many kinds, or if they have a largely patchwork self, they may be unable to resist the demands of the peer group. Even though they are aware of the risks involved, they rationalize, "I am grown up and have the right to do as I please."

Stress Reactions to Loss (Type B Stressors)

Regardless of its source, the experience of loss gives rise to depression, usually involving the symptoms of low mood, negative attitudes, and decreased energy level. Depression in young people can range from the normal and constructive to the dysfunctional and destructive. Loss stressors include not only the dissolution of their parents' marriage, but also the loss of friends necessitated by the family relocation often associated with divorce. Other losses experienced by teenagers include the loss of grandparents through death, and the loss of boyfriends or girlfriends as a result of quarrels, disenchantment, or new attachments.

Since the 1980s there has been a growing recognition among clinicians of the prevalence of affective (emotional) disorders among adolescents. In part this new recognition is the result of better diagnostic procedures and the fact that health services now reach a larger percentage of the population. But it is probably also an index of the increased incidence of these disorders in the teenage population. That is to say, because adolescents in the postmodern world experience more loss than was true for teenagers in the modern world, they necessarily suffer more depression than did earlier generations of young people.

As illustrated in the initial discussion of responses to loss in the preceding chapter, some adolescents handle loss by repression and denial. Yet not dealing directly with the emotions associated with loss leaves these hurtful feelings unresolved; they often emerge at a later time to cause delayed pain and suffering. This sequence of events is the dynamic behind many of the so-called "post-traumatic stress disorders" wherein the individual suffers an emotional reaction long after the event is past. For example, young people who have been sexually abused as children may repress the experience but engage in such dysfunctional behaviors as substance abuse, running away, and delinquent behavior as adolescents (Pokorny 1992).

In some types of loss experience, the denial and repression may appear in delayed acting-out behavior that attempts to redress the earlier deprivation. Such behavior is not uncommon in young women whose fathers left the family when they were young and who never fully dealt with their feelings about the separation. Such young women often become seductive with older men and seem in constant search of the father they lost when they were small. Here is the reply of one teenage girl to the question, "How do you think not having a father in your house for most of your life affected you?"

I know me, and I can see it in my sister, too. I'm always looking for some guy I can confide in. Maybe a teacher. Not so much a teacher, but like this couple I worked for this summer. I'm really close with them. They're young and the guy couldn't be my father because they're too young, but I can confide in him. . . .

My little sister falls in love with her teachers. She finds reasons to stay at school a lot. If I were her, if I really wanted to see my father, I'd get mad and call him up. But I don't think she ever does. (Jackson and Jackson 1981)

Other adolescents with a patchwork self deal with their separation and loss by reversing roles and taking on parental responsibility for the remaining parent who is treated as the child. In adolescence, however, young people realize that they have not only lost their parent, but also their own childhood. It is then that dysfunctional symptoms appear:

Kathleen entered therapy at age 15, feeling down and hopeless, desirous of help and agreeing with her teacher's concerns about her academic struggles and the problems she had handling her work. She was a white, upper-middle-class adolescent, who had experienced great stress for many years, dating back to her parents divorce when she was ten. . . . At the onset of treatment Kathleen described her sadness and despair as the current distance and perpetual conflict between her and her mother and new stepfather. This conflict took the form of cold estrangement and overly controlled silences, which alternated with her mother's total dependency on Kathleen. In Kathleen's words, "I've been her mother for so long, her moral support. Look at these notes I left her daily, written when I was ten, eleven and twelve. I can't believe I wrote this stuff constantly. Isn't it terrible for any little girl to feel so worried and responsible?"

These are the notes of childhood that Kathleen shared:

Dear Mom,

    I want you to make sure that you are going to be all right. I just want to say that when you walk in the door of the lawyer's office, put some pride in you. Don't let Dad overcome you. Stand straight like a soldier. Think of yourself that you're the right one. Just wanted to give you some tips.

    Love,
    Kathleen

Dear Mom,

    I don't want you to feel badly. I know this is a very sad time for you, but keep your spirits up. The world is not at an end yet—you've got to think happy. I love you very much. You're the best mother that ever was and that's the truth. You're very special to me. Don't be sad. I love you. Roses are red, violets are blue, sugar is sweet and so are you. Keep your spirits up.

    Love,
    Kathleen   (Mishne 1986)

Prematurely taking on the mothering and caring role also interfered with Kathleen's effective identity formation. She began to do poorly in school despite her high level of intelligence and it was her school problems that initially brought her into therapy. In some respects, Kathleen dealt with the loss of her father from her mother's perspective and never attended to her own feelings of anger and separation. In adolescence, however, she began for the first time to confront her own feelings.

It is important to say here that depression is a natural and healthy response to loss, whether this is a loss due to separation—occasioned by divorce, by moving to another state or country, or by the death of a loved one. We all suffer depression at times. We usually handle it by talking about the loss with friends and relatives, thinking about the good and the bad times, and, in general, gradually letting go of the relationship. In clinical depression, however, the individual does not attempt to "work through" the emotions of loss, but rather, seeks to escape them through behaviors such as substance abuse or sexual promiscuity. Young people with a patchwork self are more likely to respond dysfuntionally to loss than are those with an integrated sense of self and personality.

The most extreme reaction to the experience of loss is suicide. One concrete evidence of the increased number of losses experienced by postmodern teenagers is the fact that the suicide rate for this age group has more than tripled over the last three decades (*Health United States 1990*). Currently, more than 5,000 young people between the ages of 10 and 24 take their own lives each year. Sadly, this number probably underestimates the actual number of deaths of this kind. These figures do not include the many deaths recorded as accidents (single-person car crashes, drownings, overdoses) which are not classified as suicides because of the stigma associated with that term (Tishler 1992).

Among 10- to 24- year olds, males are three times more likely to commit suicide successfully than are females. This is explained by the fact that young men are more likely than young women to shoot themselves. Young women, in contrast, more often use drugs or medications in their attempts; these are less immediately lethal and leave more time for discovery and countermeasures. A 1991 survey conducted by the Centers for Disease Control of almost 12,000 adolescents across all fifty states, Puerto Rico, and the Virgin Islands revealed that 27% had seriously thought about killing themselves the preceding year and that one in twelve had attempted suicide. Overall, there have been very large increases in the numbers of young people who think about, who make attempts at, and who succeed in taking their own lives (Saltzman et al. 1991).

Theories of suicide range from the sociological to the biological. French sociologist Emile Durkheim argued that suicide was the result of a condition that he termed *anomie*—a form of withdrawal that separated the individual from social contact and created a sense of isolation from the rest of society (1950). Many psychological explanations of suicide start from Freud's theory of melancholia and attribute suicide to the loss of love and to the victim's feelings of guilt, deprivation, and rejection in relation to important persons in their lives (1925). Those who propose a biological explanation look at the extent to which suicide runs in families and find this to be far greater than chance would predict (Tishler and McKenry 1981). In all probability, sociological, psychological, and biological factors are all involved, but the increase in suicide rates for adolescents over the last few decades suggests that the social factors coincident with the ascendance of postmodern society certainly play an important role.

This multilevel explanation of suicidal behavior is supported by psychologist Norman Farberow's 1985 review and summary of the literature on adolescent suicide from ten countries:

Those feelings and behaviors considered most significant were the feelings of depression and hopelessness and the behaviors of withdrawal, isolation,
and a previous suicidal history. Poor interpersonal
relationships were seen in a number of the cases and
these young people had few friends and a history of
school difficulties. Some adolescent suicides, especially boys, were good students, but, as loners, they
attracted little attention, presented no school problems and were often practically unknown by teachers and peers. The area of family and parental
interaction contributed the greatest number of significant factors. The studies reviewed reported
disturbed relationships with parents, violence and
physically abusive incidents between parents and/or
between parent and child, parental alcoholism and
suicidal behavior, and general parental discord.

While every suicide is unique, the pattern of disturbed
development, the resulting patchwork self, and the real, or
perceived, sense of overwhelming stress all contribute to
the mindset of both those adolescents who attempt suicide
and those who succeed.

Stress Reactions to Failure (Type C Stressors)

The postmodern American high school, with its large
size and large classes, works against teenagers' construction of an integrated sense of self, and identity. In addition
to making young people more vulnerable to stress by not
supporting healthy identity formation, schools add to
young people's burdens by creating unnecessary stresses of
their own. To be sure, there are many excellent private and
public middle, junior high, and high schools around the

nation that support young people's growth and development. These schools, sad to say, make up only a small proportion of the secondary schools in this country. Below are some of the complaints that teenagers voice about the stressors encountered at school:

> Trying to get through school is a tough problem. The teachers seem to give too much homework, the classes seem too hard, and the only thing likeable in school is lunch-time. Most teenagers get tired of school by their senior year in high school. This causes many problems with future education. The teen is so burnt out with school that he doesn't even want to go to college.
>
> School is one of the main problems teenagers have. Homework is very hard to keep up, and seems to pile up rapidly when one has five or six classes. This causes many kids to feel restricted and to feel an urge to ditch school for some free time. When one feels held down, he tends not to do well, and grades often turn out very badly. Some feel that grades are a big problem. (Brondino et al. 1988)

Others who want to enjoy all of the material things that are constantly being advertised to teenagers get caught in a struggle between the demands of work and school:

> A big problem teenagers have is keeping up with their homework, and some say, "Who cares about homework? I want some CASH!" So that's exactly what they do; they work all the time and never find any time for homework. All they're thinking of is their car expenses, clothes, etc. They're not thinking

of what their Mom and Dad will do if they don't get
good grades. For most, it's no more car and no more
dates. (Brondino et al. 1988)

Teenagers who are particularly vulnerable to demands
that are forseeable and unavoidable are those who are
angry or frightened. The contemporary overemphasis upon
grades combined with the relative anonymity and coldness
of large schools often encourages these teens to escape into
time-consuming jobs and eventual school failure and its
negative consequences. But there are other Type C stressors
that evoke dysfunctional reactions among teenagers who
have not attained an integrated sense of self. For all too
many adolescents, the home, as well as the school, presents
a whole menu of stressors. We need to look at some of the
ways angry and frightened teenagers react to the inordinate
demands for adaptation made by school and home.

Reactions of Angry Teenagers

Young people who are failing at school often feel that
it has nothing to offer them and see no reason why they
should waste their time going to class or doing homework.
Their anger at the demands of schooling is often projected
upon society at large. They come to regard rules and limits
as challenges, as something to be broken, rather than as unavoidable limitations demanded in return for the benefits
offered by society. These benefits—food and shelter, sanita-
tion, recreation facilities, and the rest—are simply taken for
granted. Not surprisingly, many of these angry teenagers
break the law and are adjudicated as delinquent. Delinquency is a legal not a psychological term; the psychological diagnosis for many young people who repeatedly break
the law is that of *conduct disorder*.

Studies of adolescents who have become delinquent

suggest that such young people share certain characteristics. In most cases, delinquents have experienced school failure and are likely to be on the lowest academic track. They also tend not to be involved in school activities and to drop out as soon as this is possible. Delinquents also tend to have a poor sense of self and are less apt than their more well-put-together peers to see themselves as competent and successful (Arbuthut, Gordon, and Jurkovic 1987).

In addition, delinquents are likely to come from homes characterized by violence, and many are victims of child abuse and/or neglect. Also common are conflicts between parents, poor communication, and harsh punishment. Finally, parents' preoccupation with their career and personal problems (which young people perceive as rejection) is also common to adolescents who are adjudicated (Simons, Robertson, and Downs 1989). All of these ingredients contribute to a patchwork self that, in an angry teenager, can lead to antisocial behavior. The following case is that of a severe solitary conduct disorder:

> Butch, a 15-year-old boy, was seen for a court ordered evaluation following his alleged rape of a 12-year-old girl in his neighborhood. He vehemently denied the charge, stating that she consented willingly. His version was in marked contrast to the victim's statement, which indicated a violent, forced assault. Butch's official arrest record spanned four years and included nine previous felony charges consisting of assault and battery, burglaries, an auto theft, and shooting into a building. He had been suspended from school on numerous occasions for fighting, and at home his mother and stepfather described him as "being out of their control since he was eight." Butch's conduct problems were almost

always self-initiated and carried out in solitude.
(Myers and Burket 1992)

While Butch was a loner, the following case illustrates a milder, socially involved conduct disorder:

Betsy, a 14-year-old girl, was seen at an outpatient child and adolescent clinic for evaluation of poor school performance and problem behaviors at home. Over the past year, she had been truant sufficiently so that a decline in her grade point average was putting her at risk for failing eighth grade. At home she was openly defiant of her parents' rules, lied to them about her homework assignments and activities after school, and occasionally snuck out of the house in the middle of the night to "party" with her friends. Twice in the last six months she had run away for several days to be with her boyfriend. According to Betsy's parents, her problem behaviors began as she was entering puberty, at about 12 years of age. (Myers and Burket 1992)

As in both of these cases, anger at school, parents, and self often gets transformed into anger at authority and rules in general. In addition to breaking rules, many angry adolescents also engage in violent acts. Violence among young people is not limited to city ghettos; it is present in affluent suburbs and is engaged in by adolescents from middle- and upper-class families. Homicide is now the second most frequent cause of injury-related death, after automobile accidents for children and adolescents. Teenagers are two and a half times as likely to be victims of violent crimes than is someone who is 20 years and older (Hammond and Yung 1993).

Not all young people are equally at risk, however, either as assailants or victims. Minority males are most at risk. African-American males are nine times more likely than white American males to die a violent death. Hispanic American youth are four times more likely and Native Americans twice as likely to die violently than are white youth. For the decade from 1978 to 1988, 40% of black males who died were homicides. There are differences among minority groups in homicide patterns. Black Americans are likely to be killed by a gun, by friends, and at home. Hispanics are more likely to die from stab wounds, and to be killed on the street. Regardless of minority group, the most frequent reason given for committing violent crimes is revenge (Hammond and Young 1993).

Violence is often associated with poverty. Adolescents who grow up in poverty are likely to have a difficult time constructing a positive sense of self and an integrated sense of personal identity. Many young people from low-income families do, of course, succeed in our society. But, in most cases, these adolescents have the love and support of their caring, if impoverished, family. Where such family support is absent, the frustration of being poor in an affluent society sets the stage for young people to act out their anger at one another and at society.

Reactions of Frightened Teenagers

Some adolescents grow up in a home where a parent is alcoholic, abusive, rejecting, or some combination of these. Young people who have to live with this type of unhappy family life react with one of several patterns. Among teenagers whose parents are alcoholic, some choose the path of accepting the deviant behavior of their parents as the norm. They avoid the behavior by denying it. Other adolescents, whose parents are extremely abusive and rejecting, may simply leave home and become runaways.

Many adolescents growing up in dysfunctional families regard the circumstances as not only foreseeable but as unavoidable as well. As a result, many teenagers living in homes with an addictive parent accommodate to the parent's aberrant behavior as if it were normal (Whitfield 1991). Moreover, this pattern of co-dependence described earlier deprives young people of the time and the materials needed to construct a healthy sense of self and identity. In addition, teenagers growing up in addictive homes have acquired a strange sense of normality. They may think it is the norm to have a parent come home and fall dead drunk on the living room floor, where he or she stays till morning. Likewise, the trademarks of the patchwork self—low self-esteem and conflicting attitudes, beliefs, habits, and values—are particularly striking in adolescents who grow up in addictive families.

Other teenagers whose parents are physically and/or verbally abusive become so fearful of further harm that they run away from home. For most runaways, their home is a war zone. In one survey, among adolescents in homeless youth shelters, 62% of the females and 46% of the males had experienced some form of parental abuse. Although children at all age levels are abused, 24% of the fatalities and 46% of the serious injuries attributable to abuse are incurred by adolescents from 12 to 17 years of age. It is estimated that some 25% of runaways have been sexually abused (Farber 1987).

Running away, of course, does not solve adolescents' problems. Instead it carries them into environments with new and daunting demands for adaptation. Arriving in a strange city with no money, no job, and no skills, young people are often unaware of the help that is available from runaway shelters across the country. Out on the streets and alone, teenagers are easy prey for the smut vultures: "There are people who are good at spotting confused kids like that in urban areas," says Veronica Reed of San Francisco's Huckleberry House. "They come up and tell them how they can make some money" (1983).

Many runaways become prostitutes because it is the only way they can make money and survive. The case of Cathy is typical:

> I started turning tricks when I was thirteen. I never had sex till then. He was nice, about 50 I guess. I didn't have to do anything bad. I didn't know anything about sex. Every time I was with a trick I was scared. I felt bad, always being with someone I didn't know, because you don't ever know if you'll end up dead or beat up or something. I tried to get jobs. I had applications but I always was too young or something. There ain't much younger girls can do. (Rader 1982)

Dotson Rader, who has studied runaways by talking with them on the streets, has this to say about the fate of many of these young people:

> There are local and national call services and "buy-a-kid" rings from which customers can purchase a runaway child for a night or permanently. In New York, runaways told me that the cost of buying a child for life was $5,000.00. In San Diego, I interviewed a runaway who had been sold by his grandfather for $500.00.
>
> Many runaway children don't live long.... 150,000 disappear each year. They also suffer from

malnutrition, drug related disorders, sexual dysfunction and having little access to health care (runaways
don't have health insurance), from disease of all
types. A major cause of death among boys engaged
in prostitution is rectal hemorrhage. (1982)

The stories of runaways tear at our hearts and sympa-
thies as much as the stories of those who commit crimes of
violence arouse our anger and frustration. We cannot color
all teenagers with the same emotional crayon. Some deserve our understanding, others our justifiable anger, and
still others our compassion. They all need our help. As I
have argued throughout this book, the causes of much
teenage misery are societal as well as familial. Both indi-
vidually and as a society, we must reinvent adulthood and
assume the responsibility for providing the care, guidance,
values, and direction that adolescents need to acquire a
healthy sense of self and identity. These things take time.
Yet many young people need help now. [In the Appendix I
have listed a number of programs and services available to
help troubled teenagers and their families.]

A far better remedy, however, is prevention. And while
we can never entirely eliminate the stressors affecting
youth (nor should we want to) we should work toward reducing them to manageable and constructive levels and to
helping young people to cope. These issues will be taken
up in the next chapter.

CHAPTER 10

Helping Teenagers Cope

The new morbidity and the epidemic of teenage problem
behavior in America today is deeply troubling and threatening. When homicide is a leading cause of death among
youth, and when a third of high school seniors report having five or more drinks within a two-week period, we have
a dangerous social problem that is getting out of hand. Our
perception of adolescents as being sophisticated and competent to deal with the postmodern stressors of increased
freedom, loss, and failure has too often led us to abrogate
our responsibilities to youth.

The problem will not go away and will only get worse
if we don't take some concerted action. While there have
been a number of calls to action, such as *Beyond Rhetoric: A
New American Agenda for Children and Families*, the final report of the National Commission on Children (1991), and
the annual *State of America's Children*, published by the Children's Defense Fund (1994), federal funds for children and
youth have been cut rather than increased. Legislators, if
not child advocates, seem to have accepted the perception
of young people as competent and sophisticated and not in
need of any special treatment or consideration.

Societies, no less than individuals, always wait too

long before confronting serious problems—in the hope, perhaps, that the problems will go away or get better by themselves. When this does not happen, as it rarely does, we are forced to take action as the problem becomes so damaging that it can no longer be ignored. I hope and pray that this will not happen with the children and youth of our country. Even without support at the legislative, media, and business levels, there are things that we can do as parents, educators, and health professionals to help the young people in our care grow by differentiation and integration—the best preparation for coping successfully with the stressors of their postmodern world.

Before looking at what we can do, however, it is important to acknowledge what we cannot do. We cannot turn the clock back to the modern world of nuclear families and protected children and youth. Nor are we going to reverse the second sexual revolution that made premarital sex socially acceptable first for adults and now for teenagers. We are not going to get that genie back in the bottle. Nor is there any way we can alter the pace of technological change, the computer revolution, or the Internet and World Wide Web communication explosion. Other changes, such as the deteriorating environment, diminishing natural resources, and the disappearance of species, are, however, foreseeable and avoidable correlates of an expanding human population. It will take the highest qualities of our humanness to take both caring and preventive action.

It should be emphasized that not all of these changes are bad or harmful. Computers have significantly recast the way in which we live and the ways in which we pursue our occupations. For example, some 30 million people now work part or full time in their homes—thanks to computers, fax machines, and networking software. This means that many more parents are home more hours of the day than was possible when most people worked in factories. This certainly can benefit children and youth. Likewise, medical science and nutrition have greatly extended our life span. Jet travel has made the whole world accessible to families and individuals of even modest means. If there are negatives to our postmodern world, there are many positives as well.

While we cannot, as individuals, alter the course of social events in the larger world, we can influence the events in our own miniature worlds of home, school, and community. In these circumscribed worlds, we have to look at ways of helping adolescents cope effectively with the negative stressors of postmodern life. We can do this both by helping young people attain a differentiated sense of self and identity, and by reducing some of the stressors that we ourselves impose.

Encouraging Growth by Integration

What Parents Can Do

It is important to begin this discussion of what parents can do by stating firmly that *parents make a difference in children's lives*. In these postmodern times when we are ready to see children as competent and teenagers as sophisticated, it is easy to believe that we play a minor role in their development. This belief is enhanced if our children are in out-of-home care from an early age and if, thanks to divorce, we see them only on weekends or during the summer. Yet all of our clinical experience and our research data are consistent in making one resounding point: parents are the single most powerful, nonbiological influence on their children's lives.

Parenting is, therefore, a very important responsibility. But it need not be an onerous one. One does not have to change personality or learn a whole new set of complicated techniques to do a good job. Parents with many different personality types and styles can all be sensitive, caring, and wonderfully effective parents. It is important, however, to gain some general knowledge about child growth and development, such as I have tried to provide in this book. Such knowledge helps us to see the world from the adolescent's point of view, and that is the first step to effective and rewarding parenting. Knowing about child growth and development, and de-centering from our own point of view, is the all-important first step toward helping young people grow by differentiation and integration rather than by substitution.

The second step in helping young people develop a healthy sense of self and identity is to be *adults* to our children. Children and adolescents are the young of our species and like the young of all species have to learn from adult guidance and direction. Being an adult simply means recognizing that children and adolescents need to be socialized and that such socialization is neither instinctual nor acquired spontaneously, without instruction. This is easy to appreciate when it comes to bowel and bladder training and weaning, but less so when it comes to manners and morals. Yet it is our responsibility to teach our children to say "please," "thank you," "excuse me," and "I'm sorry" at appropriate times. We have to teach children about lying and stealing, about property and privacy rights, and the limits of freedom.

In our postmodern world, however, I often find that parents are reluctant to assert their adultness, to set limits and teach manners and morals. Perhaps because many postmodern parents spend less time with their children and adolescents—most often to maintain a standard of living that could once be maintained with shorter hours and with a single parent working—they are reluctant to say or do anything negative in the little time available. Indeed, I find many parents worry that their children will not "like" them and in this way put themselves at their children's mercy. This is not healthy for either parent or child. It is an abrogation of our adulthood and blocks the child's ability to grow by differentiation because the child adopts, by substitution, an air of adult authority.

Being an adult to children and adolescents does not mean being an ogre or a drill sergeant. It does mean that we recognize young people's need to be socialized and that we accept responsibility for that socialization. We can set limits with love and caring. When setting a time for adolescents to come home, for example, many teenagers will complain and say, "You don't trust me." In reply we might say something like, "You may see it as my not trusting you enough, but if I didn't set a time limit you could equally well accuse me of not loving you and caring enough about you." When we set rules and limits with love and caring, we give young people the opportunity to argue with us but also to internalize those rules so that they can later regulate their own behavior.

And adolescents do appreciate the fact that we care enough about them to risk an angry confrontation. As several teenage boys said to me in relation to a peer who had ready access to his parents' liquor cabinet, "I guess his parents don't love him or they would say no, wouldn't they?" One father told me the following story:

> My wife and I set a firm curfew for our daughter. She didn't like it and gave us a hard time about it. But we stood firm, and despite her complaints she did come home when she was supposed to. One

night when she came home from a party she was wearing a little smile, almost a grin. When I asked her about it, she said, "Oh, Dad, you remember Barbara and Jean who are always teasing me about coming home early. Well they were bragging about not having to go home when these two creeps came along and started bothering them. I told them I had to go home but they were stuck!

When I talk to parents about being adults to their children and about setting rules and limits with love and caring, some parents respond by saying, "It doesn't do any good, they do what they want anyway." On further exploration, I often find that these parents have set rules that they could not enforce and which their teenagers broke with impunity. These parents seem to throw up their hands and believe that because they can't control everything the teenager does, they can control nothing. Even if we can't regulate all of our teenager's behavior, nor should we want to, we can regulate some things. We may not, for example, be able to prevent teenagers from smoking when they are with friends. But we can still say, "I don't want you to smoke because it is bad for your health. I know that you can smoke when you are elsewhere. But each time I find out about it, you will be grounded and have your allowance cut in half." Just because we do not have total control doesn't mean that we have no control.

Many postmodern parents fail to assert their adultness out of sheer exhaustion. Working long hours at a stressful job can leave parents reluctant to face confrontations with their teenagers at home. They feel that they lack the energy to get into fights about curfews, clothing, friends, and so on. Unfortunately, backing away from rule setting only sets the stage for more difficult and angry confrontations later. If there was ever a time when we needed to call upon our energy reserves, this is it. On the other hand, if we are so tired and stressed out, that a confrontation will lead to an angry shouting match, it is best to keep it short and to the point. "Please be home at twelve. If you are not you will be grounded for a week. We can argue about it later and then you can tell me what a meanie I am. Right now I am exhausted."

Some parents tell me that they cannot assert their adultness, say no, and set limits, because the teenage peer group is too powerful. There is no denying the power of the peer group, particularly in early adolescence, and especially when the pressure comes from other parents as well as from the peer group itself. In some communities, for example, one group of parents encourages their daughters to date at age ten. Other parents then have to deal with their own preteen daughters' requests to date. But giving in to pressure is still another abrogation of our adulthood. In such cases a general rule to follow is *deal with principle, not with pressure*. Dating by ten-year-olds is developmentally inappropriate because it encourages them to skip the all-important chumship stage in which young people learn social skills with peers of the same sex that they can then extend to peers of the opposite sex. The principle is that skipping stages is harmful.

Teenagers and preteens will fight limits and rules and may say hurtful things about our cruelty, our lack of feeling and understanding, and our failure to appreciate how times have changed and how different things are today from when we were growing up. At a deeper level, however, teenagers know that a parent risks this vilification out of love and caring, and they do appreciate it. They simply have a very peculiar way of showing this appreciation. Many of my college students tell me how much they welcomed, in retrospect, the rules and limits set by their parents. The frequency with which I hear such stories from both parents and young people is testimony to the underlying strong desire of adolescents to live in an orderly, caring world.

Accordingly, even though being adult is difficult and it is easier to give in, we should stick to the principles we believe in. By keeping to the tenets we hold dear, we provide the experiences adolescents need to attain an integrated sense of self and identity. Perhaps this is what Ralph Waldo Emerson had in mind when he wrote, in his essay "Self Reliance":

> A political victory, a rise of rents, the recovery of a sick friend, or some other external event raises your spirits and you think good days are preparing for you. Do not believe it. It can never be so. Nothing can bring you peace but yourself. Nothing can bring you peace but the triumph of principle. (1909)

If we give in to pressure, rather than making the matter one of principle, we only set ourselves up for more of the same in the future. Blackmail begets blackmail.

Basing our responses on principle can be useful in other situations as well. For example, a parent told me the following incident about her teenage son: "I asked him not to play his stereo loud, but he just doesn't listen." Her solution was to move to another part of the house where she could avoid the din. Yet there is a matter of principle here as well. Our freedom stops when it impinges on the freedom of someone else. One might say to a teenager, "When you exercise your freedom to play your stereo loud and I am around, it interferes with my freedom to do the work I have to do. You can certainly play it loud when I am not in the house, but please turn it down when I am here." By basing our argument on principle we appeal to the adolescent's sense of justness and fairness. If we simply complain that the noise bothers us, we make it a personal issue rather than one of principle, and our objection loses force.

Principles can be used in a variety of innovative ways to deal with common issues raised by teenagers. For example, one parent I know solved the problem of messy rooms by adopting a principle of reciprocity. She told her teenage son, "Look, I really don't like your messy room, so I will help you clean up your room if you will help me clean up mine." By turning a personal complaint ("I don't like your messy room") into a matter of principle, ("You help me and I will help you"), she transformed the issue into a principle of mutual cooperation rather than of individual unhappiness. Basing rules and limits on general principles, rather than upon personal feelings or inclinations, renders the issue less emotional and encourages the adolescent to argue at a higher level and without personal recrimination.

Dealing with conflictual issues on the basis of principle has other implications as well. Although it is not always easy, it is important to look for principles even when the teenager says or does things that are personally hurtful. One mother was shattered when she inadvertently heard her daughter call her "frumpy." While she was tempted to retaliate with a verbal attack of her own, she refrained. Instead she said, "I heard what you called me and I didn't like it. Calling people names behind their backs is unfair; it doesn't give them a chance to defend themselves. If you have a complaint about me, tell me to my face and I will tell you whether or not I think it is justified. It will, however, also give me an opportunity to tell you what I don't like about you." When we deal with adolescents on the basis of principle, rather than from emotion, we are asserting our adultness in a way that is helpful to the young person's struggles in identity formation.

At this point I have to say that asserting our adult-ness and operating on the basis of principle rather than emotion is in many ways a return to modern advice giving to parents. Modern writers such as Gesell and Ilg (1956) and Fraiburg (1959) gave parents descriptions of how children grew and developed; they argued that parents, armed with that knowledge, could tailor-make their parenting to the individuality of their child. In effect, modern writers for parents tried to answer the question: *How do children grow and develop?* They gave parents basic principles of growth and development but few prescriptions. In addition, they did not tell parents that if they did or said something wrong, they might harm their child's budding personality.

All of that changed when we entered the postmodern era of the permeable family. Parenting is now seen not as a matter of unlearned intuition, but rather of learned technique. Consequently the advice for parents has been translated from answering the question: *How do* children grow and develop, to answering the question: *How to?* This is the emphasis in books like Ginott's *Between Parent and Teenager* (1969), Gordon's *Teaching Children Self Discipline* (1989), and Faber and Mazlish's *How to Talk So Kids Will Listen: How to Listen So Kids Will Talk* (1980). While the emphasis upon technique is valuable to the extent that it builds upon the distinction between the child's actions and his or her personality, it is also limited. Those who write about techniques give parents no information about child development. Their advice suggests that one size fits all. There is no way to individualize techniques.

The problem with techniques that are not founded on a basis of child development and knowledge of the individual is that they can misfire. For example, in the book *How To Talk So Kids Will Listen*, Faber and Mazlish suggest that parents describe situations that elicit their emotions rather than attribute blame. They give the example of a mother who sees her two children come into the house covered with green watercolor paint, and she says; "I see two boys with green paint on their hands and faces." But the authors also point out that this descriptive technique can fail:

> It is possible to use this skill in a way that can be irritating. For example, one father told us he was standing near the front door on a cold day and said to his son who had just entered, "The door is open." The boy countered with, "So why don't you close it?" (1980)

One problem with techniques is that they are just that, techniques. They are not founded on the basis of established psychological research and theory nor upon moral or ethical principles. Sometimes they work, sometimes they don't. Children, moreover, are deprived of the tailor-made parenting strategies that come from applying general principles of development to the unique individual child. Another problem with techniques is that those who advocate them suggest that if they are not used, children's sense of self will suffer.

One implication of many of the postmodern parenting books is that children and adolescents should never feel bad about themselves. Yet we are all human, we all make mistakes, do the wrong thing, and say the wrong thing. At such times it is entirely appropriate to feel ashamed and guilty. Erik Erikson (1950) makes this very clear when he says that a certain amount of guilt is healthy as long as it is less powerful than our sense of initiative. Clearly children should not be made to feel guilty when they do something by accident. But when children do something purposely cruel or intentionally nasty, their deeds *should* be tied to their motives. The principle here is one of justice, that malicious words and deeds have consequences for those who employ them.

When my sons were young, one of them told a joke that involved a minority stereotype. I told him that I did not think the joke was funny and that I was disappointed in him for having told it. I stated the principle that it was wrong to make fun of people on account of their race or religion because this denies their individuality and encourages hatred. We have all too many examples from all over the world of peoples warring with one another because of their race or religion. Although my son meant no harm by the joke, I felt it was important for him to feel badly about having told it. I hoped my response would make him think seriously before telling such a joke again.

Being a parent is not easy, and being the parent of a teenager is perhaps the hardest of all. Yet teenagers can be wonderfully enthusiastic, loving, and caring. That is why knowing about child development is so important. It helps us to take distance from the immediate strains and stresses of a particular stage and recognize it as such, a stage that will be all too quickly passed through. Now that my own children are grown, their childhood seems to have been but a short moment of time, a dream. I look back at all of the issues that I thought were so momentous at the time and they all seem so insignificant now. Often when things get tight it is useful to think, "How will I feel about this next year or five years from now?" Taking distance allows us to be adults to our teenagers and to operate on the basis of principle rather than emotion. Fortunately, there are a number of books today that try and provide parents with both child development and techniques. T. Berry Brazelton's book *Touchpoints* (1992) and my own *Parenting Your Teenager* (1994) are examples of the new trend toward combining child development with helpful techniques.

In talking about being an adult to young people, I am saying that we often need to exercise *unilateral* authority. We all have to obey unilateral authority in order to live in a society. We may not like paying income tax or property tax or even sales tax, but we do so because the state has unilateral authority to levy taxes. Likewise, we may not like speed limits, but the state has the unilateral authority to establish and to enforce them. When we set rules and limits, when we teach manners and morals, we are exercising unilateral authority. As parents, we can exercise this authority with love and caring and not in the impersonal way such authority is exercised by the state.

It is also important, however, to engage in *mutual* authority as well. Mutual authority is that which exists between equals such as friends or between husband and wife. With mutual authority all parties have a say both in the setting up of the rules and in assuring that they are followed. With respect to our children, we should exercise mutual authority when it comes to matters of taste, style, and interest. A child should have the choice of what to order at a restaurant, what sports to engage in, and what musical instrument to play.

In my work with parents over the years, I find that one of the hardest things for them to do is to distinguish between unilateral and mutual authority and to use each appropriately. Some parents go overboard in exercising unilateral authority—they give teenagers little choice even in matters of food or dress. Other parents go to the opposite extreme and make everything a matter of mutual authority—they give their adolescents too much choice in all domains. The most effective parents are those who are flexible in their use of unilateral and mutual authority and who use both types of authority appropriately and with warmth and love.

In addition to the flexible use of unilateral and mutual authority, another characteristic of effective parents is their sense of humor. Such parents do not take themselves or their teenagers too seriously. They tend to see the trials and tribulations of adolescence as just that—a troublesome time that will pass. Such parents accord teenagers a special place, and they can balance the headaches teenagers provoke against the pleasures of their special charm and creativity. We don't really appreciate our teenagers until they leave the house, and the noise, the bustle, the coming and going, the exuberance, and the low moods are gone and the house is strangely, and sadly, silent.

What Schools Can Do

Since the 1960s educational reforms under one label or another have come and gone, and yet little has really changed in education. This is the conclusion of Richard Gibboney in his book, *The Stone Trumpet: A Story of Practical School Reform 1960–1990* (1994). The failure of most of the more than seventy different reform initiatives during the last thirty years has had many different political, economic, and social causes. As I argued in the education chapter, the major reason for this failure is that the schools are stuck in the modern paradigm while children and youth are already postmodern. On the other hand, those reforms that do start from postmodern premises, such as Sizer's Coalition for Effective Schools, can be effective (1992).

Despite the resistance to genuine reform in education, there are things that teachers can do. Like some parents, some teachers believe that if they cannot do everything, they cannot do anything. The choice is somewhere in between. As Sizer makes so movingly true in his book *Horace's Compromise* (1984), even when a teacher makes some concessions to the large classes and the boredom of students, there are still things you can do. Teachers, like parents, have to be adults to their students and set the expectations and limits that are appropriate for this age group. Teachers, like parents, tell me that this is difficult to do, and for many of the same reasons. And my answer is comparable as well: *Even if we can't do it all, we can do something*. With teenagers in the classroom, setting limits is difficult because these are often taken as challenges. It is sometimes just asking for trouble if we insist that students do not chew gum or whisper.

On the other hand, if we set rules and limits that are based on principle rather than on what annoys us, we are on safer ground. "In this class if you do the work, you get the grade; if you don't do the work, you don't get the grade." And/or "If homework is done neatly and on time, you get the grade; if it is late or looks like something written by a parakeet with ink on its claws, you get marked down." In the same way, if some students are creating a commotion, it is best to start from principle: "You are certainly free to talk to your friends when you are outside the classroom, but inside the classroom talking to your friends interferes with other student's freedom to study or to listen."

Students are more willing to be governed by principle than they are by personal preferences. We can still set rules and boundaries in our own classroom, and we can still communicate our love for and excitement about the subject matter we teach. And we can still give words of encouragement to those young people who use them to build their sense of self and identity. Teaching is still one of the most rewarding of professions. Here is how one teacher described those rewards:

> I want to say what it has meant to me to spend my professional life as an educator in the public schools, to convey the truly inexplicable, incomparable exultation I felt when I taught a pipsqueak of a child how to read. I want others to know the pride I felt when one of my students was accepted at an Ivy League College—a student who learned to cope with long division because I tutored him during recess so that other students wouldn't know how scared he was of math. . . . And what about the high school valedictorian who told me on graduation night that she remembered the first day she saw me in 3rd grade wearing my kelly green dress, and every time she sees that color she thinks of me and that class. . . . And the note I found on my car one day from a mother who admonished me for driving with a dirty windshield. She cleaned it for me, she said, because I had opened the windows on the world for her twins.
>
> Teaching hasn't been all wonderful, of course. Some terrible soul-searching mornings I was caught between my own daughter—coughing and wanting Mommy to stay home with her—and twenty-three students primed for a field trip they couldn't take without me. Occasionally "idiot" proclamations from on high forced me to use strategies in my classes that I considered educationally unsound.
>
> There were some children, parents, and colleagues whose concepts of right and wrong were diametrically opposed to my own. And I believe, even now, as an administrator with a good salary, that my

compensation is considerably less than it would have been in industry or in almost any other comparable profession. I also believe that, in the world outside of public school, I never had much status as a teacher. . . . There were fights I couldn't settle, students I couldn't help, mothers who thought I was too soft or too strict, fathers who thought I gave too little homework or too much. . . .

As you can see, I have my retirement speech practically all written. But how can I retire? The phone is ringing, the problems keep pouring in; three people are waiting to see me. . . There's so much to do, I don't have time to retire right now. (Fisher 1988)

It is due to the dedication and hard work of teachers such as Eleanor Fisher that so many young people get not only a fine education, but also adult support that encourages healthy identity formation.

In addition to exerting our adulthood, setting limits and standards, and helping individual students when we can, there are some structural changes that would also improve the educational quality of our high schools. Although the postmodern perception of adolescent sophistication is often exaggerated, as I have argued in this book, it is also true that young people today are more sophisticated in some ways than were their peers of the modern era. The fact that large numbers of teenagers are sexually active is a case in point. It seems to me that high schools must recognize this sophistication in ways that older adolescents will appreciate and that will provide a marker that sets them apart from young adolescents.

One way to accomplish this is to make the last two years of high school more like a junior college. Courses could be offered three times a week; students with an advisor could arrange their own schedules and select their own course pattern. With such an arrangement juniors and seniors would be able to exercise more freedom over their school day than is true for the freshmen and sophomores. Such an arrangement would give eleventh and twelfth graders additional mutual authority in keeping with their own sense of sophistication.

Stress Management

Even teenagers who are able to attain a healthy sense of self and identity can be overwhelmed by the magnitude of the psychological stressors of postmodern society. In addition to helping them attain an integrated sense of self and identity, we can also provide guidance in developing strategies for dealing with the three major stress situations. These are general strategies, or guidelines, and have to be adapted to the particular situation.

Type A: Foreseeable and Avoidable Stressors

The emotions elicited by Type A stressors are anxiety and worry. As we noted in Chapter 2, worry is the product of thinking in a new key and the accompanying ability to think about the future. Many adolescents who can foresee a danger and recognize its avoidability may still wonder about the mechanics of it. A teenage girl, for example, knows that a boy whom she does not like is going to ask her out, and she knows that she is going to have to refuse. She is a sensitive and thoughtful young woman and worries about how she is going to turn him down without hurting his feelings. Another teenager has let homework pile up for so long that his or her grades will fall if the work doesn't get done. For all Type A situations, there is a useful

formula that can reduce the related anxiety.
1. Identify and label the type of stressor
2. Consider all the available options
3. Take action
It is relatively easy for teenagers to learn to identify the type of stressor they are dealing with, but sometimes they need help in imagining all of the available options. Indeed, this is where most young people run aground. We can help them to appreciate that we all have many more options than we realize, we just need the time to think about them. The failure to consider all of our available options is amusingly illustrated in this anecdote from social psychologist Daniel Yankelovitch:

> A patient in psychotherapy . . . a woman in her midtwenties, complained that she had become nervous and fretful because life had grown so hectic—too many big weekends, too many discos, too many late hours, too much talk, too much wine, too much pot, too much love making.
>
> "Why don't you stop?" asked the therapist mildly. Her patient stared back blankly for a moment and then her face lit up, dazzled by an illumination. "You mean that I really don't have to do what I want to do?" (1981)

For the girl who is worried about turning down an invitation, what are some of her options? Decline with dismissal ("I'm busy. Don't bother calling me again."); decline with encouragement ("I'm busy, but I would like to go out with you. Please call again."); decline without comment (I'm busy that evening and can't go out with you."). In this instance, the last response might be the preferable. Teenagers often feel that they have to explain everything; in fact by saying less they say more. A good rule is that the less explanation the better. In this case the young woman communicates that she credits the young man with sufficient intelligence and good sense to draw his own conclusions. Once a teenager decides on a course of action, much of the anticipatory anxiety is dissipated.

The teenager who lets his work pile up should follow the same approach. In this instance, he has at least three options: don't do the work and accept the low grades; do the work right away and rescue the grades; postpone the work a little longer. It is clear that the second option would be the most stress-reducing alternative. But here we run into a more complicated but not unusual problem. What do we do as parents if our teenager chooses to procrastinate and not do the work? The temptation, of course, is to make the teenager's problem into our problem and to worry about what will happen if the work does not get done. Although it is impossible for parents not to become emotionally involved in this state of affairs (probably one of the reasons it happened in the first place), we should again base our reaction on principle rather than emotion.

In this situation, we can look to the outside world and to the workplace for guiding principles. In many respects, going to school and doing homework is like having a job. When you take a job, you accept the responsibility of doing the required work. If the work is not done, you lose the job. If we wish to prepare our teenagers for the real world, we have to say that doing their homework is their responsibility and if they do not do it, they will have to pay the consequences. Schooling is the occupation of young people, and their performance of this activity should be treated accordingly.

Although this may seem a little harsh and hard hearted, it is in young people's best interest as well as our own. It helps them to grow by differentiating situations in which they are responsible and those in which they are not. In making choices about available options, for ourselves as well as for our children, it is often helpful if we can find a guiding rule or principle.

At this point it might be useful to say something about parental pressure on young people to take lessons or to participate in sports. Many adults tell me that in retrospect they wish their parents had made them take music lessons so that now they would be able to play the piano, violin, or guitar. Others say that they are glad their parents made them take lessons. These reactions seem to be an argument for parents taking a more active role in pushing their children. My own feeling is that in both types of memory the adult is overestimating the role of parents and underestimating the role he or she might have played as a child. When parents pressure young people into doing something they have no liking or aptitude for, it is unlikely that such pressure will ensure that the adolescent acquires the skills in question. Likewise, adolescents who did succeed with lessons did so not because their parents pressured them but because at some level they had a talent for the instrument and enjoyed playing it. Parental intervention is all-important in the areas of manners and morals, but much less so in matters of taste, interest, talent, and preference.

Type B: Unforeseeable and Unavoidable Stressors

Some stressors can be neither predicted nor avoided. The best protection against this type of stressor for teenagers, as for all of us, is a perspective on life as a whole. Many different writers have attempted to offer perspectives that help us deal with situations in which "bad things happen to good people." William James wrote, "Be willing to have it so." Acceptance of what has happened is the first step to overcoming the consequences of any misfortune.

The Greek philosopher Epictetus wrote almost twenty centuries ago, "There is only one way to happiness, and that is to cease worrying about things that are beyond our will." These two writers express the same essential truth: some things in life cannot be changed. Both sayings are simple and honest truths that can make sad and unhappy moments a little easier to bear.

Young people are receptive to the wisdom of adults. Many of us, now that we are grown, continue to repeat the sayings we heard from our parents and teachers when we have to deal with unforeseeable and unavoidable stressors. I still recall that when I learned that my father had cancer and broke into tears in front of one of my professors, he said, "It is all right. Sometimes all that you can do is cry." Now when I have students in similar circumstances I say the same thing. What that teacher did was give me permission to feel sad, and to express my feelings. At such times, one of the most important gifts we can give young people is the *permission* to express their feelings.

Giving teenagers words or phrases that help them put Type B stressors in perspective, or that enable them to accept their feelings as healthy and acceptable, can help them get over some of life's rough spots. It is important to say these things even if the young person seems not to be paying attention. Yet they are listening and they will recall what we say at these moments for a lifetime. One final bit of wisdom speaks to both Type A and Type B stressors; it was written by the theologian Reinhold Niebuhr:

> God grant me the serenity
> To accept the things I cannot change
> The courage to change the things I can
> And the wisdom to know the difference.

Sometimes too, words are not enough. Teenagers are never too old for a hug. And sometimes, both at happy and sad times, we need to show our sharing of their joy or sadness by holding them. Once they grow big, sometimes bigger than we are, we may mistakenly assume that they no longer need the physical contact that was so much part of our interaction when they were young. Certainly we don't want to hug young teenagers in front of their friends. But at home, at times, giving our teenagers a hug may be the best way to help them deal with an unforeseeable and unavoidable stressor.

Type C: Foreseeable and Unavoidable Stressors

In most cases what is foreseeable and unavoidable has to do with actions we have to take or with work that must be done. The best way to help adolescents deal with this type of stress is to help them acquire good work habits. There are several constructive work habits that we can pass on to young people to help them better manage the stress of foreseeable and unavoidable tasks. But we need to remember that example is the best teacher and if we ourselves follow good work habits our children will be more inclined to do likewise.

One effective work habit is to do *first* the thing that you wish to do least. This also contributes to the quality of the work. In most things, the excellence of what we do depends upon the amount of preparation we put into it, and it is often the preparation that is most onerous. Whether we are preparing the walls for painting or the soil for our garden, the fun part—the actual painting or planting—always has a much better outcome when we take more time in doing the less rewarding preparation. Learning this habit takes effort in the beginning, but once acquired, it brings many rewards later in life. The person who works in this way is respected as efficient, reliable, and conscientious.

A second habit is to plan the work to be done each day and to set specific goals. When he was a teenager, famed Swiss psychologist Jean Piaget wrote a book entitled *Reserche* that outlined a plan of work for his whole life. To a remarkable degree, he fulfilled that plan. He set himself a daily goal as well. Each morning Piaget rose at five o'clock and wrote the equivalent of five printed pages each day. He kept to this regime throughout his entire life and authored over a hundred books and more than a thousand articles. George Bernard Shaw also set himself the goal of writing five pages every day. He did this for nine years while working as a bank cashier and piling up rejection slips. He earned only thirty dollars from his writing during those nine years.

A third good work habit is to do each task as if it were our *last*—to give every job we do, whether small or large, important or unimportant, our full attention and effort. It troubles me to go into a store and to see teenagers, or adults for that matter, who are more interested in talking to their peers than they are in doing the job they were hired to do. I recall, in contrast, watching a janitor at Logan Airport in Boston. He was sweeping the floor and emptying the trash barrels. It was not a prestigious job to say the least, but he obviously took pride in what he was doing and was noticeably pleased with the neat clean look of the trash barrel after he had emptied and relined it. This man knew the secret of taking pride in his work. The pride comes not from the prestige of the job but rather from the knowledge that we have done the very best that we know how. Even in these postmodern times, taking pride in the simplest as well as the most complex task is a reflection of an integrated sense of self and identity.

Although most Type C stressors have to do with tasks that need to be done, others relate to situations that may be unpleasant but that cannot be avoided, like spending time with people we detest. One strategy that is useful in dealing with this type of stressor is to imagine the worst possible outcome of the situation: "What is the very worst thing that can happen?" Once we think through what the worst possible eventuality could be, some of our anxiety is diminished. Part of the anxiety has to do with leaving the worst possible outcome unimagined and therefore more dire than is true in actuality. Once we know what the worst is, we often find that reality is far less serious than we had imagined.

Type D: Unforeseeable and Avoidable Stressors

Up until now I have avoided discussing the fourth type of stressor, those events that are unforeseeable but nonetheless avoidable. At first this type of stressor would seem to be impossible: how can we prepare for something that is unforeseeable if we don't know what it is? But we do know in a general way. We know that we will die, that we will experience successes and failures, pains and pleasures, tragedies and comedies. These unforeseeable events are not really avoidable but they can be made less traumatic and disorienting if we prepare for them in a general way. And the preparation for Type D stressors is a spiritual conviction, or a religious faith.

In these postmodern times we have become more secular than ever before. Yet as humans we have a deep need for spiritual as well as physical nourishment. Many young people are turning back to religion for this nourishment, others to cults and even to martial arts programs that have a moral component. As I described in an earlier chapter, young adolescents are deeply religious in a personal rather than in an institutional sense. This speaks to their hunger for ideals and values, their recognition that life needs to be sustained by more than the foul language, the sex, and the violence that they are fed daily by the media. A spiritual awakening, a sense of wonder at the miracles of life and nature and of awe at the power of human goodness and depravity of human evil, provide young people with a broader perspective on life as a whole.

It is true that religion has often been abused and employed in exploitative and hateful ways. But the fact that religion has been abused does not mean that religion itself is exploitative and hateful. The examples of religious figures such as Christ, Moses, Buddha, and Mohammed, and the late Mother Teresa give young people the sense that a moral and unselfish life is possible despite the most extreme adversity. If we do not have a religious faith ourselves, we should not deny it, nor denigrate it to our adolescents. Fortunately, an increasing number of institutional religions are responding to the needs of postmodern families and youth.

It should be said too, that many modern social scientists had little use for religion. Freud called it an "illusion" and Marx called it the "opiate of the proletariat." In the postmodern world, however, we recognize that social science itself is subjective and reflects the biases and perspectives of those who create it. Social science, so quick to deny the transcendence of religion, did not hesitate to raise its own laws and principles to the plane of universality. Today we recognize that religion and social science are simply different narratives and that each has its own claim on truth. As humans we have deep-seated desires both to know and to believe. In modern times both religion and science tried to answer these needs. Today, we can accept the fact that both needs are important but are perhaps best met by different, rather than the same, narratives.

A sense of spirituality, of something greater than ourselves, is all important for contemporary adolescents. Vanishing markers, family permutations, and inhospitable schools have taken away many of the supports young people need to attain an integrated sense of self and identity and have contributed to the increase in patchwork selves and to the new morbidity. When we behave as adults, set limits and standards, and operate on the basis of principle and not emotion, we are acting spiritually. In so doing we let young people know that there is a place for human values in postmodern society; and, most importantly, that there is a place for them as well.

Appendix

Services for Troubled Teenagers

Parent Self-Help Groups

Parents Anonymous, Inc.
675 West Foothill Boulevard, Suite 200
Claremont, CA 91711
(909) 621-6184

Toughlove International
P. O. Box 1069
Doylestown, PA 18901
(800) 333-1069

Toughlove Canada, Inc.
Box 101
Sackville, NS B4C 2S8
(902) 864-7894

Parents, Families, and Friends of Lesbians and Gays (P-FLAG)
1101 14th Street, NW, Suite 1030
Washington, DC 20005
(202) 638-4200
www.pflag.org

Substance Abuse

Teenagers are welcome at Alcoholics Anonymous meetings, and
in larger cities there may be groups organized for young people.
For teenagers affected by someone else's drinking, usually a
family member's, there are Alateen meetings. For a local group,
contact:

Al-Anon Family Group Headquarters
P. O. Box 862, Midtown Station
New York, NY 10018
(800) 356-9996

National Institute on Drug Abuse
National Institutes of Health
5600 Fishers Lane, Room 10A-39

Rockville, MD 20857
(301) 443-6245
www.nida.nih.gov

National Parents' Resource Institute for Drug Education
(PRIDE)
10 Park Place, Suite 540
Atlanta, GA 30303
(404) 577-4500
recorded information on drugs: (800) 677-7433

National Family Partnership
11159-B South Town Square
St. Louis, MO 63123
(314) 845-1933

Runaway Services

In addition to the national hotlines listed below, many cities and
states have their own services for runaway youth and their families.

National Runaway Switchboard
3080 North Lincoln Avenue
Chicago, IL 60657
(312) 880-9860
Crisis hotline: (800) 621-4000

Youth Development, Inc.
P. O. Box 178408
San Diego, CA 92177-8408
(619) 292-5683
Crisis hotline: (800) MISS-YOU

Suicide Prevention

Almost every state now has one or more suicide hotlines and
suicide prevention centers. Your local phone directory or opera-
tor can provide the number for your area. The following groups
work on the problem nationwide.

Youth Suicide Prevention
65 Essex Road
Chestnut Hill, MA 02167
(617) 738-0700

Samaritans
500 Commonwealth Avenue
Boston, MA 02215
(617) 247-0220

References

Abbot, John. 1995. "Children Need Communities." *Educational Leadership*, 52:8, 6–10.

Adger, Hoover, Jr. 1991. "Problems of Alcohol Abuse and Other Drug Use and Abuse in Adolescents," Seventh Conference on Health Policy, *Adolescents at Risk: Medical and Social Perspectives*, edited by David Roger and Eli Ginsberg. 1–23. Cornell, N.Y.: Cornell Medical College.

American Psychiatric Association. 1993. *DSM (Diagnostic and Screening Manual DSM) III*. Washington, D.C.

Angel, Ronald, and Jacqueline Angel. 1993. *Painful Inheritance*. Madison, Wis.: University of Wisconsin Press.

Anon. 1983. "Dear Jill." *Teen Magazine*, February.

Arbuthnut, J., D.A., Gordon, and George Jurkovic. 1987. "Personality." In *Handbook of Juvenile Delinquency*, edited by Herbert Quay. New York: Wiley.

Aristotle. 1941. "Rhetorica." In *The Basic Works of Aristotle*, edited by Richard McKeon. New York: Random House.

Balk, David. 1995. *Adolescent Development: Early Through Late Adolescence*. Pacific Grove, Calif.: Brooks/Cole.

Bandini, Linda. 1992. "Obesity in the Adolescent." In *Adolescent Medicine: State of the Art Reviews*, vol. 3, no. 3, edited by Michael Nussbaum and Johanna Dwyer. 459–472. Philadelphia: Hanley & Belfus.

Bandura, Albert. 1964. "The Stormy Decade: Fact or Fiction." *Psychology in the Schools* 1:224–231.

Barnicle, Mike. 1982. "Why They Hate School." *Boston Globe*, September 12.

Bidwell, R. 1988. "The Gay and Lesbian Teen: A Case of Denied Adolescence." *Journal of Pediatric Health Care* 2(3): 33–39.

Blume, Judy. 1970. *Are You There God? It's Me, Margaret*. New York: Dell.
_____. 1971. *Then Again, Maybe I Won't*. New York: Dell.

Boyer, Ernest. 1983. *Highschool*. New York: Harper & Row.

Brazelton, T. Berry. 1992. *Touchpoints*. Reading, Mass.: Addison-Wesley.

Brondino, Jeanne, et al. 1988. *Raising Each Other*. Claremont, Calif.: Hunter House.

Brooks-Gunn, Jean, and Diane Roble. (1983). "The Experience of Menarche from a Developmental Perspective." In *Girls at Puberty*, edited by Jean Brooks-Gunn and Anne Petersen. New York: Plenum.

Brown, Jane, Bradley Greenberg, and Nancy Beurkel-Rothfuss. 1993. "Mass Media and Sexuality." In *Adolescent Medicine: State of the Art Reviews,* vol. 4, no. 3, edited by Victor Strassburger and George Comstock. Philadelphia: Hanley & Belfus.

Brown, Robert. 1992. "Psychosomatic Problems in Adolescents." In *Adolescent Medicine: State of the Art Reviews,* vol. 3, no. 1, edited by Robert Brown and Barbara Cromer, 87–96. Philadelphia: Hanley & Belfus.

Buchanan, C., E. Maccoby, and S. Dornbusch. 1992. "Adolescents and Their Families after Divorce: Three Residential Arrangements Compared." *Journal of Research on Adolescence,* 2:261–191.

Bureau of Labor Statistics. 1990. *Handbook of Labor Statistics.* Washington, D.C.: U.S. Government Printing Office.

Children's Defense Fund. 1994. *State of America's Children 1994.* Washington, D.C.: Author.

Cobb, Nancy. 1995. *Adolescence: Continuity, Change and Diversity.* Mountain View, Calif.: Mayfield.

Cobb, Nathan. 1982. "Who's Getting High on What?" *Boston Globe,* October 10

Coleman, M., and L. Ganong. 1991. "Remarriage and Stepfamily Research in the 1980s." In *Contemporary Families: Looking Forward, Looking Back,* edited by A. Booth. Minneapolis: National Council of Family Relations.

Coles, Robert, and George Stokes. 1985. *Sex and the American Teenager.* New York: Harper.

Collins, Maryanne. 1981. "One Breast Larger in Young Girls." In *The Parent's Guide to Teenagers,* edited by Leonard Gross, 257. New York: Macmillan.

Comstock, George, and Victor Strassburger. 1993. "Media Violence." In *Adolescent Medicine: State of the Art Reviews,* vol. 4, no. 3, edited by George Comstock and Victor Strassburger. Philadelphia: Hanley & Belfus.

Connor, Steven. 1989. *Postmodernist Culture.* Cambridge, England: Basil Blackwell Inc.

Costa, Arthur. 1985. *Developing Minds.* Alexandria, Va.: Association for Supervision and Curriculum.

Cox, June, Neil Daniel, and Bruce Boston. 1985. *Educating Able Learners.* Austin Tex.: University of Texas Press.

Cross, Wilbur. 1979. *Kids and Booze.* New York: E.P. Dutton.

Danziger, Paula. 1973. *The Cat Ate My Gymsuit.* New York: Dell.

DeBono, Edward. 1988. *CoRT Program.* San Diego, Calif.: Pergamon Press.

Devine, J. 1984. "A Systemic Inspection of Affectional Preference Orientation and the Family of Origin." *Journal of Social Work and Human Sex* 2:9.

Devlin, B. 1995. "Why Do We Believe?" *Mad* magazine, March/ April, 27–28.

Dewey, John. 1938. *Experience and Education.* New York: Macmillan.

Dreyer, P. 1982. "Sexuality during Adolescence." In *Handbook of Developmental Psychology*, edited by Benjamin Wolmann, 559–601. Englewood Cliffs, N.J.: Prentice Hall.

Durkheim, Emile. 1950. *Le Suicide*. Glencoe, Ill.: The Free Press.

Elkind, David. 1994. *Ties That Stress: The New Family Imbalance*. Cambridge, Mass.: Harvard University Press.

_____. 1994 *Parenting Your Teenager*. New York: Ballantine.

Elkind, David, and Robert Bowen. 1979. "Imaginary Audience Behavior in Children and Adolescents." *Developmental Psychology* 15: 38–44.

Ellsworth, Daniel. 1988. *Poor Support: Poverty in the American Family*. New York: Basic Books.

Emerson, Ralph Waldo. 1909. "Essays and English Traits," vol. 5. In *The Harvard Classics*, edited by C. Eliot. New York: Collier.

Ephron, Delia. 1981. *Teenage Romance: or, How to Die of Embarrassment*. New York: Ballantine.

Erikson, Erik. 1950. *Childhood and Society*. New York: Norton.

_____. 1968. *Identity: Youth and Crisis*. New York: Norton.

Faber, Adele, and Elaine Mazlish. 1980. *How to Talk So Kids Will Listen: How to Listen So Kids Will Talk*. New York: Avon.

Farber, Eleanor 1987. "The Adolescent Who Runs." In *Youth at High Risk*, edited by B. Brown and A. Mills. Washington D.C.: U.S. Government Printing Office.

Farberow, Norman. 1985. "Youth Suicide: A Summary." In *Youth Suicide*, edited by Michael Peck, and Robert Litman, 191–203. New York: Springer.

Fisher, Eleanor 1988. "On Being Not Quite Ready to Retire." *Educational Leadership*. 43 (8):82–84.

Fisher, Martin. 1992. "Medical Complications of Anorexia and Bulimia Nervosa." In *Adolescent Medicine: State of the Art Reviews*, vol. 3, no. 3, edited by Michael Nussbaum and Johanna Dwyer, 487–502. Philadelphia: Hanley & Belfus.

Freud, Sigmund. 1925. "Mourning and Melancholia." In *Collected Papers of Sigmund Freud*, edited by Joan Riviere. London: Hogarth Press.

Fromm, Erich. 1969. *Escape from Freedom*. New York: Avon.

Fuchs, Victor. 1988. *Women's Quest for Economic Equality*. Cambridge, Mass.: Harvard University Press.

Fugua, N. 1995. Lonely. *Teen*, April 24.

Gardner, D., and Y. Larsen. 1983. *A Nation at Risk*. Washington, D.C.: U.S. Office of Education.

Gardner, Richard. 1973. *Understanding Children*, 51–52. New York: Aronson, Inc.

Gesell, Arnold, and Frances Ilg. 1956. *Youth: The Years from Ten to Sixteen*. New York: Harper & Row.

Ghai, Kanika, and Robert Rosenfeld. 1994. "Disorders of Pubertal Development." In *Adolescent Medicine: State of the Art Reviews*, vol. 5, no. 1, edited by Joseph Sanfilippo, Jordan Finkelstein, and Dennis Styne, 19–36. Philadelphia: Hanley & Belfus.

Gibboney, Richard. 1994. *The Stone Trumpet: A Story of Practical School Reform 1960–1990*. Albany: State University of New York Press.

Gilligan, Carol, Janie Ward, and Jill Taylor. 1988. *Mapping the Moral Domain*. Cambridge, Mass.: Harvard University Press.

Ginott, Chaim. 1969. *Between Parent and Teenager*. New York: MacMillan.

Glick, P. 1989. "Stepfamilies and Stepchildren: A Brief Family Profile." *Family Relations* 38:24–27.

Goffman, Erving. 1969. *Strategic Interactions*. Philadelphia: University of Pennsylvania Press.

Gordon, Thomas. 1989. *Teaching Children Self Discipline*. New York: Random House.

Greenberg, Bradley, Jamie Brown, and Nancy Beurkel-Rothfuss. 1986. *Media, Sex and the Adolescent*. Cresskill, N.J.: Hampton.

Haggarty, Robert, Kenneth Roughman, and Barry Bless, eds. 1975. *Child Health and the Community*. New York: Wiley.

Hall, Granville. 1924. *Confessions of a Psychologist*. New York: Appleton.

Hamburg, David. 1992. *Today's Children: Creating a Future for a Generation in Crises*. New York: Times Books.

Hammond, S., and B. Yung. 1993. "Psychology's Role in the Public Health Response to Assaultive Violence among Young African American Men." *American Psychologist*, 48:142–54.

Hass, Aaron. 1981. *Teenage Sexuality*. New York: Ballantine.

Health United States, 1990. Hyattsville, Md.: National Center for Health Statistics.

Heron, Ann. 1983. *One Teenager in Ten*. Boston: Alyson.

Hetherington, E. M., M. Cox, and R. Cox. 1982. "Effects of Divorce on Children and Parents." In *Nontraditional Families*, edited by Michael Lamb. Hillsdale, N.J.: Erlbaum.

Howard, Marion. 1992. "Delaying the Start of Intercourse Among Adolescents." In *Adolescent Medicine: State of the Art Reviews*, vol. 3, no.2, edited by Susan Coupey and Lorraine Klerman, 181–194. Philadelphia: Hanley & Belfus.

Hunter, Madeline. 1984. "Knowing, Teaching and Supervising." In *Using What We Know About Teaching*, edited by Peter Hosford, 175– 76. Alexandria, Va.: Association for Supervision and Curriculum.

Hyde, Janet. 1990. *Understanding Human Sexuality* (4th ed.). San Francisco: McGraw-Hill.

Inhelder, Barbel, and Jean Piaget. 1958. *The Growth of Logical Thinking from Childhood to Adolescence*. New York: Basic Books.

Insel, Paul, and William Roth. 1994. *Core Concepts in Health*. Mountain View, Calif.: Mayfield.

Jackson, Michael, and Bruce Jackson. 1983. *Doing Drugs*. New York: Martins/Marek.

Jackson, Michael, and Janet Jackson. 1981. *Your Father's Not Coming Home Anymore*. New York: Ace Books.

Jackson, Shirley. 1960. *Come Along With Me*. New York: Viking.

Jenkins, Esther, and Carl Bell. 1992. "Adolescent Violence: Can it Be Curbed?" In *Adolescent Medicine: State of the Art Reviews*, vol. 3, no. 7, edited by Robert T. Brown and Barbara Cromer, 71–86. Philadelphia: Hanley & Belfus.

Johnston, Lloyd, and Patrick O'Malley. 1991. *Drug Use, Drinking and Smoking: National Survey Results from High School, College and Adult Populations, 1975–1990*. Washington, D.C.: National Institute for Drug Abuse.

Kierkegaard, Soren. 1945. *Stages Along Life's Way*. Princeton: Princeton University Press.

Kleen, F. 1982. "Stepfamilies Growing Common, Pose a Host of Problems." *The Wall Street Journal*, December 23.

Knowles, John. 1960. *A Separate Peace*. New York: Macmillan.

Kohut, Heinz. 1972. "Thoughts on Narcissistic Rage." In *Psychoanalytical Study of the Child*, 37: 360–398. New York: International Universities Press.

Koss, M. 1988. "Hidden Rape: Sexual Aggression and Victimization in a National Sample in Higher Education." In *Rape and Sexual Assault* vol. 2, edited by A. Burgess, 3–25. New York: Garland.

Landau, Elaine. 1983. *Why Are They Starving Themselves*. New York: Julian Messner.

Landers, Ann. 1983. "Grandfather Feels Ashamed." *Boston Globe*, July 24.

Lasch, Christopher. 1977. *Haven in a Heartless World*. New York: Basic Books.

Lash, Scott. 1990. *Sociology of Postmodernism*. London: Routledge.

Lifton, Robert. 1976. "Proteus Revisited." In *Adolescent Psychiatry*, edited by Peter Feinstein, 21–35. New York: Jason Aronson.

Longway, L., et al. 1983. "Young Fu." *Newsweek*, January 17.

Louv, Richard. 1990. *Childhood's Future*. New York: Houghton-Mifflin.

Madaras, Lynda. 1991. "The Changes of Puberty." In *Teens: A Fresh Look*, edited by Anne Pedersen and Peggy O'Mara, 53–71. New York: W.W. Norton.

Marsh, J., and M. Wirick. 1991. "Evaluation of Hull House Teen Pregnancy and Parenting Programs." *Evaluation and Program Planning* 14:49–61.

McCoy, Kathleen. 1982. *Coping with Teenage Depression*. New York: New American Library.

McCullers, Carson. 1946. *The Member of the Wedding*. New York: Bantam.

Mead, George. 1934. *Mind, Self and Society*. Chicago: University of Chicago Press.

Mechanic, D., and S. Hansell. 1989. "Divorce, Family Conflict and Adolescents Well Being." *Journal of Health and Social Behavior* 20:105–116.

Mishne, Judith. 1986. *Clinical Work with Adolescents*. New York: Free Press.

Morley, Christopher. 1939. *Kitty Foyle*. Philadelphia: Lippincott.

Morris, Naomi. 1992. "Determinants of Adolescent Initiation of Coitus." In *Adolescent Medicine: State of the Art Reviews*, vol. 3, no.2, edited by Susan Coupey and Lorraine Klerman, 165–180. Philadelphia: Hanley & Belfus.

Muro, Ann. 1965. "Cecilia Rosas." *New Mexico Quarterly* 4 (Winter).

Myers, W. C., and R. Burket. 1992. "Current Perspectives on Adolescent Conduct Disorder." In *Adolescent Medicine: State of the Art Reviews*, edited by Robert T. Brown and Barbara Cromer, 61–70. Philadelphia: Hanley & Belfus.

National Center for Education Statistics. 1995. *Projection of Education Statistics to 2005.* Washington, D.C.: U.S. Department of Education.

National Commission on Children. 1991. *Beyond Rhetoric: A New American Agenda for Children and Families.* Washington, D.C.: U.S. Government Printing Office.

National Commission on Excellence in Education. 1983. *A Nation at Risk.* Washington, D.C.: U.S. Government Printing Office.

National Educational Goals Panel. 1991. *The National Educational Goals Report.* Washington, D.C.: U.S. Department of Education.

Norman, Jane, and Myron Harris. 1981. *The Private Life of the American Teenager.* New York: Rawson-Wade.

Oaks, Merilee. 1982. Quoted in McCoy, Kathleen *Coping with Teenage Depression*, 232–36. New York: New American Library.

Offer, Daniel and Judith Boskin. 1975. *From Teenage to Youngmanhood: A Psychological Study.* New York: Basic Books.

O'Malley, Patrick, Lloyd Johnston, and Jerald Bachman. 1993. "Adolescent Substance Use and Addictions: Epidemiology, Current Trends and Public Policy." In *Adolescent Medicine: State of the Art Reviews*, vol. 4, no. 2, edited by Manuel Schydower and Peter Rogers, 227–248. Philadelphia: Hanley & Belfus.

O'Neil, J. 1994. "Aiming for New Outcomes: The Promise and the Reality." *Educational Leadership* (51)5: 12–17.

Parent. 1983. "Helping a Teenager Grow Up Gradually." *Boston Globe*, July 8.

Pascal, Frances. 1994. *Sweet Valley High: The Boyfriend War.* New York: Bantam.

Peck, Michael, Norman Farberow, and Robert Litman. 1985. *Youth Suicide.* New York: Springer.

Perlmutter, C. 1982. "Competitive Sports." *Children* 35–38.

Phelps, L., et al. 1993. "Figure Preference, Body Dissatisfaction, and Body Distortion in Young Adolescence." *Journal of Adolescent Research* 8:297–310.

Piaget, Jean. 1950. *The Psychology of Intelligence.* London: Routledge & Kegan Paul.

Pill, J. 1990. "Redefining the Family." *Family Relations* 39: 186–193.

Pokorny, Susan. 1992. "Inappropriate Sexual Behavior: One Gynecologist's View." In *Adolescent Medicine: State of the Art Reviews*, vol. 3, no. 2, edited by Susan Coupey and Lorraine Klerman, 339–57. Philadelphia: Hanley & Belfus.

Quint, J. 1991. "Project Redirection: Making and Measuring Difference." *Evaluation and Program Planning* 14: 75–86.

Rader, D. 1982. "Children on the Run." *Parade* magazine, September 5.

Randall, Vera. 1978. "Waiting for Jim." In *Adolescence in Literature*, edited by Thomas Gregory. New York: Longman.

Rappucci, N., and J. Haugaard. 1989. "Prevention of Child Sexual Abuse: Myth or Reality." *American Psychologist* (44)10: 1274.

Ravitch, Diane. 1983. *The Troubled Crusade*. New York: Basic Books.

Reed, V. 1983. "Shelters and Streets Draw Throw-Away Kids." *New York Times*, June 3.

Rogers, Peter, and Hoover Adger. 1993. "Alcohol and Adolescents." In *Adolescent Medicine: State of the Art Reviews*, vol. 4, no. 2, edited by Manuel Schydlower and Peter Rogers, 295–304. Philadelphia: Hanley & Belfus.

Roth, Philip. 1969. *Portnoy's Complaint*. New York: Random House.

Salinger, J.D. 1951. *The Catcher in the Rye*. Boston: Little, Brown.

Saltzman, L., P. O'Connell, P. J. Meehan, and J. A. Lamb. 1991. "Attempted Suicide Among High School Students—United States: 1990." *MMWR* 40:633–635.

Selye, Hans. 1976. *The Stress of Life*, rev. ed. New York: McGraw Hill.

Sheridan, Richard. 1909. *The School for Scandal*. In *The Harvard Classics*, vol 18, edited by C. Eliot. New York: Collier.

Shorter, Edward. 1975. *The Making of the Modern Family*. New York: Basic Books.

Simons, J. F., R. Robertson, and W. Downs. 1989. "The Nature of the Association Between Parental Rejection and Delinquent Behavior." *Journal of Youth and Adolescence* 18:297–310.

Sizer, Theodore. 1984. *Horace's Compromise*. New York: Houghton Mifflin.

_____. 1992. *Horace's School*. New York: Houghton Mifflin.

Smoll, Frank, and Ronald Smith. 1991. "Stress and the Adolescent Athlete." In *Adolescent Medicine: State of the Art Reviews*, vol. 2, no. 1., edited by Paul G. Dyment, 51. Philadelphia: Hanley & Belfus.

Sorenson, S. and P. Bowie. 1994. "Violence and Youth: Psychology's Response, vol 2." In *Papers of the American Psychological Association*, edited by L. Eron and J. Gentry. Washington, D.C.: American Psychological Association.

Spanier, G., and P. Slick. 1981. "Marital Instability in the United States: Some Correlates and Recent Changes." *Family Relations* 30:329–38.

Sperling, Edward. 1981. "Psychological Impact of Small Penis." In *The Parent's Guide to Teenagers*, edited by Leonard Gross, 255. New York: Macmillan.

Stein, E. 1982. "Have Horror Films Gone Too Far?" *New York Times*, June 20.

Strassburger, Victor, and Alison Reeve. 1991. "The Adolescent with Chronic Pains: Principles of Psychosomatic Medicine." In *Adolescent Medicine: State of the Art Reviews*, vol. 2, no.3, edited by John Kulig, 677–96. Philadelphia: Hanley & Belfus.

Strommen, E. 1989. "You're a What? Family Reactions to the Disclosure of Homosexuality." *Journal of Homosexuality*. 18:37.

Sturdevant, Marsha, and Gary Remafedi. 1992. "Special Health Needs of Homosexual Youth." In *Adolescent Medicine: State of the Art Reviews*, vol. 3, edited by Susan Coupey and Lorraine Klerman, 331–338. Philadelphia: Hanley & Belfus.

Tishler, Carl. 1992. "Adolescent Suicide: Assessment of Risk, Prevention and Treatment." In *Adolescent Medicine: State of the Art Reviews*, vol. 3, no. 1, edited by Robert I. Brown and Barbara Cromer, 51–60. Philadelphia: Hanley & Belfus.

Tishler, Carl, and P. McKenry. 1981. "Adolescent Suicide Attempts: Some Significant Factors." *Suicide and Life Threatening Behavior* 11:86–92.

Toth, Susan Allen. 1981. *Blooming: A Small Town Girlhood*. Boston: Little, Brown.

Trussel, J. 1976. "Economic Consequences of Teenage Childbearing." *Family Planning Perspectives* 10(4):184–90.

U.S. Department of Commerce: Bureau of the Census. 1990a. *Current Population Reports: Household and Family Characteristics*. Washington, D.C.: U.S. Government Printing Office.

U.S. Department of Commerce: Bureau of the Census. 1990b. *Current Population Reports: Marital Status and Living Arrangements*. Washington D.C.: U.S. Government Printing Office.

U.S. Department of Health and Human Services. 1990. *Healthy People, 2000: National Health Promotion and Disease Prevention Objectives*. Washington D.C.: U.S. Government Printing Office.

Visher, Emily, and John Visher. 1988. *Old Loyalties, New Ties*. New York: Brunner/Mazel.

Voydanoff, Patricia, and Brenda Donnelly. 1991. *Adolescent Sexuality and Pregnancy*. Newberry Park, Calif.: Sage.

Weiner, Irving. 1992. *Psychological Disturbance in Adolescence*. New York: Wiley.

Weir, Don 1983. "Shyness." *Young Miss*, February.

Whitfield, C. 1991. *Co-dependence*. Deerfield, Fla: Health Communications Inc.

Whittemore, H. 1982. "The Competitors." *Parade* Magazine, April 11.

William T. Grant Commission on Work. 1988. *The Forgotten Half: Non-College Youth in America*. Washington, D.C.: William T. Grant Foundation.

Wilson, Kenneth, and Bennett Davis. 1994. *Redesigning Education*. New York: Henry Holt & Co.

Winnicott, D. W. 1987. *The Child, the Family, and the Outside World*. Reading, Mass.: Addison-Wesley.

Winship, Elizabeth. 1983. *Reaching Your Teenager*. Boston: Houghton-Mifflin.

Wood, A. 1982. "Stepparents: How to Deal with Them." *Seventeen*, February.

Wurtman, Judith. 1981. "Persistence of Childhood Chubbiness." In *The Parents Guide to Teenagers*, edited by Leonard Gross, 217. New York: Macmillan.

Yankelovitch, Daniel. 1981. *New Rules*. New York: Bantam.

York, Phyllis, and David York. 1982. *Toughlove*. New York: Doubleday.

Permissions Acknowledgments

Index

A

Academic performance, 163–165
Actions
    accountable for, 96
    responsibility for, 217
Activity markers, 115–120
    age changes in, 118
    beauty contests and pageants, 117–118
    consequences of vanishing, 119–120
    playing games on their own, 117
    religious activities, 118–119
    sports, 115–117
Adolescence
    changing perceptions of, 3–8
    elimination of age period, 3
    golden age of, 3–5
    literature glorifying, 4–5
    social science depiction of, 4
    social sophistication, 5
    stereotypic depiction of, 16–17
    technological savvy, 5
Adolescents
    access to adult-rated materials, 123
    emancipation, 16–17
    guilt, 249–250
    held accountable for actions, 96
    immaturity of, 14, 120
    media images of, 127–128
    parents sharing feelings with, 143
    perceptions of sophistication, 143
    premarital sex, 6
    premature adulthood, 7

social perceptions of, 121
societal view of, 6
sophistication of, 9, 14, 120
transition to adulthood, 5
universality, 179
Adult information markers, 123–124
Adult-rated materials, 123
Adulthood
    adolescent transition to, 5
    premature, 7
Adults
    hypocrisy and deceitfulness of, 33
    resisting authority of, 210
    See also Parents
Advertising campaigns, 130–131, 132–133
Age dynamism, 119
Aggression, 123
Aid to Families with Dependent Children, 158
AIDS, 9
    homosexuality and, 76
    new morbidity, 24
Alcohol
    abuse, 220–223, 239
    new morbidity, 23
Alcoholism, 223
American Psychiatric Association, 74
Angry teenagers, 210–212
    delinquency, 232–234
    failure reaction, 232–235
    violence, 234–235
Anomie, 229
Anorexia nervosa, 218–220
Antisocial behavior, 233–234
Anxious teenagers, 202–206
    coping, 256–258

fads, 83–85
parents, 85
peer groups, 84
rules of, 87

F

Fads, 83–85
  acceptance by peer groups,
    84, 85
Failure reaction, 230–238
  angry teenagers, 232–235
  frightened teenagers, 235–238
  school and stress, 230–231
  work and school stresses,
    231–232
Families
  emotional conflicts, 17
  kinship structures, 13
  nuclear, 10–11
  permeable, 10, 13, 135–162
  postmodernity changes in,
    121
  togetherness, 11
Family finance markers,
  123–124
Farberow, Norman, 229–230
Faultfinding. *See* Criticalness
Flashbacks, 79
Forgotten half, 170
Formal operational thinking, 27
  gender differences, 30–31
  language use, 32
  syllogistic reasoning, 27
  symbolic logic, 27–28
  thinking about thinking,
    39–40
  wordplay, 29–30
Formal operations, 16, 28–29
Freedom
  anxious teenagers, 217–220
  conforming teenagers,
    220–224
  impinging on other's
    freedom, 246–247
  type A stressors, 216–224
Friends, 85
Frightened teenagers, 212–214
  abusive parents, 236

accepting deviant behavior
  as norm, 235–236
failure reaction, 235–238
runaways, 236–238
Fromm, Erich, 217

G

Gangs
  absence of religious training
    and, 53
  replacing family with, 142
Gardner, Richard A., 116
GAS (General Adaptation Syndrome), 191
Gender differences and formal
  operational thinking, 30–31
Gesell, Arnold, 11
Gibboney, Richard, 252
Gilligan, Carol, 31, 179
Girl Scouts of America, 4
Girls
  first sexual experience,
    105–107
  masturbation, 69, 70
  puberty, 56–72
  romantic, 104
Global economy, 9
Goals
  public approval of, 111–112
  work habits, 262
Growing up today
  societal dangers, 8–9
  violence, 8
Growth, 18–22
  calendar energy, 193
  differentiation, 18–20
  encouraging by integration,
    241–256
  integration, 18–20, 21–22
  substitution, 20–22, 21–22
Guilt
  adolescents, 249–50
  parents, 249–50
  romantic attachments, 36

H

Hall, G. Stanley, 69–70
Heavy metal music, 29